PRAISE FOR ANTONIO LOPEZ

With a kind of stubbornness that bordered on obsession, Antonio Lopez and his wife set a big and luminous goal for themselves—and then went out and achieved it. For young parents everywhere who want their kids to have authentic adventures and a sense of wonder beyond the world of screens and likes and cursors, here's a bright, handy primer on what to do and where to go. For Lopez, "America's Best Idea" became *his* best idea for how to raise a family while keeping the heart and soul recharged.

— HAMPTON SIDES, NEW YORK TIMES BESTSELLING AUTHOR OF *IN THE KINGDOM OF ICE* AND *THE WIDE WIDE SEA*

NATIONAL PARKS

NATIONAL PARKS

A Family Travelogue Adventure Through All 63 US Parks

PART 1

ANTONIO LOPEZ

ISBN: 978-1-61153-703-1 (paperback)

ISBN: 978-1-61153-704-8 (ebook)

ISBN: 978-1-61153-715-4 (large print)

Library of Congress Control Number: 2025913747

National Parks: Part One is published by: Torchflame Books, an imprint of Top Reads Publishing, LLC, 1035 E. Vista Way, Suite 205, Vista, CA 92084, USA

www.torchflamebooks.com

Cover design and interior layout: Jori Hanna

Cover photos courtesy of Antonio Lopez

To my Mother,
for her grace, wisdom, & Kindergarten lessons,

...

And to all the mothers who left us too soon

CONTENTS

INTRODUCTION

How do your adventures start? Our only child had just been born, and we were looking at our first holiday season and the end of the year with a newborn. My wife Liz and I knew things would never be the same. We feared we wouldn't be great parents, but more importantly we feared our son would grow up so fast we would not remember—or as people say, "It goes by quickly." We wanted to spend every second with our newborn. Perhaps we could be the family that would spend 90 percent of our time together before our son was twelve, like the statistics promise, and still spend time together afterward when he gets busy with his own life.

Time is the most precious thing we own. To live in the present, to live in the moment is worth working for. It takes time and practice. It may be the equivalent of self-actualization. With a small family, time was slowing down and speeding up, all at the same time. We wanted to slow down everything, but in today's world that is almost impossible.

The world keeps on turning. Our family, our faith, our God, our work, and more goals that just keep coming. Our son went from one month to six months to . . . we are counting in years. We want every minute to count with him!

As the time with our son made us slow down, we took every moment to appreciate our little miracle. Our son Logan was born a little after 3:00 a.m. on a Saturday. In an age of Google, Wikipedia states that on this date close to three hundred landmarks in sixty countries, from the pyramids in Egypt to the Eiffel Tower in Paris and the Empire State Building in New York, were lit up in blue—the official color of the United Nations—to commemorate the seventieth anniversary of the world body. Being born on the day that the world lit up their most sacred landmarks was a day that made our hearts and souls light up as well. If the word joy had a color, it would be that same blue.

As a father, who was I now? As a couple and now a family, how would we live, give back, and most importantly, raise our son?

As of this writing, with my now three-year-old son by my side watching *Peppa Pig* and *Paw Patrol,* the October hues of Santa Fe drifted from yellows and oranges in the Aspen tree groves that outline our views. The monolithic grays and whites of snowcapped peaks remind me of all those hues of a New York City winter. Things as simple as getting the mail turned into gigantic occasions with a little boy discovering the world.

He was barely two months old that winter in 2015. I drove down to our mailbox, combined with many other mailboxes, about a quarter of a mile from our home. Catalogs for Christmas shopping had arrived, full of interesting gifts to buy for the holidays. One of these catalogs was called MADE. When I looked through it, I felt that tingling feeling when you know something as simple as a catalog for the holidays is very different.

Their website told me more:

> MADE has quickly become the hotspot gift-buying shop for locals as well as visitors. MADE is located in the Gaslight Alley in Jackson Hole, Wyoming. A small and unique shop, MADE is filled with handmade usable items from over 360 artists from across Wyoming and the USA . . .

It didn't take long to make a list of too many MADE items that I wanted to buy. The problem was . . . now we had a baby. We couldn't just buy anything, right? Wrong! We settled on a map of all fifty-nine national parks. The price for shipping and handling was steep: a quarter of the price of the map itself! But we did our homework. Amazon didn't have such a great map like the one in the MADE catalog. We chose the MADE map.

Ideas started percolating as we waited for the package to arrive. We had our goal.

We were ready for our next adventure as a family. The map came equipped with fifty-nine separate pine-tree stickers to mark the parks families visit, to remind them they were there. This was amazing!

Instead of pinning this map to a wall in a room we rarely went to or in a dark corner of our large garage, I immediately framed the map and mounted it in our living room right below the television.

Our goal was simple: to visit all fifty-nine national parks with our son by the time he reached the age of eighteen. To be precise, before he went off to college. That would be the framework for the family adventures to knit us together for good.

Now we knew how we could spend our time as a family. My wife and I are avid marathon runners. We had seen many states running in half-marathons or marathons. We had also been to many state and national parks. We didn't know if our child would be a long-distance runner like we were, so instead we had a goal of traveling our country and going to all the national parks.

When I started writing this book, there were fifty-nine national parks, and that has increased to sixty-three. Perhaps by the time I finish this book, it will be a hundred. This was our family travel goal, and we would start as soon as possible.

Goals are very interesting things. Our son might not remember his early trips except through the photos and our stories. As he grows, the adventures we will enjoy as we travel park to park and live in the outdoors with him will be amazing!

PETRIFIED FOREST NATIONAL PARK

OUR FIRST NATIONAL PARK WAS PETRIFIED Forest/Painted Desert National Park in Northeastern Arizona. It's 297 miles and a four-hour-and-forty-minute drive from Santa Fe. Our son was three months old. My wife's parents accompanied us in another vehicle as we set off on our maiden voyage. We didn't know how the trip would be with a newborn, so we were very cautious. The park was a circular loop, almost a figure eight, so given the winter conditions we would just drive through and stop at certain locations to see the scenery.

We left the comfort of our adobe home in Santa Fe and took to the road at around daybreak. The sunrise was pink, orange, and shots of red. Getting onto Interstate 25 and onto Interstate 40 in Albuquerque was less busy than expected, and we crossed into Arizona without any baby glitches. Liz was breastfeeding and cuddling all the way. We gassed up in a small town and entered the national park around 10:30 a.m. Mountain Time.

When we arrived at the park, I jogged to the restrooms since the gas station's were, should I say, not inviting. The park's restrooms were very clean and quite cold. That's the thing about most outdoor national park restrooms. One, they are always clean. Two, given the season, they are always cold or hot! Not a perfect system, but they beat going at a gas station.

There's something about entering a national park. At this park there was an entrance. We had bought an annual national park pass for seventy-five dollars for entry into all national parks. Some parks have entrance fees, and this one would have been twenty dollars per vehicle. The gentleman at the guard's gate punched our pass, unremarkable for him, a celebration for us!

To enter a park is to feel like it is your own, our own as taxpayers. The parks are owned by all of us. They have their quirks and idiosyncratic characteristics, but at heart, they are ours to keep and cherish.

Joe and Josie, Logan's grandparents, took pictures of us at the entrance with our three-month-old son. The Petrified Forest National Park has a large, graceful brick wall at the entrance to the visitor center with the national park sign and its name. It's the largest sign of all the ones I've seen in the country, and it was a perfect backdrop for our first stop. We took about an hour's break and went into the movie that was playing in their small auditorium. Logan slept as we watched how the climate changed and who had roamed these parts in the past in search of unique scenery.

We learned Petrified Forest National Park is located in Navajo and Apache counties in Northeastern Arizona. Growing up, my parents always said my great-great-grandmother was Navajo and grew up in Gallup, New Mexico. Perhaps my ancestors walked through this land.

Named for its large deposits of petrified wood, the park covers two hundred and thirty square miles (six hundred square kilometers), encompassing semidesert shrub steppe, as well as highly eroded and colorful Badlands. Painted Desert was declared a national park in 1962.

The United States has sixty-three protected areas known as "national parks" (fifty-nine when we started this adventure . . .) that are operated by the National Park Service, an agency of the

Department of the Interior. National parks must be established by an act of the United States Congress. A bill creating the first national park, Yellowstone National Park, was signed into law by President Ulysses S. Grant in 1872. The Organic Act of 1916 created the National Park Service "to conserve the scenery and the natural and historic objects and wildlife therein, and to provide for the enjoyment of the same in such manner and by such means as will leave them unimpaired for the enjoyment of future generations." Many current national parks had been previously protected as national monuments by the president under the Antiquities Act before being upgraded by Congress. Seven national parks (including six in Alaska) are paired with a national preserve, areas with different levels of protection that are administered together but considered separate units. Thirty states have national parks, as do territories of American Samoa and the United States Virgin Islands. California has the most (nine), followed by Alaska (eight), Utah (five), and Colorado (four). The largest national park is Wrangell-St. Elias in Alaska. At more than eight million acres (32,375 square kilometers), it is larger than each of the nine smallest states. The next three largest parks are also in Alaska. The total area protected by national parks is approximately 52.4 million acres (212,000 square kilometers).

As we watched the movie in the Painted Desert with our slumbering newborn, we saw that this desert landscape averaged about fifty-four hundred feet (sixteen hundred meters) in elevation; the park has a dry, windy climate with temperatures that vary from summer highs of about one hundred degrees Fahrenheit (thirty-eight degrees Celsius) to winter lows well below freezing. More than four hundred species of plants, dominated by grasses such as bunchgrass, blue grama, and sacaton are found in the park. Animals such as pronghorns, coyotes, and bobcats are seen on very few occasions. More often visitors drive into and occasionally run into deer mice, snakes, lizards, seven kinds of amphibians, and more than two hundred species of birds. There are so many birds because it is a windstream to their migratory patterns. Although, many birds make this park their permanent residence.

The Petrified Forest is known for its fossils, especially fallen trees that lived in the Late Triassic period, about 225 million years ago. The sediments containing the fossil logs are part of the widespread and colorful Chinle Formation, from which the Painted Desert gets its unique name. Around sixty million years ago the Colorado Plateau, of which the park is part, was pushed upward by tectonic forces and exposed to increased erosion. Most of the park's rock layers above the Chinle have been removed by wind and water. Many petrified logs are all over, scattered around the park. Paleontologists have been unearthing and studying the park's fossils since the early twentieth century.

As we stepped out of the movie that most national parks have for their respective grounds, we were reminded of the winter conditions outside. In the sun it felt almost warm, but in the shade and under the clouds it was around freezing. We drove the road that connected the park's main veins. We stopped at various vistas for places to click our smartphones. The various colors of the earth are hard to put into words. Do you recall playing marbles? The earth's tones are much like those exotic marbles rolling in the distance.

What stood out the most were the petrified trees. They blended into the earth like dinosaur toenails that had been clipped millions of years ago. At certain stops, it felt like a natural museum. The petrified trees had been exposed to the earth's torturous environment over millions and millions of years, and we felt like the first visitors to see such miraculous sights. Hundreds of years ago this land was filled with petrified trees.

In addition to petrified logs, fossils found in the park include Late Triassic ferns, cycads, ginkgoes, and many other plants. Faunas include giant reptiles called phytosaurs, large amphibians, and early dinosaurs that inhabited these lands all those millions of years ago. Compared to the size of our baby, these logs looked like fallen trees, iced into Earth's rotating cycle.

There's magic in visiting national parks in the winter months. At many of these stops, we were the only living beings for miles and miles. On occasion we would run into a car of a retired couple looking out the window, possibly traveling back to Phoenix. On one specific stop, there was an elderly man with two canes and Boston Red Sox and Patriot attire. The teams had recently won the World Series and Super Bowl. I asked him if he wanted a picture of himself with a prehistoric background. He was surprised and happy with the helping hands of my father-in-law and myself, ladies staying warm in the heated cars. Our new friend told me that he was traveling across the country from New England and had never been in Arizona. This was his first stop in the Grand Canyon State. My father-in-law carried on a conversation with him, and they gave each other that look—the look that says, "Hey, we're in the same generation, and we're doing the same thing at this point in time." However, my father-in-law, Joe, had been here once before.

Petrified Forest is one of those places that if you are driving seventy-five miles per hour on the highway going from point A to point B, you will definitely miss it. At that speed, you'll fly by the park in a matter of minutes.

SOMETIMES THESE PARKS ARE VERY HARD TO FIND. THE one or two signs on the side of the highway are small, and when I say small, I'm talking about very small lettering, and they are usually old signs. Old as in three to four decades old!

Marketing for the national park system is a foreign idea. These parks are like a secret. I wonder what my life would have been like if I had never bought that national park map?! In my lifetime I'd driven by this national park at least ten times and never noticed it. If I had known it was out there, I probably wouldn't have stopped by myself.

I usually drove in this area between the ages of nineteen and twenty-four, driving from college in San Diego and back home to Albuquerque. This was my route of choice.

Parks for some may be a place to go by themselves. For me, it became a place to take family. I might have felt a bit lonely on those many trips back home and to college if I had stopped by myself. What would I have thought? What would I have had to tell? Whom would I have told?

Back in my twenties, the drive took twelve hours if I only stopped for gas. Usually I'd leave San Diego at 4:00 p.m. and get to Albuquerque around 4:00 a.m. That meant I'd pass this place by the highway around midnight, long after the park had closed. My whole life I had no idea this place existed.

I think we go through life really not knowing our surroundings. How many times do we get into our routine and just pass by? For once in my life the world stopped and I looked. I looked into nature. I saw the future that lay before me. It was time to take notice. My life had just changed before my eyes.

As I stepped back into reality, my baby boy was crying. He needed something. My wife jumped into the back seat, unplugged him from his car seat, and held him close to breastfeed him. He settled happily. He was good!

Before we got too far from the park, we went to a store that sold petrified wood from private lands outside the park. The lands around the park have such logs and wood. After polishing, they shone bright as any gem I had seen in my life. Who knows how old they are? One would say thousands if not millions of years. I bought a pair that could act as bookends, which now sit on our fireplace mantle, except for the holidays. They remind me of the balance of time and man's need to consume. They also remind me of greed. What if everyone wanted one of these polished petrified logs? There would be no Petrified Forest.

As we drove past the forest, I had images of ancient cultures. I grew up just a few hours east of this national park in the largest city in New Mexico, Albuquerque, yet in thirty-six years I had never stopped by this sacred land. As we got on the road to Phoenix, we drove through a snowstorm through the Arizona mountain towns in and around Flagstaff. More than an inch of snow fell in a few hours. I worried for a split second as I looked in my rearview mirror and saw my precious baggage. Our son was sound asleep. I wonder what three-month-olds dream about? Perhaps they drift off into their past life experiences. What were our past lives? The past life of the forest we had just come from has a long history. Had we been here before?

The park's earliest humans arrived at least eight thousand years ago. That's six thousand years before Christ! Holy shit! In and around two thousand years ago when Christ was walking in the Middle East, the people of this land grew corn and built pit houses in what would become the park. Later inhabitants built aboveground homes called pueblos. The changing climate caused the last of the park's pueblos to be abandoned by about 1400. More than six hundred archeological sites, including petroglyphs, have been discovered in the park.

In the sixteenth century, Spanish explorers visited the area, and by the mid-nineteenth century a US team had surveyed an east-west route through the area where the park is now located and noted the petrified wood. Roads and a railway came next. Before the park was protected, many of the large-scale fossils were removed by tourists. Theft of petrified wood remains a problem in the twenty-first century.

My problem, as my wife would say, was going off on tangents. My current tangents were worrying about the snow falling gently in the sky and the half-marathon I was going to run the next day.

We ascended the mountainous passage that would lead us into the city and valley we call Phoenix. We checked into our Downtown Phoenix sky-rise hotel. I had run the Rock 'n' Roll Arizona half-marathon many times, but this was my first half-marathon as a father. Before Logan was born, I had three serious conversations with my wife:

1. I would try to shift to a healthier diet.
2. We needed to start saving for college.
3. I would either stop running or hire a coach.

I hired a coach. He was a former US Olympian in the triathlon, a few years my senior. Man was he the best coach I've seen in my life, but WOW, at $250 per month he was expensive.

I was in the best shape of my life. This half-marathon was my first test! My time was 1:19:01. That's 6:01 per mile. Wearing bib number 1084, I placed sixty-ninth out of 13,104. For my age group, I was third out of 785 men my age.

To me this was a huge step in the right direction. I hadn't run this fast in a decade. But in the back of my mind, I still knew how it was to run 1:08 in the same event in a half-marathon right out of college in the summer of 2004. Everything is relative. Running is relative. If you take one step in the right direction, you can call it a success.

It's a great message that from the ashes rises a strong bird. My long-distance running has always been this way. As a child I spent many weeks in the ER due to asthma. My father and mother worried about me.

My mother was my kindergarten teacher, and after that first year of school she could no longer protect me every moment. She by far was my best teacher! She taught all her students, no matter their skill level, how to read. This may sound like the main objective of kindergarten, but many go without learning to read until much later, and sometimes not at all.

My dad was also once a teacher. He went to medical school and became an emergency room doctor. Due to my illness with asthma, he became an expert on the disease. Many of his colleagues said I would not be able to lead an athletic life. They were wrong.

I excelled in all kinds of outdoor activities. The many parochial Catholic schools in Albuquerque fed into one coed Catholic high school. In my first semester of high school, I ran cross-country and quickly became the school's best cross-country runner. Unfortunately, I sat on the bench in basketball and baseball. The silver lining was that I could concentrate my energy on running full-time. My high school coach from Mississippi had run at the University of New Mexico. Through his teachings, I became the state champion in the eight-hundred-meter, mile, and two-mile run. I got an $8,000 athletic yearly scholarship to attend the University of Notre Dame. It was a big deal. I was on the cover of the local sports pages for my accomplishments. In my last weeks of high school, I did too much. I won three state championships, got my first girlfriend of high school, and crashed my parents' 1992 Ford Explorer Eddie Bauer. Then it was off to Notre Dame.

My sister graduated from ND. She encouraged me to attend. She's now an anesthesiologist. It worked for her. I wish she would have warned me about the winter tundra there. Fall semester was great. Our cross-country team was the Big East Champion and finished eighth in the nation at the National Championships. Being a freshman, I ran on varsity for each meet, but my coach made me be the alternate at the National Championships and gave the seniors one last chance for glory. This didn't sit well with me. I've never mentioned this to anyone. But that one decision was enough for me to drop out of college a few months later.

It just wasn't fair! I later fell into a deep depression. I returned to Albuquerque where I was an ND dropout delivering pizzas in rough neighborhoods and motels across town. Running ceased to exist.

I felt encouraged to pick up my running. I did. I won every road race I could find in Albuquerque. From the 5K, 10K, and even the half-marathon. It was too easy! I needed more challenges. I was taking two classes at the University of New Mexico at the large Kirtland Air Force Base (the largest employer in ABQ). I got two As, which combined for a 3.2 GPA at ND and a 4.0 GPA at UNM. That was my first year of college.

I got into every college I applied to and decided to attend the University of Arizona, as they had an almost equivalent running program to ND. When one of my best friends invited me to the University of San Diego for her spring break, I was thrilled by what I saw. My depression ended the moment I was in Southern California. Life was different there. Worries were different. If life was not peachy, you could just go to the beach; and for me that meant a six-mile run by the Pacific Ocean. USD, if you haven't been there, is like a resort. It is, in my opinion, the most beautiful place on Earth. It also houses an Institute for Peace and Justice. It's really my Zen place.

At U of A in Tucson I was taking two chemistry classes with labs and getting in around a hundred miles of running per week. Arizona in the summer meant 106-degree heat, week after week. I had to run at 5:00 a.m. or midnight. I ran most of my life away from midnight to 1:30 in the morning. That was after studying, say, from 8:00 p.m. until around midnight. My collegial roots came back. But I kept hearing *San Diego*. This time, when I visited, I made a stop at the cross-country coach's office.

Coach Richard Cota was a high school history teacher with a collegiate coaching problem. At Notre Dame my coach was getting paid six figures. He had also been there for almost two decades. USD paid Coach Cota around $10,000 per year. USD did not have a track and field team, and the job was only for the fall semester. Coach Cota's office had no windows. It was about ten square feet. This was different from the multimillion-dollar facilities at Notre Dame. He put it simply, "Antonio, running is like dessert. Life is large. You have your main course, and after that, running is your dessert."

That's what I needed to hear. I didn't want running to be my everything. At times, if I didn't want to run, I didn't have to. He offered me an athletic scholarship of $17,000 per year. That was more than double ND's offer, and the U of A coach was just going to give me room and books. It was an easy decision to make. I wanted to be where the weather was seventy degrees every day, a 10K run on the beach was a daily routine, and running did not have to be my life.

A gift from God can be a blessing and a curse. Sometimes having a talent takes away your life. My 4:17 mile in high school at a mile above sea level in Albuquerque was among the top fifty times across the country. I wouldn't make the same mistake again. I wouldn't have to take it too seriously. Running could be my dessert.

The Painted Desert

A petrified forest

SAGUARO NATIONAL PARK

MONDAY AFTER THE ROCK 'N' ROLL ARIZONA HALF-marathon in Phoenix is always on Martin Luther King Jr. Day. It's a great day to spend in the warmer weather of Arizona's seventy degrees versus the thirties or forties in Santa Fe. A lot of folks think all of Arizona and New Mexico are always absolutely warm or hot. Not the case! The high elevation in New Mexico, coupled with the mountain towns and their ski basins, makes it a good two to four months of winter in this new global warming environment. So onward we drove south from Phoenix to Tucson. Our next national park was Saguaro.

Saguaro National Park is close to Tucson, Arizona. We got to Tucson and spent the night in a hotel next to the University of Arizona. I spent the summer of 2000 living in the Apache-Santa Cruz dorm at U of A. It was a lovely campus.

A lot of memories came back to me as we turned off the highway. We had dinner at In-N-Out Burger. We don't have any in New Mexico, so it was a treat. The lighting in these burger joints is very bright, and I remember our Logan crying a lot. He didn't like the bright lights. We ate fast, slept in our hotel, and checked out early to hike in Saguaro.

We took a main entrance to the park, one of many entrances available. The roads through the small town and scattered trailer parks are hot and dusty. We were driving in January, and I thought about how hot it must have been in July when my family had to move from Tucson back to Albuquerque before I was born. In the 1970s my father was one of the first few Hispanic physicians in the Southwest. After medical school at the University of New Mexico in Albuquerque, he got a residency in pediatrics at the University of Arizona in Tucson, where he moved with my mom and two sisters. My sisters were very young. The heat was a lot different in Tucson compared to Santa Fe, where both my parents grew up. The story was that the heat was too much for my mother, so my dad transferred back to UNM in ABQ for a residency in emergency medicine.

That was that. I would grow up as a New Mexican rather than an Arizonan all because Tucson was too hot. I totally understood my mother's pain when I lived here in the summer of 2000.

The silver lining was the monsoon season. It's more like a monsoon weekend. The sky opens and pours out almost all the rain this part of Earth will see for one whole year, drenching us like a few hours of nonstop showers!

If you've never experienced the monsoons of Tucson, Arizona, believe me, you're missing an amazing show. It makes your world stop for at least a day. You must stop everything and ponder the wonder of Mother Nature. I've only experienced Mother Nature's force like this while skiing in the Rockies and surfing the Pacific and Atlantic.

After the rains come thousands if not millions of frogs. They are everywhere! Even the streets needed to close for the duration.

We arrived at Saguaro on Monday, January 18, 2016, at around 3:00 p.m. It was warm, and I was comfortable wearing swimming trunks and a Brazilian "Neymar" soccer jersey I'd bought in Brazil the prior year. Our four-year-old Jack Russell terrier mix Krug had come along on this trip. He was happy to stretch his legs in the parking lot of the Arizona-Sonora Desert Museum there at the national park. It was a lovely museum with a few trails to walk. Dogs are usually not allowed, so we loaded ourselves and Krug into the car again. Most parks have different trails, so we all brainstormed and drove to a few hiking trails.

The five of us and one dog got out of the cars and started our journey into the national park. The trail was so easy to navigate, and all the saguaro cacti were amazing. They are out-of-this-world crazy. It reminded me of a Dr. Seuss book or movie. The saguaro can grow up to forty feet tall. That's like a four-story building. For most small towns in Middle America, that's as high as their tallest downtown buildings. While walking among these wonders, one sees how birds and other animals have made them their permanent home. In 1994 Saguaro National Park was designated to help protect the saguaros and their habitat. Saguaros have a relatively long lifespan, often exceeding 150 years. At around seventy-five to one hundred years of age, they grow their first side arm. Arms are developed to increase their reproductive capacity, as they lead to more flowers and fruit. Inside the saguaro, there are many "ribs" of wood, which form something like a skeleton, with the individual ribs being as long as the cactus itself and up to a few inches in diameter. The spines, or prickly points, on a saguaro are extremely sharp and can grow up to 2.8 inches long.

The flowers of saguaros appear from April through June and are white and waxy, opening well after sunset and closing in midafternoon. In June ruby red fruits pop up around the plant, allowing birds to perch and eat in the hot summer air. The plant is highly evolved and appears quite alien in nature. Imagine for just one moment if they became alive and started walking. That would be an interesting television or streaming series.

As our family climbed to the top of a small southwestern mound overlooking thousands of saguaros, it again made us feel like we were on another planet. Our baby was taking another nap, and it was about time to head back to the car and get on the road for a seven-hour drive back home.

As we got toward the bottom, we had an opportunity with our

little Logan for a family photo. Even our dog was part of the new family tradition.

Saguaros

GUADALUPE MOUNTAINS NATIONAL PARK

For Mother's Day in 2016 we decided to drive to El Paso, Texas. It was my wife's first Mother's Day. Liz was raised in a small town called Alamogordo, New Mexico, about ninety miles from El Paso. Now at the age of thirty-six she was a mother for the first time. We stayed in the tallest hotel in Downtown El Paso and celebrated with a walk downtown and dinner at a fancy restaurant. There was a mariachi celebration going on, with music, dancing, and a parade with horses stepping high down the middle of the street. We had our baby in a LÍLLÉbaby carrier and Krug on his leash. It was one of the first times our dog encountered horses, and he went crazy barking and jumping at them. The baby laughed, and we vowed to make sure our dog was far away from any more horses.

El Paso was also a very interesting political environment. It was the Trump verses Clinton war zone. The border was a toxic place for cultural conversations. For us it was normal, and we walked up and down the streets with our baby in tow.

Our family snuggled that night and got up early on Mother's Day to explore our third national park together. Guadalupe Mountains National Park, in the Guadalupe Mountains, is just east of El Paso,

Texas. The mountain range includes Guadalupe Peak, the highest point in all of *big* Texas at 8,749 feet above sea level. The mountain range rises three thousand feet above the desert around it. It's a landmark for travelers on the route along the Butterfield Overland Mail stagecoach line, which loops through Texas on its way from St. Louis to San Francisco.

Guadalupe National Park was established as a national park in 1972, seven years before my wife was born.

The park had a small visitor center used to stage tours with a few park rangers. We got a few questions answered and walked outside and down to an arroyo. The arroyos in New Mexico that we were used to are all plain dirt. This one looked like it was right out of the Jurassic era. This was an arroyo of gypsum rocks and sand. It was not dirt brown but rather multicolored white, like marble. As I walked my family down the arroyo, it was like walking on marble cheesecake, with the El Capitan peak in the background. We circled the wagons and reflected on how Liz and I had never been here, even though she had driven around these parts for her whole life. She had never stopped to look.

We didn't do much more than this thirty-minute walk before we got back on the road for our fourth national park. We got to talking and realized some of these stops at national parks might be rather short. This was one of them.

If you hike for a few hours, there is some great camping at Guadalupe. This would have been tough with a six-month-old baby. Maybe another year.

The drive to our next national park, Carlsbad Caverns, was only twenty-five miles.

Holding my World below the highest peak in Texas. Guadalupe Peak

CARLSBAD CAVERNS NATIONAL PARK

As we drove across the state line back into New Mexico and up to the parking lot of Carlsbad Caverns, a lot of cars were already there. Many signs said we had to check our pets into the boarding house, as it was too hot in the vehicles for them. I checked our dog into his kennel. It was already hot, and it was only early in May—Mother's Day to be exact.

Carlsbad Caverns National Park is in the Guadalupe Mountains in Southeastern New Mexico. It is one of two national parks in our home state, and in 2016 when we visited it was the only national park in New Mexico. White Sands Park was not yet designated as a national park, so to us it was a point of pride for our home state. Carlsbad Caverns became a national park in 1995, when Liz and I were in high school. We grew up four hours apart and didn't meet until we were in our twenties. As a vacationing family of four (three humans and one dog, in a kennel on this day), we were happy to be at the cave entrance. Both Liz and I had been here as children, and it hadn't changed much, except for an elevator. We decided to keep it old school and walk down the cavern walkway.

We forgot how long this walk was. We were also carrying a baby boy. The most popular route, the Big Room, is the largest single cave chamber by volume in North America. The trail from the top is about 1.25 miles, so when you get there, it feels as if you are in the largest cathedral you can imagine, its dome soaring 255 feet above you. Instead of religious artifacts, art, and statues of saints, Mother Nature was its designer. It is a masterpiece, weaving large limestone chambers almost four thousand feet long, 625 feet wide, and as high as a twenty-five-story building. Imagine vacationing in a desert town in Europe and taking an elevator twenty-five stories high to get to the top of the cathedral. You feel the impact of this enormous space, and you also sense the difference in air pressure, the moist environment, and the artificial lighting. It's like a journey to the bottom of the world with a theatrical spectacle to think, pray, and marvel at the wonders of our Earth. It is out of this world. A must-see.

As we walked up the path, I realized carrying a sleeping baby was tough. I had run many marathons, but this was a different exercise. It was a meditation on keeping the baby sleeping and weight lifting all at the same time. I sensed during this fourth national park adventure that fatherhood would be a similar balancing act—an act to please my spirit, keep the peace, and walk where we had in the past with a new perspective. This would be our legacy!

The Caverns Sign

The Cave entrance

ROCKY MOUNTAIN NATIONAL PARK

BIRTHDAYS ARE A YEARLY REMINDER THAT WE ARE A BIT more mature. Some say older, but in today's politically correct environment "older" is sometimes hinted as incorrect. On July 16, 2016, I turned thirty-six. At eighteen, growing up in Albuquerque, I could not imagine my life doubled. Here it was. I was a man doubled. Eighteen is said to be the age when you are technically an adult. What was thirty-six? I was now a husband and a new father. What should we do for my birthday?

On my birthday, we drove to Rocky Mountain National Park. We spent the previous night in a very large hotel in Colorado Springs to break up the drive. I had gone for a long run, and my wife and our newborn drove to follow me to various spots to give me Gatorade. I wanted to run twenty miles but compromised on sixteen when my legs didn't want to go anymore.

We planned to hit the road on an adventure to two more parks. I decided I would take a few days off work so we could explore some parts of the fine state of Colorado. We stopped in Denver to have lunch with one of my best friends and my aunt Flo and uncle Ken, who was born in Denver. He was nearing seventy and had seen Denver grow from a few hundred thousand people to a few million people. In 2016 Denver was one of the fastest growing cities in the United States.

Liz ordered the guacamole, as Logan loved avocados. We were busy talking up a storm when suddenly Logan started screaming. Yikes! It took us a minute to realize it was the hot sauce in the guac. He was crying and creating a scene, but everyone understood. After all, he was only eight months, three weeks, two days, and eight hours old. Oh, gosh! He was just under the age of nine months.

We ate our lunch, talked our heads off, and listened to my uncle's tales of the park then and now. Both my friend, aunt, and uncle had not seen Logan, and they were excited for us to be a family. My friend was in his forties and had never had a child. My aunt had a daughter, my cousin, from a previous marriage that Uncle Ken had raised as his own. He did not have a biological child. They all liked our goal of visiting the national parks and were happy to see us. We departed the parking lot together and waved our goodbyes.

Rocky Mountain National Park was about an hour-and-forty-minute drive from the bustling city of Denver. It's about 78.1 miles from downtown to the park. The traffic from Denver thinned as the rain started to pound our windshield just north of Boulder. I had never driven north of Boulder, so this was new to us.

We stopped for the night, checking into a nice, newly remodeled motel and took a dip in the hot tub. The couple in the hot tub were also visiting the park and had been on a day's long hike. They liked that we were starting our national park adventure with the baby, even as young as he was. Logan, meanwhile, was splashing, gurgling, and delighting our new friends.

The next morning, we ate our continental breakfast and, after a morning run, drove to the park. We were on the trail by 9:30 a.m. It was July 17, 2016, and the day after my birthday could not have been more perfect.

A shuttle waited at the parking lot to take us to our hiking trail. Krug was with us. As I opened our car, our dog ran off to see the mountain. We saw a sign that dogs were not allowed, but we didn't want to keep him in the motel room. So back into the car he went. A park ranger lady came up to us. She said, "I don't mean to worry you, but dogs don't do so well in cars. It's not a policy, but make sure you leave the windows down."

We thanked her, and before we left the car, we did leave the windows down. That left me a little uneasy. Although our dog in the past had done okay with the windows down, it still bothered me that we couldn't bring him along. I understood the rules. The day was not going to be too hot, about eighty or so, and we were at 9,475 feet above sea level. We left Krug behind reluctantly. He watched us go, his head hanging out the window sadly.

Once we got on the trail, I could understand why this park was one of the most popular in the world. The eastern and western slopes of the Continental Divide separate the western and eastern rain runoff, running directly through the center of the Rocky Mountain National Park. The Colorado River is in Rocky Mountain's northwestern region. The park includes many mountains, alpine lakes, and a variety of wildlife within various climates and environments, from wooded forests to mountain tundra.

The history of Rocky Mountain National Park began when Paleo-Indians traveled along what is now Trail Ridge Road to hunt and forage for food. Ute and Arapaho people subsequently hunted and camped in the area. In 1820 or so, the Long Expedition, led by Stephen H. Long, for whom the Longs Peak was named, approached the Rocky Mountains via the Platte River. Settlers began arriving in the mid-1800s, displacing the Native Americans, who mostly left the area voluntarily by 1860, while others were removed to reservations by 1878. In the 1870s prospectors came in search of gold and silver. Their hopes for a gold dream of prosperity did not come true. The boom ended by 1883 with miners deserting their claims and returning to their place of origin.

The railroad reached Lyons, Colorado, in 1881, and the Big

Thompson Canyon Road—a section of U.S. Route 34 from Loveland to Estes Park—was completed in 1904.

The Rocky Mountain National Park Act was signed by President Woodrow Wilson on January 26, 1915, establishing the park boundaries and protecting the area for future generations. Enos Mills was a prominent individual in the effort to create Rocky Mountain National Park.

Enos Abijah Mills (1870–1922) was an American naturalist, author, and homesteader. He was the main public figure behind the creation of Rocky Mountain National Park. Enos was born into a family of ten brothers and sisters in Pleasanton, Kansas. He moved to Colorado in 1884 at the age of fourteen. He had an unidentifiable illness, which was later discovered to be an allergy to wheat, and was advised to move to a higher elevation, an accepted treatment for the times. At age fifteen he made his first ascent to Longs Peak. Over the course of his life, he made the adventure more than forty times by himself and nearly three hundred additional times as a guide. He built his homestead near Longs Peak and the town of Estes Park at the age of fifteen, completing it at age sixteen.

I don't know about you, but I was just selling sneakers at Foot Locker at the age of sixteen. This guy moved away from home, built a home, and hiked to mountaintops. That's courageous.

Mills loved the mountains, and his travels through the West led him to California, where he met John Muir. Muir inspired Mills to focus on sharing his love of nature.

At the time, there were no limits on what people could do in the mountains. Miners dug into the earth, loggers felled huge swaths of trees, and tourists pulled whatever they wanted of the plants and wildflowers along the hiking paths.

Mills took his lead from Muir, who had established Yosemite National Park to protect the sequoias. Mills led the fight to preserve the Rocky Mountains as a national park too. He used his speeches, his writings, and photography to lobby for the park, and in 1915 Congress created the Rocky Mountain National Park. Mills was called the "Father of Rocky Mountain National Park" by *The Denver Post*.

The 1920s saw a boom in building lodges and roads in the park, culminating with the construction of Trail Ridge Road to Fall River Pass between 1929 and 1932, then to Grand Lake by 1938.

Rocky Mountain National Park encompasses 265,461 acres of federal land, with an additional 253,059 acres of US Forest Service wilderness adjoining the park boundaries. The Continental Divide runs generally north-south through the center of the park, with rivers and streams on the western side of the divide flowing toward the Pacific Ocean, while those on the eastern side flow toward the Atlantic. The park contains approximately 450 miles of rivers and streams, 350 miles of trails, and 150 lakes. The headwaters of the Colorado River are in the park's northwestern region.

Rocky Mountain National Park is one of the highest national parks in the nation, with elevations from 7,860 to 14,259 feet. The highest point is Longs Peak. The Civilian Conservation Corps built the main automobile route, Trail Ridge Road, in the 1930s. Trail Ridge Road is the highest paved through-road in the country, with a peak elevation of 12,183 feet. There are more than sixty mountain peaks over twelve thousand feet high. They provide some of the best scenic vistas in the world.

In 1976 UNESCO (United Nations Educational, Scientific, and Cultural Organization) designated the park as one of the first World Biosphere Reserves. These reserves are designated as sites for learning and managing ecological systems and biodiversity.

As we boarded the bus to our trailhead, I noticed how busy this park was. It was like being at Disneyland for naturalists and nature enthusiasts.

We got off the bus and started walking. Now I know why it was so busy. It was a mountainous paradise. Trees, lakes, streams, waterfalls, flowers, animals, and people were everywhere. There are five regions to Rocky National Park. We were in Region 4. This region is known as "Heart of the Park" and is known for its great climbs or hiking. Region

4 has easy road and trail access, great views, and lake hikes, including the most popular trails. We walked around Bear Lake, Dream Lake, and Nymph Lake. We stopped often to take pictures with Logan and so he could play. At one particular stop, next to a wonderful waterfall, a chipmunk came right up to Logan's cute chubby fingers, and they instantly became best friends. Several families and hikers stopped to watch the interaction with our baby and this chipmunk. It was our son's first face-to-face encounter with a live critter in nature. Priceless.

We hiked back down, Logan now sleeping, boarded the bus, got to our car and to Krug, who was happy to see us. We walked him in the lot and to some trails nearby, giving him a good run before returning to the motel.

The next day we had an appointment to get professional family photos with a photographer who lived in the area. Our photo shoot was on another side of the park. We dressed the part of an adventurous family. Our photographer took us to wild spots off the Trail Ridge Road. He knew the places to go, stop, and take family photos. One of these photos would become our go-to family portrait for years to come. How can you put into words the feeling of being immersed in Mother Nature with your young family? These photos did the job! We thanked our photographer, who promised to send the photos in a few days, and went our separate ways.

As a family on the road, a photo shoot to boot, and spectacular views we had never seen, we were suddenly very hungry. We stopped at The Stanley Hotel for lunch. This is a famous hotel that many refer to as *The Shining* hotel from Stephen King's scary novel. We had lunch outside where every view was out of this world. My BLT was delicious.

After such a busy day, we passed out on our bed in our motel room for a good nap. It was dinnertime by the time we woke up, windy, and I only had energy for a four-mile run. We ate dinner at a unique eatery that had items on the menu from the catches by local hunters. I walked our baby around, and he laughed at all the animals on the wall, and patrons laughed with us.

We went to bed with our hearts filled with joy. We woke up early to drive to our next national park.

Rockies

ANTONIO LOPEZ

Sun Stream

A Rocky Peak

Family Valley

GREAT SAND DUNES NATIONAL PARK

COLORADO, TUESDAY, JULY 19, 2016: OUR NEXT NATIONAL park was Great Sand Dunes National Park, just north of the New Mexico state line. This park contains the largest sand dunes in North America. As we drove into the park, we didn't really see the spectacle right away. We ran into a forest that rises unexpectedly from the desert. It may be the most dramatic entry into a national park in the country.

As with many national parks, we could zip right past the entry and enter the park without stopping, no reservations needed. We had stayed in a town called Salida, Colorado, the night before, where the fast-moving Arkansas River runs right through. The closest city to Great Sand Dunes is Alamosa, Colorado. Growing up, my nana on my dad's side lived in Alamosa. I called her Nana Alamosa. Although she had been born and raised in Lamy and Santa Fe, New Mexico, her first husband died in World War II when my father and his twin sisters were very young. Nana Alamosa worked at Sears on Lincoln Avenue in downtown Santa Fe. Her second husband, also a World War II veteran, was visiting family in Santa Fe when he ran into her there. The man would go to Sears every time he was in Santa Fe. He worked for the government and owned a gas station in Alamosa. That's how my nana ended up next to Great Sand Dunes. Growing up, I never heard of this place. I don't even remember my nana or grandpa talking about it. Yet it was so close to where they lived all those years. At times, in the winter, the San Luis Valley may be the coldest place in the contiguous forty-eight states. The valley is surrounded by huge mountains that encapsulate the coldness—a different world from Santa Fe, where we live.

The sand dunes are as tall as 750 feet (229 meters) on the eastern edge of the San Luis Valley, and an adjacent national preserve is located in the Sangre de Cristo Range in South-Central Colorado. The park was originally designated Great Sand Dunes National Monument on March 17, 1932, by President Herbert Hoover. It became a national park in 2004 by an act of Congress. The park encompasses 107,342 acres while the preserve protects an additional 41,686 acres, for a total of 149,028 acres. Approximately half a million people visit every year. Liz and I had visited once before, but not with our new family. Our son Logan was now almost nine months. As we approached the parking lot, we saw some deer in the fields; the streams from the mountains above were flowing through the dunes, but there was a lot of activity. It was like parking at a Southern California beach. The lot was almost full, and people in bathing suits were carrying inner tubes from old tires, plastic snow sleds, and boogie boards. The last time Liz and I were here there wasn't this much commotion. People were frolicking in the streams and sliding down the dunes. Sandboarding and sand sledding are popular activities, both done on specially designed equipment that can be rented just outside the park or in Alamosa. They were taking Mother Nature for a ride. With a nine-month-old and a dog on a leash, we were less mobile than most visitors on this summer day. I recall the sand was hard to maneuver with shoes on, so I took them off. After three steps my feet were very hot. I ran to the water that was flowing like a river in the middle of *our* Sahara Desert.

This was Medano Creek. The creek typically has a peak flow from late May to early June. This year the runoff was good for a few more months and provided coolness for our feet. I cooled off my toes. Krug lay in the watery mud to cool his paws off too. This is where we took some very dramatic photos. Not only did we have the largest sand dunes in the hemisphere, but a large rocky mountain chain as a backdrop. Blue skies with clusters of clouds outline the dramatic hues that Mother Nature creates. The seasonal river that runs through looks like a muddy oasis that travelers stopped at to refresh during their journey.

The oldest evidence of humans in this region dates to around eleven thousand years. Some of the first people to enter the San Luis Valley and the Great Sand Dunes were Stone Age nomadic hunter-gatherers whose connection to the area centered around the herds of mammoths and prehistoric bison. They hunted with large stone spear or dart points now identified as Clovis and Folsom points. These people only stayed when hunting and plant gathering was good and avoided the region during times of drought and scarcity, especially as the winters sometimes lasted many months.

Modern American Indians were very familiar with the area when the Spanish conquistadors first arrived around the seventeenth century. The Ute phrase for the Great Sand Dunes is *saa waap maa nache* (sand that moves). Jicarilla Apaches settled in Northern New Mexico and called the dunes *sei-anyedi* (it goes up and down). Blanca Peak, which is located southeast of the dunes, is one of the four sacred mountains in the Navajo tradition. The Navajo call it "*Sisnaajini*" (White Shell Mountain).

In 1694 Don Diego de Vargas became the first European known to have traveled into the San Luis Valley. Although herders and hunters from Spanish colonies in present-day Northern New Mexico probably entered the valley as early as 1598, de Vargas and his men hunted a herd of five hundred bison in the valley before returning to Santa Fe. De Vargas, the Spanish governor of Santa Fe de Nuevo México, brought back skins and meat and many tales of a wild land up north. The days and nights were frigid.

His land fostered little change for the next centuries. Juan Bautista de Anza, Zebulon Pike, John C. Frémont, and John Gunnison all traveled through and explored parts of the region in the eighteenth and nineteenth centuries. The explorers and their servants were soon followed by settlers who ranched, farmed, and mined in the valley starting in the nineteenth century. Great Sand Dunes National Park was first established as a national monument in 1932 to protect it from gold mining and limit the potential of a concrete manufacturing business. Our visit checked off one of the most majestic parks in our land from our growing to-do list.

Check. Pinned our map. Success!

The sand mountain

Krug paws in the Medano Creek

JOSHUA TREE NATIONAL PARK

JOSHUA TREE, CALIFORNIA, DECEMBER 1, 2016: WE FLEW from Albuquerque into LAX and rented a car to drive to our seventh national park. It was an approximate three-hour drive to Joshua Tree National Park from our nation's second largest city. The city fell away to sparse desert. We had never made this drive before. Our son was now just over thirteen months old and slept most of the way. He was still dressed in his oh so cute pajamas. It was a green onesie with white stripes and puppies as the feet that matched the one on his left breast. He was truly the apple of our eyes.

We knew he would barely remember this park, but we also knew it was much easier to travel with babies under two years of age, who fly for free, and work through our vast list of national parks.

Throughout the drive from LAX to Joshua Tree, we had seen a few of the spiky, twisted Joshua trees, but as we drove on the narrow road into the park we saw masses and masses of these wonders. We stopped at the turnoff into the park for a photo in front of the handsome entrance sign.

Joshua Tree was named a national park in 1994 when the US Congress passed the California Desert Protection Act. This act created

790,636 acres of preservation. Joshua Tree takes up 429,690 of these acres.

Joshua Tree National Park encompasses two deserts, varied by elevation, which are the Mojave Desert and the lower Colorado Desert. The Little San Bernardino Mountains traverse the southwest edge of the park.

The trees all around the park looked like a groomed Hollywood set, and in fact, as we drove into a parking lot, there was a set for a photo shoot for a rock band. Our little Logan was just waking up and amazed by the noise, the bright lights, and general commotion.

We took off up the road and stopped for our own photo shoot. Liz stood ready with her smartphone as I threw our year-old baby into the air and caught him with these amazing trees in the background.

Joshua trees are the plant Yucca brevifolia. It is a plant species belonging to the genus Yucca. It is native to the arid Southwestern United States, specifically in California, Arizona, Utah, and Nevada, where it is confined mostly to the Mojave Desert between thirteen hundred and fifty-nine hundred feet above sea level. The Joshua tree barely has any leaves, just a few balls on the tips of their branches.

The name "Joshua tree" came possibly from the Mormon settlers crossing the Mojave Desert in the mid-nineteenth century. There is a biblical story in which Joshua keeps his hands reached out for an extended period of time to guide the Israelites in their conquest of Canaan. The tree's role was to guide the Mormon settlers crossing the desert with its unique shape that reminded them of Joshua's hands reaching out for an extended period of time to guide those before them.

> Then the LORD said to Joshua, "Hold out toward Ai the javelin that is in your hand, for into your hand I will deliver the city." So Joshua held out toward the city the javelin that was in his hand.
>
> — JOSHUA 8:18, NIV

Looking out at the landscape of Joshua Tree feels a bit biblical. How could anyone survive in this hostile desert?

The Natives of Joshua Tree roamed the desert between eight thousand and four thousand years before Christ. They were known as the Pinto Culture. Their stone tools and spear points, uncovered in the Pinto Basin in the 1930s, suggest they hunted game and gathered seasonal plants, but little else is known about them. Throughout the next few thousand years, four native tribes roamed this area. They were the Serrano, Cahuilla, Chemehuevi, and Mojaves. These Mojaves used the local Joshua trees and other resources in Joshua Tree National Park as they traveled along the trails between the Colorado River and the Pacific Coast.

In 1772 a group of Spaniards led by Pedro Fages made the first European sightings of Joshua trees while pursuing native converts to Christianity who had run away from a mission in San Diego. In 1823, the year Mexico achieved independence from Spain, a Mexican expedition from Los Angeles, in what was then Alta, California, is thought to have explored as far east as the Eagle Mountains in what later became the park. In 1826 Jedediah Smith led a group of fur trappers and some explorers along the nearby Mojave Trail. Others soon followed. Two decades later the United States defeated Mexico in the Mexican-American War (1846–1848) and took over about half of Mexico's original territory, including Joshua Tree National Park. Between the 1860s and 1940s, miners were in about three hundred pits in the park. On August 10, 1936, after Minerva Hoyt and others persuaded the state and federal governments to protect the area, President Franklin D. Roosevelt used the power of the Antiquities Act of 1906 to establish Joshua Tree National Monument, protecting about 825,000 acres. The monument became a national park on October 31, 1994, another reason to celebrate Halloween. Our son was born on October 24, about a week before Halloween, so this time of year has much meaning for our small family.

As we drove the entire road in Joshua Tree National Park, we made a few stops where there were hikers, bikers, rock climbers, and people camping in tents and recreational vehicles. It was December and very hot for this time of year, probably the perfect time to be in this park. As the temperature gets warm to baking throughout the year, playtime diminishes. On one of our stops, we did a two-mile circular hike. It took us around a mesa, into a mine, around an arroyo, past some petroglyphs, and back to the parking lot.

Krug was not with us since we don't fly with our twenty-pound dog, so we didn't have to worry about the arid temperatures on the long walk.

I found it amazing that text messages on my smartwatch came in while on the walk, even so remote from the big city. Since this park is in between Los Angeles and Palm Springs, one has the luxury of modern technology, unlike other parks.

We arrived at our car exhausted, very hungry, and with a baby boy still in the pajamas he woke up in two states away.

A toss into the Joshuas

The rocks at Joshua

CHANNEL ISLANDS NATIONAL PARK

We had a wonderful brunch close to Joshua Tree National Park after we left their official visitor center. It was so good, and our baby was ready to eat. We then drove more than three hours straight to our fancy hotel in Westlake Village. Presidents, dignitaries, and celebrities have stayed at the Four Seasons there, and we were amazed with our valet service, check in, the excellent holiday decorations, and our huge room.

That night we had sushi in a hotel restaurant that is among the top five in the Los Angeles area. Our son loved sushi with salmon and avocado like a true foodie.

On December 2, 2016, my family drove our rental car from the Four Seasons in Westlake Village to Ventura, California. We boarded a boat that motored to Channel Islands National Park. The boat ride was the most awesome ride we have taken before or since. The short trip should have been about thirty minutes. However, there was so much wildlife in the Pacific Ocean that the team of sailors circled around to allow the passengers to see the sea creatures. We saw pods of dolphins, sea lions, otters, and a few whales. Wow, if you have never done this, I'd say this is in my top ten of all our adventures.

Then we got to our island. An employee of the Nature Conservancy was ready to take us on a guided hiking tour of the island.

Channel Islands National Park consists of five islands of the eight Channel Islands off the Pacific Coast. Untouched by development, they took us back many centuries, as if we were seeing Southern California before people lived there.

The park covers 249,561 acres, of which 79,019 acres are federal land. The Nature Conservancy owns and manages 76 percent of Santa Cruz Island, the largest of the eight. This national park was established on March 5, 1980, and in 2018 had 366,250 visitors. In my opinion this is the best kept secret in Southern California. If I could live in any national park, this would be the one.

Juan Cabrillo first observed the islands around 1542, just fifty years after Chris Columbus came across the East Coast/Caribbean.

Research says people first roamed these islands thirty-seven thousand years ago. A burned mammoth bone was dated at thirty thousand years ago. Three islands were inhabited by an estimated two to three thousand Chumash, with dozens of villages. In my opinion, this is the most scenic Native American village in our country.

As we got off the boat with our one-year-old, we immediately felt a sense of tranquility. The Nature Conservancy lead hikers gave us instructions. We could go with them and the group or stop at any time. They would then turn around at about one to two miles away. Our group consisted of approximately twenty adults and ten children. One couple had a permit to camp for a few days and were given free range.

The first thing we noticed were the abundant island foxes. They were not shy and would come up to us and beg for food. Our guides explained their sociability compared to mainland California.

The island fox is a small fox that is endemic to the islands. Endemism is the state of a species being found in a single defined geographic location, such as an island. If you've ever seen the Disney-Pixar movie *Zootopia*, it's as if Nick Wilde was everywhere, asking us for food. They followed and were not afraid to befriend anyone. No wonder we couldn't bring our dog. Island foxes played an important role in the spiritual lives of Native Channel Islanders. The island fox is significantly smaller than the related gray fox and is the smallest fox in North America. The island fox on first sight looks RED! However, looking more closely it has gray on its head, ruddy red on its sides, white on its belly, throat, and lower face, and has a black stripe on the dorsal surface of its tail. Our son loved these foxes, and we did too.

We were hiking next to a middle-aged couple. They lived close by and had never been to this national park. We told them about our goal of visiting all the national parks with our little baby. They had grown children and had taken them to many parks as a young family. We mentioned Alaska's eight parks, and they enthusiastically shared the memories they had of visiting all eight.

Our group thinned out as some stopped to look at the most beautiful hike views in Southern California. You could see the Pacific Ocean waves below, trees climbing to the sky, a mist in the distance. The pollution was nowhere nearby, but it was a shadow over the mainland. We decided to stop at an overlook where there was about a half acre for Logan to crawl and play far enough from the overlook to be safe while we enjoyed the view. As we were talking to our friends, we saw Logan stumble and roll over headfirst in the grass. Liz and I looked at each other like we were the worst parents on the island. Lo and behold, he got right up and started laughing. It was the spirit of the fox. At that moment, I knew the fox got into him. He was smiling like he was in the best sandbox on Earth. We let the group go, and we decided to hang out here with him. By the time we left, Logan was red with dirt. He looked like a little island fox. He was tired. Harnessed to me, I could feel him fall asleep on the hike back to our beach where the boat would be waiting.

When the boat arrived, and we watched the new passengers get off, a few island foxes came to visit. At first I was very protective of our baby. Then I sensed Mother Nature would allow us to reach out.

We touched a fox. He was like a household pet asking for a treat. He looked at us like asking for food was his nine-to-five occupation.

Then we heard the call to board. On the way back to Ventura, we again witnessed the majesty of the Pacific. We saw more dolphins, fish, birds, and one large whale. We got back at sunset and walked to the beach.

While on the way to the Patagonia store in Ventura, we got into a string of fender benders on the highway off-ramp lane. Luckily, although our car incurred minor damage, we were not injured. A few of the cars behind us were significantly damaged, but, again, no one was hurt. We all exchanged driver's licenses on our smartphones and took pictures. It was another blessing from above that our baby, still sound asleep, was safe. What a day to remember!

Untouched Island

Put me down mom

Another picture guys

The Best Sandbox on Earth

ACADIA NATIONAL PARK

Acadia National Park is in the state of Maine next to Bar Harbor. Our hotel was close to the College of the Atlantic. I remember waking up before dawn to run four to six miles and thinking it was more frigid in April in Maine than February in Santa Fe. When I passed the College of the Atlantic and entered Bar Harbor, it put a smile on my face as the college campus looked like Hogwarts.

Of the nine parks we had visited so far, Acadia National Park was the most inhabited, urban park we'd ventured into. The park preserves about half of Mount Desert Island, part of the Isle au Haut, the tip of the Schoodic Peninsula, and portions of sixteen smaller outlying islands. It protects the natural beauty of the rocky headlands, including one of the highest mountains along the Atlantic Coast: Cadillac Mountain. In 2020 there were more than 2.6 million visitors to Acadia. Woven into the landscape is a historic carriage road system financed by John D. Rockefeller Jr. between 1919 and 1931. As of 2017 the park encompassed just under fifty thousand acres total.

Acadia has a rich history of Native American life. More than ten thousand years ago the Wabanaki tribe flourished in this beautiful, abundant land. In the seventeenth century, the abundance of wildlife brought fur trappers and traders from all over the world. These were the first European explorers to this part of New England. Then in the nineteenth century an influx of wealthy families built summer homes, and a wave of summer tourists came to see what the latest craze was all about. Think Aspen, Colorado, in the early 1990s. Or Austin, Texas, in the early 2010s.

This could have been the birthplace of the American conservationist. People saw others as destroying this majestic place. Urban development was on the rise. Many didn't want to see this sacred ground as the new New Amsterdam or Toronto.

Many worked to establish this first park east of the Mississippi River and the only one in the Northeastern United States. Acadia was first designated as Sieur de Monts National Monument by proclamation of President Woodrow Wilson in 1916, then renamed the redesignated Lafayette National Park in 1919. A part of me wishes it had stayed Lafayette, only because I grew up on Lafayette Drive NE in Albuquerque, New Mexico.

The park was renamed Acadia National Park in 1929. "Acadia" (French: Acadie) was a colony of New France in and around Maine. The name Acadia is primarily a female name of French origin that means "idyllic place." It originated from the Latin name "Arcadia."

Talk about an idyllic place! If this place were open—or should I say the weather were "idyllic" year-round like the Channel Islands or Southern California—it would have tens, if not hundreds of millions, of visitors per year. Maybe that's why God put such a special place in a cold environment. The moisture and snow create a garden for wildlife. The Atlantic Ocean brings sounds we'll never hear anywhere else. The mountains give views we only see in movies. Perhaps we went in the wrong month. Only 50 percent of restaurants and shops were open. We tried to eat at a famous lobster joint on the Atlantic, and the sign said it would open during the month of June. Herds of people and entrepreneurs come in for the summer months to serve the tourists from the shops and eateries. Driving through the neighborhoods we realized it's a cold and somewhat unwelcoming place.

On April 24, 2017, we went on two wonderful hikes. One was to Cadillac Mountain. They say it can sometimes take hours to get to this peak in the summer due to the traffic. It took us less than fifteen minutes. When we got out of our rental car, the wind was so blustery that we had to take turns because it was way too cold for our one-year-old. It felt like the temperature was below zero, and I bet it was.

We were standing on the highest mountain point on the East Coast. At 1,530 feet above the Atlantic Ocean, Cadillac Mountain is known as the first place in the US to see the sunrise, although that is only true for a portion of the year.

We reached the peak on Cadillac Mountain, and we realized for the sweet two minutes we could bear there in the cold, we would be by our lonesome. There would be no warm hike around the peak on this cold April day. Sometimes in parks we wish we had visited in the summer. This, however, was a dream come true. We had the mountaintop to ourselves.

On the way down we stopped at the Jordan Pond Path. This 1.5-mile hike was on an interesting foundation. The path was our favorite of the trip. We toted our son in his baby carrier around our bodies, and his warmth was enough to keep one of us warm. The path was loaded with timber used to make a path. The pond had flooded the area, and during portions of the hike, we had to walk a foot from the ground on planks of wood. The trail follows the shore of Jordan Pond, allowing iconic views of steep, glacially sculpted mountains and the glacially carved valley that is now Jordan Pond. The trail is rugged in some sections. Good footwear is recommended. Before this vacation I went to our local running store in Santa Fe, The Running Hub, and bought Nike trail shoes for me and my wife. We were wearing them, and they came in handy for sure!

If you put the Jordan Pond Path on your list, think "Walk the plank." It feels like you are constantly on a wooden plank. This hiking was so much different from hiking in the Rocky Mountains, but enjoyable. If Rocky Mountain National Park was our Venus, then Acadia was our Jupiter—both out of this world and, for the East Coast, perhaps the best national park hiking east of the Mississippi. Go on and get your hike on! We'll have to return to this one next time we visit New England.

Atop Cadillac Mountain

Jordan Pond Path

The Atlantic in Acadia

Logan hikes the Acadia trails

Where the sun rises first in the US

EVERGLADES AND BISCAYNE NATIONAL PARKS

My family went with me to a work conference in Orlando, Florida, in June 2017. While I was at my conference, Liz took our almost two-year-old Logan to Disney World. I was ready for the conference to be over as we had planned a week-long Florida national parks vacation. The weather was hot and humid, and I had to run at 5:00 a.m. to avoid dying of heatstroke. Finally, the conference was over, and we drove to the contemporary Miami South Beach hotel. We had never been to this part of Miami. As a child I once took a cruise out of Miami but really did not see the city or the culture. Liz had never been to Miami. Miami is a cultural mecca. As we drove from Orlando, passed by the colorful skyscrapers of Miami, and parked at the beach, we knew we were in for some good downtime, food, and adventures. We were right.

We checked into the SLS South Beach Miami and were intrigued. What a good pick. The pool had huge tin rubber ducky statues that our son loved. He splashed in the pool, laughing and flapping his arms as we held him. The very attractive, young, scantily clad single patrons of the hotel pool applauded, and I wondered if they loved us for the way they could see themselves in five or ten years.

The restaurant in our hotel was The Bazaar by José Andrés. Wow, was the food out of this world. They characterize it as Spanish tapas with an Asian and island taste. Our son gobbled down the dragon fruit ceviche, which was gastronomy at its finest. The pink dragon fruit foam on top of the ceviche was so wonderfully delicious. This was our son's first fine-dining experience on vacation, and he was dressed to the nines. It was very cute to see a mini me devouring fine cuisine at one of Chef Andrés's restaurants.

Our room was spacious enough for three people from New Mexico. If you aligned yourself just right, you could see the Atlantic Ocean and the hustle and bustle of Collins Avenue from our windows. Every twelve hours the three of us would walk to the beach and either dip our toes in or jump in headfirst.

Having lived in and around Pacific Beach in San Diego for five years, I knew the round-trip run was about six miles, or a 10K run. I asked my dad before I came to South Beach how long it was, and he said it was very similar. He had been here with my mom for conferences and vacation.

One morning, luckily I tucked some cash into my pockets because I tried to run the length of South Beach, and my dad was wrong. By the sixth mile I was concerned this beach would go on forever. It felt like a hundred degrees by 10:00 a.m., with 100 percent humidity. I finally stopped, got some coffee, and found a cab to jump into. Researching the beach later, I realized you could turn a round-trip run into about twenty miles. I think I ended up running about eight miles, and I was only looking for a six-miler. Sometimes on vacation it's smart to stash some cash in your pocket before you go for a run.

When I got back, my wife and son were having the time of their lives in our plush dwelling. If one could define contemporary hotel design, this hotel room was the dictionary definition for contemporary. I had to stop myself from almost passing out when I got to the room from the longer-than-expected run at a fast pace. When I finally got my bearings, I could see how my family would be if we were living in a contemporary city such as Miami Beach. Old Santa Fe does influence the classic Western lifestyle you live. I could see in my little family that they had evolved in the moment. Now we were cool. YEAH, we were contemporary.

We got ready to drive to Everglades National Park. Our one and only stop in this massive park was at the Shark Valley Visitor Center. There we walked the Bobcat Boardwalk Trail. On the trail we saw many American crocodiles and their babies. It was very hot. We also heard from some park rangers about the topography, the many animals, wildlife, and what makes this park tick.

With a two-year-old and the heat, we took it easy on this one. An average of one million people a year visit the Everglades. For some reason my imagination got the best of me while driving next to the Everglades, and for a boy from the Southwest, it's a bit different and looks to be right out of a horror movie.

What lies below the surface?

Watch out, there's a gator!

These were a couple things going through my mind. We really wanted to go on a full-day Everglades airboat ride, but our son was too young. Next time we are in South Florida we will have to book one.

Everglades National Park is the largest tropical wilderness in the United States. It is approximately 1.5 million acres. The Grand Canyon is number eleven at 1.2 million acres, and Kobuk Valley is number nine in Alaska with 1.7 million acres.

The Everglades is the third largest national park in the contiguous United States after Death Valley and Yellowstone. The park was established primarily to preserve a fragile ecosystem. This makes Everglades a bit different, as most national parks are established to preserve some unique geographic features. This park is here to save the animals, including fish and birds, and it's a significant breeding ground for tropical wading birds in North America. The park has the largest mangrove ecosystem in the Western Hemisphere. Almost forty threatened or protected species inhabit the park, including cultural favorites: the Florida panther, the American crocodile, the Florida manatee, 350 species of birds, three hundred species of fish, forty species of mammals, and fifty species of reptiles. For human life in South Florida, almost all the fresh water, which is stored in the Biscayne Aquifer, is recharged in Everglades Park.

Humans more than likely have lived here for ten to twenty thousand years. Two Native American tribes developed on the peninsula's southern tip: The Tequesta lived on the eastern side and the Calusa, greater in numbers, on the western side. The National Park Service reports there were probably twenty thousand natives living in or near the Everglades when the Spanish established contact with them in the sixteenth century. Disease, warfare (mostly from the Creek, or Muscogee, Natives), and capture for slavery were the reasons for the eradication of most of the twenty thousand Tequesta and Calusa people. Neither the Tequesta nor Calusa tribes existed by 1800. In the early nineteenth century, Creeks, escaped African slaves, and other Natives from North Florida displaced by the Creek War formed the area's Seminole Tribe of Florida. This is the famous mascot of Florida State University. After the end of the Seminole War in 1842, the Seminoles faced relocation to Oklahoma in this region's Trail of Tears. However, a few hundred Seminole hunters and scouts settled in the area and from 1859 to 1930 lived in relative isolation, making their living by trading.

In 1934 the United States made the Everglades a national park. The park was established to protect the quickly vanishing ecosystem. The ecosystem in Everglades National Park has suffered tremendously from human activity, and restoration of the Everglades is a politically charged issue in South Florida.

As we heard from the rangers at Shark Valley Visitor Center, the Everglades is always evolving. We took our two-year-old son on the Bobcat Boardwalk Trail. We were stunned by how abundant life was around us. It was crawling, flying, and swimming everywhere. I counted more than twenty American crocodiles in less than thirty minutes. Most of them were babies. I wanted to pick them up and hold them. I even got so close that my wife warned me she wouldn't go get me if the mom charged. Yikes! I kept my distance from these prehistoric beasts.

At that moment, the link between dinosaurs and I came alive. There's something about crocodiles in the wild. They just go about their business. The eight-hundred-meter or half-mile Bobcat Boardwalk Trail was just right for parents with a two-year-old son. It was a self-guided boardwalk trail that meandered through the sawgrass slough and tropical hardwood forests.

If you were to transport us from Santa Fe to its exact opposite landscape in America, it would be the Everglades. Swamp beneath our feet instead of rocky mountain, an ocean to the east and lake above, compared to dense desert and mountain topography, made this park and its prehistoric predators that sloshed around such an amazing experience. We were in another world in our own country.

That's the value of our parks. Controversy or not, national parks are worth it. Every time the Everglades makes the news, I watch and listen. I think it has more to teach us in the future than we must give it today.

As we exited the center, our tummies were rumblin'. We ate a very tasty meal at a Native American restaurant a few miles away. We saw some airboats go by. We were jealous. We will be back, if only in our dreams, Mr. and Mrs. Everglade! Glide on Mother Nature and be contemporary.

We returned to our hotel, dazzled by all we had seen. The next day we would check out and go to Biscayne National Park and thereafter to the Keys.

We went to Biscayne National Park on June 16, 2017. We drove our rental car from Miami Beach to the Dante Fascell Visitor Center, just east and on the beach of Homestead, Florida. Of all the towns and cities we had been to on our adventures, Homestead was sandwiched in between two national parks: the Everglades to the west and the Atlantic Ocean and Biscayne to the east. To me, Homestead looked like a suburb of Miami with many amenities. This park is 95 percent in the water and preserves Biscayne Bay and its offshore barrier reefs.

There is a large mangrove forest on the shore. The park covers approximately 173,000 acres.

We parked at the visitor center and were amazed at its structure. It looked like a seaside cabin mansion. It was located about ten miles east of Homestead, Florida. It had a beautiful museum that offered virtual tours through the park's four ecosystems using dioramas, audio, and videos. Logan caught on quickly. There were several films about the park. The gallery also had local artists who found inspiration in the park. We got our tickets for a guided boat ride to a few of the islands inside the Biscayne islands at this visitor center. We boarded our boat and discovered it had a glass bottom. Logan was transfixed by the sight of the fish below him. The boat would make occasional stops to explain a coral reef ecosystem, or point out a shipwreck. For those without a two-year-old, the Biscayne National Park Institute also provides eco-adventures, including snorkeling at a shipwreck on the Maritime Heritage Trail. Along the way to a secret island off the coast of Miami, I felt like a pirate from times past

Relatively speaking, the Atlantic was not as bustling or noisy as the Pacific Ocean. I found this ocean to be calm, cool, and collected. Unlike the boat ride to the Channel Islands, this boat ride did not provide the view of sea life that created the commotion of our Channel Islands ride. Our boat was headed for the Boca Chita Key harbor. At the iconic and historic lighthouse on Boca Chita Key, guides boast about the beauty and wonders of the park. Boca Chita is the most visited island in the park. As we got off the boat, we were given mosquito nets to wear. At first, we didn't put them on, but after a few minutes, we realized we were the steak on the menu, so we draped ourselves in the nets to walk around this island. We took a path to a beautiful beach. I put a pair of goggles on and went for a dip. It was splendid. Fish were abundant, and it seemed the coral reef life was throwing a New Year's party just for us. I took a few seashells and aged coral. As I got a bit more adventurous, I started to swim among the mangroves. Liz waved to me and said our time was up; she and Logan were heading back to the boat reluctantly.

I waved them off, saying I would catch up. I imagined myself as the lone discoverer of this beautiful island and picked up a few of the seashells I was stepping on. Suddenly I realized I was alone on the beach, and the family that was in the waterway with me was gone. I started to skip along, jog, and ended up sprinting at full speed. As I got a half mile in, I realized I was way too late. I could be left behind for mosquito meat. As I rounded the corner to see the boat ready to cast off, the captain of the boat announced on her intercom, "Hurry up, we are about to leave you!"

Everyone was laughing as I dragged my sandy, mosquito-bitten self onto the boat. My wife said I was only a few minutes late, but it felt like an eternity to her with everyone seated and watching for me.

The treasures in my pocket were well worth the holdup.

For the island, the holdup for becoming a national park was perhaps the island itself; Biscayne took longer to formalize as a national park by law, mostly being part of the ocean floor.

Originally proposed for inclusion in Everglades National Park, Biscayne Bay was eventually removed from the list of Everglades. The area remained undeveloped until the 1960s. The plan was to develop it as a port for cargo and goods. Through the 1960s and 1970s, two fossil-fueled power plants and two nuclear power plants were built on the bay shores. There was angst and backlash against development, which led to the 1968 designation of Biscayne National Monument. The preserved area was expanded to its 1980 redesignation as Biscayne National Park. Its land and sea areas are now accessible only by boat.

There were approximately 470,000 visitors in 2018. This park was established about eighteen days before I was born in 1980. I guess you could say we connected. It's always good to connect to nature that is similar in age to you. But it's been here forever.

Yes, please. Consider my opinion to give the utmost preservation in the country—and perhaps the world—to every national park designation. This designation alters an ecosystem from point of inception to present day.

This newly designated national park, like me perhaps, has an ecological advantage. What could upset this balance? Perhaps a change to the law? Perhaps a natural disaster? Perhaps an uncontrolled predator? Perhaps a lion?

On the way back we were given a tutorial on the lionfish. The lionfish is not a native species to this ocean and is killing other species. Indo-Pacific lionfish have spread to Biscayne from the Caribbean Sea. In some areas, they are as abundant as native grouper species. Sightings of lionfish in Biscayne occurred as early as 2008, yet lionfish were rare until 2010. Some park rangers and many locals actively remove lionfish from Biscayne whenever possible. This was a major problem and culprit of Biscayne when we visited. It's interesting that this park was the first park in our adventures to have an invasive number-one enemy.

Florida politicians usually have a number-one enemy, and it was interesting to point a finger to this park for removal of the lionfish. It makes a lot of sense. Lionfish are voracious predators and compete for food resources of commercially and ecologically important fish like the snapper and grouper in Biscayne Bay. Lionfish also have venomous spines that can cause intense pain, swelling, headache, nausea, paralysis, and convulsions. They are also not timid. Imagine the tentacle of a lionfish creating paralysis in a snapper. That snapper would be more susceptible to predators. Finally, the lionfish has few natural predators in the Atlantic Ocean. There's even a phone number to call if you see them in Biscayne. The rangers will input that data for lionfish hunters, who attempt to keep their numbers as low as possible.

As we got back to the visitor center, we had lionfish on the mind. It's very interesting how a fish can cause so much damage. I guess it's like when a line of ants enters our home. It's usually around the change of seasons from winter to spring or spring to summer. They become invasive, and we must get rid of them. They become our common enemy.

As we exited the park we saw the beautiful cement and red brick Biscayne National Park sign welcoming visitors in. I wrote about the large sign at Painted Desert in Arizona. If that sign was the tallest, this sign was the most elegant. A sculptural masterpiece, it shows a three-dimensional underwater coral reef. Fish and fauna represent the site as an underwater park. That's exactly what Biscayne is. This is perhaps the best national park sign we have seen. As we clicked our iPhone to take many pictures with our son next to the sign, we slowly but surely realized again that we were being eaten alive by the mosquitos. Yes, we did have repellant on, but they still loved us. We ran from the sign to our car and were dismayed to see that we left one door open. As we were driving away, we discovered there were hundreds of mosquitos in our car. HELP! With the windows down to flush them out, we drove to Key West, Florida, and onto Dry Tortugas National Park.

Mosquitos are everywhere

See the swimming alligator?

DRY TORTUGAS NATIONAL PARK

THE DRIVE FROM MIAMI TO KEY WEST, FLORIDA, TAKES about four hours without stopping. We stopped for lunch and a little sightseeing. My parents had told me that this was one of the most scenic drives in America. It was, and to this day, I don't know if I've been so entertained by any of the drives for our national park vacations. We felt like we were on a cruise out at sea.

There are very interesting Keys from mainland Florida to Key West. Along the way you see tourist attractions, restaurants, apartments, middle-class neighborhoods, and neighborhoods with large mansions. If the man-made structures don't grab your attention, then it may be the different color blue of the ocean, the wind hustling along the gulls in the air, or one's imagination about how big the ocean really is. Every day when I look at the mountains, they look back at me and say, "How insignificant you are, Antonio." The ocean was saying the same thing to me. This must be the feeling past explorers and current fishermen have.

We finally got to our hotel in Key West, Florida. One immediate feeling was that this island was on "island time," like the first time I went to Hawaii. Driving around, I could also feel the significant military presence with bases in every direction. The population of Key West in 2019 was approximately twenty-five thousand, with five thousand, or 20 percent of the population, military.

Everything in Key West is expensive; the cost of living is extremely high. In 2017 the homes for sale that I saw walking the neighborhoods well exceeded $1 million for about twelve hundred square feet. Living in Santa Fe is a bit more expensive than average, but here in Key West it's normal to feel poor seeing yachts, tiny million-dollar homes, and a tropical paradise. We visited the Ernest Hemingway Home and Museum and could only imagine what it might have been like to live among many cats in this Spanish Colonial architecturally designed mansion.

If Miami was on the move, Key West was laid-back. The food was divine, and we ate and walked among other tourists for hours our first night at the Sunset Pier. Like the first light at Acadia, the day's last light on the Sunset Pier was breathtaking. We remembered freezing in Maine in April, and the heat in Florida at sunset on this day in June was tolerable. Tomorrow we were in store for another adventure of a lifetime.

Early in the morning on June 16, 2017, we boarded the Yankee Freedom ferry for a two-and-a-half-hour boat ride to Dry Tortugas National Park. It was by far the longest and most luxurious of the boat national parks (Channel Islands, Biscayne, and Dry Tortugas). The Yankee Freedom is a high-speed, state-of-the-art, all-aluminum catamaran. The boat is powered by twin Caterpillar engines that give her a speed of more than thirty miles per hour. The distance between Key West and Dry Tortugas is 67.9 miles. Our son, of course, took a few naps. We moved from inside to outside, from the front to the back. Every place we sat had an impressive view. The Yankee Freedom provided lunch on the way, as well as snorkeling and fishing gear for our visit to the park.

If you're a photographer, this is your national park. Dry Tortugas National Park is in the Gulf of Mexico. The park preserves Fort Jefferson, where we landed, and the seven Dry Tortugas islands. The archipelago's coral reefs are the least disturbed of the Florida Key reefs. In 2018 only 56,810 people visited Dry Tortugas. We must convince more people to see this fabulous place. Pound for pound this may be the most spectacular park I've ever been to. If I could camp anywhere in the world, it would be here for one reason only: THE STARS. With no population nearby, I'm told this is the best place in the country to see the stars.

The park is 99 percent underwater, and its total boundaries are 101 square miles, or ten million acres. If humans could live in water, this would be the most visited park. The highest elevation of this park is ten feet above sea level. Some people on our boat were camping for a few days or a week. They packed coolers with tons of food and drinks. If I were a Floridian, this would be at least an annual camping vacation. Or perhaps in a busy decade, a camping trip once every five years.

Please, please go visit this park. Even though the park is 99 percent underwater, the park will give you an unforgettable vacation.

Dry Tortugas National Park is noted for abundant sea life, tropical bird breeding grounds, colorful coral reefs, and legends of shipwrecks and sunken treasures. The park's centerpiece is Fort Jefferson. Fort Jefferson is a massive but unfinished coastal fortress. It is the largest brick masonry structure in the Western Hemisphere and is composed of more than sixteen million bricks.

Before this massive structure was built, the first European to see Dry Tortugas was Juan Ponce de León, who visited on June 21, 1513. He caught 160 sea turtles there and called the island Tortugas, or the Spanish name for turtles. The island is the second oldest surviving place with a European name in the US. Florida was acquired from Spain by the United States in 1822. Dry Tortugas was seen as a strategic point for the control of the Straits of Florida and the Gulf of Mexico.

The construction of Fort Jefferson began in 1847. Work was half complete in 1860. This bastion was in Union hands throughout the

Civil War and later was used as a prison until it was abandoned in 1874.

Dr. Samuel Mudd, famous for being the doctor who treated John Wilkes Booth in the wake of President Abraham Lincoln's assassination, was imprisoned here for conspiracy with three others until early 1869, when he was pardoned after averting a viral outbreak. During the 1880s, the Navy established a base for coaling (refueling) and a wireless (radio) station here. During World War I, a seaplane base was established in the islands, but it was abandoned soon thereafter. From 1903 to 1939 it became the best equipped marine biological station in the tropical world.

Fort Jefferson, with its 47,125 acres, was designated a national monument by President Franklin D. Roosevelt under the Antiquities Act on January 3, 1935. The monument was expanded in 1983 and redesignated as Dry Tortugas National Park on October 26, 1992, by an act of Congress. Dry Tortugas National Park is managed by the staff of Everglades National Park. The park was established to protect everything in the park, including the islands, marine ecosystems, Fort Jefferson, submerged cultural resources such as shipwrecks, and to allow tourism in a regulated manner.

We took an hours-long stroll and wound up on a snorkeling beach about a mile away from the boat. The views were to die for. As I swam with my mask, snorkel, and flippers around the fort, surrounded by other snorkelers, I saw the immense abundant life in the gulf. Millions of fish swam in the coral that had been structured on man-made brick from the fort on the ocean floor. It was a pleasure of colors, sights, and swimming creatures. As I returned to Liz and Logan, she handed our baby off to me, and she went for a snorkel. About ten minutes later I could sense a flurry of fish and their babies surrounding me and my son. Liz floated to the top at just the right moment. I asked her what was happening, and her motherly instincts set in. She asked me to check Logan's diaper. By golly, he had pooped his pants. The fish were eating his poop that was now floating from his diaper. We all got out and rested for a long moment and began to giggle at how resourceful

Mother Nature was. The fish were probably eating breast milk and dragon fruit ceviche. Good for them.

Soon a group of three other tourists asked about the snorkeling. I was too embarrassed to tell them about Logan's mishap, so I stalled them by asking if they could take a family photo of us. We handed them our phones, and the process of fumbling with flippers took a good five minutes. We answered their questions about the wonderful snorkeling and created enough of a delay for the waves to clear the water. We laughed all the way back to the boat.

We had about thirty minutes until our boat arrived, and there were fishing poles we could try to fish with. I cast out a few times and then helped someone nearby bait his rod. He ended up catching a two-foot sea bass. If I had another hour, I bet we would have had sea bass for dinner.

All along Key West are places to fillet the fish you catch. There are also statues of famous swordfish caught here. We boarded our Yankee boat and took a snooze, our dreams built from the images of this beautiful park. Sometimes I wake up and look at that picture of the three of us in flippers not only to laugh but realize it's about the story sometimes more than the location. We were very young once, and this was the place where it occurred. Thank you, Tortugas. Your beautiful island will live in my dreams forever.

Snorkeling in the Gulf of Mexico

Fort Jefferson

It's windy, Dad.

DEATH VALLEY NATIONAL PARK

TO SAY THE LEAST, WE HAD NO IDEA ABOUT THE complexity of Death Valley National Park. To say it's complex is an understatement. I don't know if anyone really says, "I'm going on vacation in Death Valley." Or for that matter, "I'm going to the hottest place on Earth for fun." We never would have until we were trying to travel to all the national parks. As usual I looked at half-marathons across the country and found one in Death Valley on Saturday, December 2, 2017. We flew from Albuquerque, New Mexico, to Las Vegas, Nevada, and rented a Jeep. The drive to our hotel, The Ranch at Death Valley, was just over two-and-a-half hours. We stopped once on the way to the hotel at Zabriskie Point. Zabriskie Point is a part of the Amargosa Range in the east portion of Death Valley. This outlook has been one of my most memorable. The smell was of the desert, and the wind full of salt and sand had a unique tickle to the nose. From this point, we could see many of the colors of the rainbow in the hills of the badlands. The striped hills are composed of sediments from Furnace Creek, a lake that dried up five million years ago. There are many sub-colors of brown, gray, and black from the dried-out lake bottom. In the distance are large mountains, giving off blue, orange, and red colors from the sun going down. This is a special place for sunrises and sunsets. It looks like hoodoos are boiling in the ground with peach and brown colors. Liz took a classic picture of Logan in my arms—perhaps one of the last baby photos of him, as he grew into a toddler on this trip. He was just two years, one month, and one week old. Every so often, this picture stops me in my path to the garage or home office. I just look at it and smile.

The point was named after Christian Brevoort Zabriskie, who was the vice president and general manager of the Pacific Coast Borax Company in the early twentieth century. Zabriskie's twenty mule teams transported borax from its mining operations in Death Valley. From the lookout point, it did seem like a lot of chemicals and borax were below. Borax first came into common use in the late nineteenth century when Francis Marion Smith's Pacific Coast Borax Company marketed and popularized a large variety of applications under the 20 Mule Team Borax trademark, named for the method by which borax was originally hauled out of the California and Nevada deserts. Applications for borax included metal soldering, glaze and enamel manufacturing, tanning of skins and hides, artificial aging of wood, a preservative against wood fungus, analytical chemistry as a buffering agent, and pharmaceutic aid as an alkalizer. Like Silicon Valley for the computer and information age, this was borax valley for the industrial age.

There was no borax around as we checked into our unique hotel. At first glance we noticed the Furnace Creek Golf Course on sprawling lawns. I wondered how they kept the course so green in this desert. The hotel has an ever-refreshing eighty-seven-degree spring-fed pool that we could enjoy.

The night before the marathon and half-marathon, we were served a pasta dinner with many runners, their families, and guests of the ranch. That night's rest was splendid.

The alarm went off early, and we all got up and drove half an hour to the start of the race. That was when I realized we were in a very large park. I had read it was the largest in the contiguous forty-eight states. I, however, didn't realize it took a long time to drive anywhere on the park's map. The commute to work in this park would be eternity.

Death Valley National Park straddles the California and Nevada borders. It is located east of the Sierra Nevada mountains. The park occupies the zone between the arid Great Basin and Mojave deserts. Death Valley is the hottest, driest, and lowest national park in the contiguous United States. The park is approximately 3.4 million acres. In 2018 there were nearly 1.7 million visitors. That would be two acres per every visitor in 2018. That's more acres than most people own in their life.

The 2017 Death Valley Half Marathon started at 8:00 a.m. at the bottom of Titus Canyon. It was an all-uphill run to the turnaround point and was downhill from that point to the finish, the exact place of the starting point. The scenic Titus Canyon started in Beatty, Nevada, where the start of the marathon was an hour before. In the first few minutes I knew I was likely to get second place in the half-marathon. How did I know? Well, the runner in front of me was about a quarter of a mile ahead, and the person behind me was about as far back. I settled into second place by mile one and was already happy with the placing. The trail quickly turned into a canyon that was cut into the steep face of the Grapevine Mountains. It was twenty to fifty feet wide at points and made of limestone rock formations with petroglyphs on its walls. Native plants and wildlife filled the canyon. The sand was soft and at points hard to race in. From time to time I would jump off a few rocks to catapult my velocity. As we got close to what I felt was our turnaround point (6.6 miles), a few marathon runners started to pass us going downhill. A few more minutes went by, and another handful of marathon runners passed by. I got a bit nervous that a few things didn't feel right. Things were not right. The volunteers did not get to the turn around point fast enough with the sign to have us turn around. So, the leader, myself and the lead pack ran longer than expected. Another half marathon runner and I took it upon ourselves to run downhill and start the second half of our half marathon. He was with me for about half a mile, and then I really put on the wheels. I wanted to win this half-marathon. I figured the leader would find out at some point that he had run too far. He was way ahead of me from the start. I could not see him or yell at him. I calculated that at his speed, he may pass me to reclaim his lead. So the best thing to do was to run like I had to win by a few minutes. A few minutes downhill turned into an all-out sprint. I was probably running at an eight-to-ten-minute pace uphill, and now I was running a six-to-seven-minute pace. The emotions, pace, and environment put me in a headspace that reminded me of competing in cross-country in college.

It was fun! I was on my way to victory. I kept chugging along and didn't know I was going to win until the last steps of the race. The crowd of a few dozen cheered me on. I was exhausted, and the organizers handed me a few awards. I quickly saw my family cheering and applauding.

As we walked to our SUV to go back to the hotel, I heard the crowd cheer on the second-place half marathon runner. It was the guy who was waiting at the turnaround point. As we got on the desolate desert road, I explained the race chaos to my wife. She couldn't believe it. We unloaded our son, got lunch, and slowed the day down. I took some time to go to the natural hot springs pool. A handful of runners from the half-marathon and marathon were swimming and chatting about how the race was a bit chaotic because of the absence of the half-marathon turnaround. I didn't chime in. It sounded like they were thinking the same thing I was. For a few short hours, it was posted on the organizer's website that I had won the half-marathon.

Then the next day, they created a separate half-marathon group for few of us, besides the guy who was way ahead of all of us. That guy ran 1:58, and they listed him as the winner for the half-marathon runners. He probably convinced them of his win and to change the results. Who knows how much longer he ran? For a few years my time was still up, but when I recently checked it, it was not there. Where do all our times go with the passage of time? I forget if I was under two hours or just above. I want to say I ran somewhere in the 1:50 to 1:55 time. Nonetheless, as a runner, you get used to things like this.

Volunteers often tell you to run the wrong way. A cop did this to about ten runners in front of me at the 2005 Philadelphia Marathon; they went the wrong way, and by the time the cop figured it out, I was the first person he guided the right way (despite being in eleventh place). So I was in first place for a moment before the top ten runners caught me. In the case of Death Valley, the volunteers just didn't drive from the start of the marathon in time to put up the half-marathon turnaround marker before the first few runners got there. Timing is the name of the game in long-distance running. The course for this race has changed from Titus Canyon to the location at the hotel/resort we stayed at. The race was moved to the road. I'm glad I got to run thirteen-plus miles in a beautiful canyon in this huge national park.

Mistake or not, the race was fun, worthwhile, and very enjoyable. I went through so many emotions. They ranged from a content *second place is great* to *no, I'm not the first loser* to angry: *Did I run too much? Why wasn't the sign up?!* Euphoric: *Yes, another victory.* Controversial: *Maybe I wasn't the winner.* And finally, content again: *I'm glad I can finish a half-marathon today.* All the normal roller-coaster emotions for a marathoner.

Sleep came easy that night. We slept in. When we got on the road, we shifted to vacation mode. Who could survive in this desert? Native Americans could.

Native American groups inhabited Death Valley as early at 7000 BC, most recently the Timbisha around 1000 AD. Also, a few European Americans were trapped in the valley in 1849 while looking for a shortcut to the gold rush. Remember the San Francisco 49ers? One who died in this valley on their way to the gold fields gave the name to the park. That's why it's called Death Valley. You may run out of water, and this valley may be the last thing you experience. Perhaps that's why the SUV of volunteers were handing out water bottles to the marathon runners. The thought of death is not easy, and it goes through one's mind in a marathon, perhaps more so in Death Valley. Maybe that's why I ran the half.

Death Valley had several short-lived boomtowns in the late nineteenth and early twentieth centuries to mine gold and silver. Tourism expanded in the 1920s when resorts were built around Stovepipe Wells and Furnace Creek. We stayed at the resort in Furnace Creek.

Death Valley was declared a national monument in 1933 and became a national park in 1994.

The rocks in this park have been aged to 1.7 billion years old. Talk about longevity! If only these stones could talk. It's also a great place to see the stars, and in 2013 this park was designated as a Dark Sky Park.

Our first stop on Monday was to Badwater Basin. This basin has a walking path that leads to the lowest point in America and North America. The sign reads "282 feet below sea level." On the mountain above we saw the sea level point.

Right above this lowest point and about a forty five minute drive from the resort is the famous Dante's View. We drove to this high point and were awestruck at the views. The Badwater Basin looks like a giant's salt closet, perhaps where a giant was leaving their kill to preserve. The land is salted below. This peak is towering 5,575 feet above Badwater Basin on the ridge of the Black Mountains. One might have a religious experience from this peak.

The weather was quite nice in December. Summer temperatures commonly run above 120 degrees Fahrenheit in the shade, with overnight lows dipping only into the nineties. During the summer it is one of the hottest places on Earth, like the deserts of the Middle East and the Sahara. On the afternoon of July 10, 1913, the National Weather Service registered a US record-high temperature of 134 degrees Fahrenheit at Furnace Creek. Imagine what it might feel like to run a marathon in that temperature?

We spent the rest of our days in the park zooming past the desert, walking with our son, and taking it easy. From time to time, I think about climate change. The entire American Southwest one day may resemble Death Valley National Park. By that time, we might not be alive. I wonder how Death Valley will be in the future.

Half Marathon Start

Dante's View

Badwater Basin – Lowest point in North America

GRAND CANYON NATIONAL PARK

ARIZONA IS SUCH AN INTERESTING STATE. ON SATURDAY, February 3, 2018, I ran the Sedona marathon. We had never been to this beautiful place. Wow, talk about a town you can write home about. Running 26.2 miles in Sedona gave me perspective of this sacred place.

By the halfway point I was in second place. Somewhere in my brain, I thought, *I could win this one.* I've only won one marathon in my life. Could this be number two? But my pace started to slow. When the fourth or fifth person passed me, I knew it was over. No victory today. Around mile seventeen I hit a wall in this very hilly marathon. I had to walk a few miles at the end. Volunteers on the course warned me and the runner who ultimately finished second about upcoming hills. We ran together as numbers one and two for fourteen miles, and we ignored them. We kept upping the pace from eight minutes a mile to six-and-three-quarter minutes a mile, pacing each other. They screamed, "It's a hilly one, slow down," as if they knew our pace was right for a straightaway but not right for this challenging route to our destination. My wife and son were waiting for me, and with his BOB stroller, they encouraged me to jog the last half mile, which I did with them. It must have been weird to see a grown man, staggering as if he is about to drop, running beside a tough wife pushing her baby in a stroller at the end of the marathon. I ran the slowest marathon of my life to this point in 3:36. This earned me ninth overall. A total of 188 marathon finishers had an average finishing time of 5:11 that year. Ninth out of 118 was still respectable in spite of it all.

I was in a haze. I should have gone Jeep four-by-four riding with other tourists instead. A dozen Jeeps taking tourists around the hilly mountains passed us on the dirt roads as we ran. We certainly ate a lot of their dust. At times I could hear them apologizing as they blew past us at thirty miles per hour, slowing their earlier fifty miles per hour.

My runner's high was slow and painful that day. However, at the age of thirty-seven, I was determined to run one marathon a year. I'm glad I accomplished that early in 2018. This year would prove to be one of my longest and toughest.

In 2018 my family would travel to five national parks; my mom would come down with symptoms of Lou Gehrig's Disease (ALS); and life would take on a different meaning.

The day after the Sedona marathon we drove to Grand Canyon National Park.

Arizona's nickname is the Grand Canyon State. Most of Grand Canyon National Park carves its way through Arizona. We drove my 2001 Nissan Xterra for its last long-distance trip from Santa Fe. Seventeen years and 150,000 miles . . . if this vehicle could talk or, for that matter, write, we'd have a great novel from all the places it took us.

We stayed in a nice, quiet lodge on the South Rim of the Grand Canyon. It was like a little town, with a lot to see and do at this national park. We settled in for a week. It was time to take it easy after my marathon and for a vacation in February. We would have never in a hundred years thought about vacationing in February before our national park adventures. This turned out to be a wonderful silver lining for this adventure.

The next morning we grabbed breakfast in a cafeteria-style

restaurant steps from our hotel. We passed many deer on the way, unafraid of humans and probably waiting to be fed.

Breakfast was *too* good, as there were many delicious options. I was post-marathon, likely to eat everything I could. My wife was breastfeeding, so she was eating for two, and Logan was at that age when he ate about half of what he reached for. The rest came to me. The deer didn't get any of it; our bellies did. Sorry, deer.

After breakfast we passed the deer and headed to the South Rim. It was about a half a mile walk from our cafeteria. There was something very collegial about this place. I always felt like I was learning, and it was a real community. Everyone ate together, everyone lived next to each other, and everyone hiked together. We stopped and looked at the angelic views, truly one of the top-ten views in the whole entire world. Even seeing the spectacular views from the mountains of a handful of ski resorts we had seen, this one was out of this world. I could stare at this view for a lifetime. I'll bet this little village probably has a lot of workers who live here just for the views.

I'm what they call a *Burqueño*. I was born in the big, big city of Albuquerque. I can't believe I'm writing this, having lived in New York City, but it took me thirty-seven years to finally see the Grand Canyon in person. Some people from around the world see the Grand Canyon in their first week in the US. Why hadn't I been here? That's a question we all must ask ourselves about some of the national parks. We have so much beauty within our reach. Why don't we take the opportunity to see it?

We hiked the Bright Angel Trail for approximately one-and-a-half miles down and one-and-a-half miles up. The entire trail goes all the way to the Colorado River, which can take nine to twelve hours. Talk about a marathon. My attention span was about as long as it takes me to run my slowest marathon, around three or four hours. Our hike that day was almost three hours.

Bright Angel Trail is the most popular hiking trail into the Grand Canyon. This may be one of the most popular trails in all the national parks. Sometimes I think of it as the Blue Angel Trail in my head, one that lets hikers walk in the footsteps of Native Americans, canyon miners, pioneers, and early tourists as they descend into the canyon's depths. The trail provided big views, morning and afternoon shade, rest houses, vault toilets—everything we could want for what was a great first trail to hike on our first day in the canyon.

Logan woke up in the morning and watched *Peppa Pig* for an entire hour. It was the first time he had immersed himself in *Peppa Pig*. Soon I could tell by his sounds, words, and body language that he was ready to go and have a great hiking day.

At one point on our approximate five-kilometer hike, Logan asked to stop and play with a dinosaur, a car, and excavator toys in the sand. This was his big sandbox. Amazing!

The busy trail was full of happy people seeing the most glorious views; they were delighted to see our little Logan playing happily too. They always complimented him, us, or all of us. At times he'd spend twenty minutes in a corner on the trail playing with his toys in his ginormous sandbox, greeting strangers walking over him and laughing. Come to think of it, this park is a tremendous sandbox for all of us. Maybe that's it. These parks offer an unusually large sandbox for all the big kids. It's that simple.

It only took me fourteen national parks with my two-year-old son and lovely wife to figure it out.

IT'S HARD TO WRAP MY HEAD AROUND THE SIZE OF THE Grand Canyon because it is so vast. How do you think about a place like this, its chasms stretching far into the distance? How do you understand how small you are as you stand next to its edge?

The park is more than 1.2 million acres and had six million visitors in 2017. This is the second most visited national park, after Great Smoky Mountains National Park. The park's most sought-after view is of the Gorge of the Colorado River. It is considered one of the

Wonders of the World and was designated a World Heritage Site by UNESCO in 1979.

The history of this wonderful place is also interesting. Native Americans inhabited many areas at least four thousand years ago, and there is evidence of their presence as long as 10,500 years ago. Ancestral Pueblo peoples developed this area when they became less nomadic and more dependent on agriculture. Drought in the late thirteenth century likely caused many to move away. Paiute, Cerbat, and Navajo peoples also settled in the Grand Canyon only to be later forced onto reservations by the United States government. I once had a coworker who grew up close to the Grand Canyon. His mother was Native American, and his dad was white. He told me that as a Native he could hunt on Native land but not national park land. He said the deer would be so plentiful in the park that all he had to do was wait by the border. It made for easy pickins'.

In September 1540, under direction of Francisco Vásquez de Coronado, García López de Cárdenas led a party of Spanish soldiers with Hopi guides to the Grand Canyon in search of the Seven Cities of Gold. After that expedition, about two hundred years passed before anyone chronicled the Grand Canyon.

Around 1869 U.S. Army Major John Wesley Powell led the Powell Geographic Expedition through the canyon on the Colorado River. This was a great survey of the canyon's geology and helped advance the science for geologists to come. The promise of copper renewed interest in the area, and some settlements were established along the rim in the 1880s. However, as with everything in America, tourism became more profitable than mining.

By the turn of the twentieth century, the Grand Canyon was a well-known tourist destination. In 1901 the railroad came to the South Rim from Williams, Arizona, and tourism increased exponentially.

As for politics, Theodore Roosevelt created the Grand Canyon Game Preserve by proclamation on November 28, 1906, and the Grand Canyon National Monument on January 11, 1908. Some Senate bills to create a national park were defeated in 1910 and 1911. I'd like to have been in the rooms to hear why. Perhaps mining? Was it the local politicians and their business-oriented power brokers back home? I bet it was.

Finally, on February 26, 1919, with Congressional approval, President Woodrow Wilson created Grand Canyon National Park. One year after we visited the Grand Canyon, on February 26, 2019, the park celebrated one hundred years as a national park. We celebrated its ninety-ninth year!

The week went by quickly, but time felt eternal in the Grand Canyon. Our small family took in many places, views, and the vistas from the South Rim. One afternoon we took a bus tour to many stops. We became one with the millions of years of history written by Mother Nature. This was truly a magnificent preserve.

Early one morning we met with a talented photographer. We hired a photographer in Rocky Mountain National Park when Logan was a baby, and those pictures were so emblematic of his babyhood. He wore a cute Hawaiian shirt to that photo shoot.

The photographer lived near the South Rim but had flown back from the East Coast where she was visiting her parents. I hired her from a website I found of photographers in the area. She was approximately our age, and from the get-go, she was firm and efficient, while the morning was a bit cold and breezy. We got spectacular pictures of Liz and I swinging our son back and forth. We took off our jackets for this picture, and the canyon background with the hues of the morning sunrise made it look like the middle of spring instead of February. Brrr! There was no snow on the ground, but we quickly put on our jackets. Then we changed our clothes a few times in the car and took some photos with the jackets.

This sunrise with my baby in my arms sits on my desk to this day. It looks as if all 1.2 million acres are just below the picture. Now I know why so many families have their most memorable family photos from this park. We were very happy with hiring a photographer because, to be frank, it's hard to juggle a baby, the cliff edge, and taking photos with our smartphone. And dangerous.

Every year a few people fall to their deaths taking selfies or not staying safe on the edge of the South Rim. Even in some of the best settings, there is no protection between you and a fifteen-story fall. Please be careful when taking pictures at this national park. Photographers can be expensive, but they beat the most expensive ride: a helicopter ride to the emergency room.

We'll have these photos for the rest of our lives hanging on shelves, offices, and our home. One day, four years after our photo shoot, Logan brought a friend home from kindergarten at lunch. His friend said they went to the Grand Canyon, and Logan said he went there too. I immediately took the large photo off our hall wall and showed him. "That's you, Logan!" Perhaps he remembered that trip. I remembered what a cute baby he was. One day I hope my family walks all the way down the Bright Angel Trail to the Colorado River.

Inside a Utah Juniper Tree

South Rim Smiles

FLIGHT

Looking into the Canyon

ZION NATIONAL PARK

FROM FEBRUARY UNTIL APRIL, I GOT MYSELF IN PRETTY good race shape. We flew to Las Vegas, Nevada, with my in-laws for the Zion National Park Half Marathon. Vegas to Zion is about a three-hour drive with a family, maybe two-and-a-half hours if you rush it. My beautiful bride and I planned to run the half-marathon while Joe and Josie looked after Logan. We rented a fabulous Airbnb about twenty miles from the park, in between Hurricane and La Verkin, Utah. These were quintessential small towns. There was a delicious barbecue restaurant in Hurricane. That would be for after the half-marathon, a couple times.

I had not really spent any time in Utah other than the Salt Lake City airport; this was my first experience in Utah. Our rented home was new and fabulous. The owners lived next door and had retired here and were raising one of their grandsons who looked to be about seven or eight. Someday I'd be playing catch with Logan in the yard like they were. This home offered the luxury of a new home with a Ping-Pong table in the garage.

The regular Zion Half Marathon was usually run on the main road in the national park, but that road was under construction, so they moved it to a private ranch just on the boundaries of the park.

We woke up early for the 2018 Zion Half Marathon on Saturday, April 28. The road to the half-marathon was mostly up a sandy, rocky mountain. The 2018 Zion Half Marathon was on the west side of the park and ran along Smith Mesa Road, located north of Virgin, Utah. Throughout the length of the course, runners and spectators saw amazing views of the west side of Zion National Park.

For this event there were 2,729 runners. Estimating one-and-a-half cars for every runner would total around four thousand cars. It was bumper-to-bumper traffic, and the ranch was now full of cars. Cows roamed around, and I got the feeling I wasn't in Kansas anymore. It looked like the race was leading us to the Wizard of Oz.

I recall going out very fast and rounding the first curve with a few cows in the way. Wow, was this the way to experience a national park. The visibility was fifteen miles on this clear day, and we had a long view into the park. The excitement put me in between some experienced runners. I reached my goal and hadn't felt this way since the Chicago Marathon in October 2016. The last few miles were an uphill struggle on a dirt ranch road at about a twenty-five-to-thirty-degree angle with loose ends falling all over the place. Those loose ends were mostly manure, hay, rocks, and sediment. I caught a few runners on this hill as they started walking. Rounding the curve, I was finishing with the first overall female runner, and many observers were definitely cheering her on. She passed me with about half a mile to go. I don't believe I got caught by anyone in this race as I went out somewhat conservatively from the thirty or so runners in front of me and gradually picked up the pace.

I finished with a time of 1:29, good for ninth overall and second in my age group of thirty-five- to thirty-nine-year-olds at my old age of thirty-seven. My pace was 6:52 minutes per mile for 13.1 ranch miles. I felt like a cowboy. I lassoed in about ten runners the last 5K or so.

Liz had a spectacular run as well. For her first half-marathon since giving birth, she ran 1:57, or 8:57 minutes per mile, and placed eleventh in her age group (thirty-five to thirty-nine) of 307 women in that division. We were both happy to see that Logan was in good hands with his grandparents. I caught glimpses of Logan and his nana and grandpa in various places in the park throughout the race.

The view of the landscape for 13.1 miles of the course was amazing. I wished we could camp here. The race started at 8:30 a.m., and awards were a few hours later. I remember going up to the podium with a two-year-old in my arms to stand on the second-place box in my age division. I don't know if I'll ever have such a spectacular half-marathon.

We were off the ranch by noon, home sweet home, and ready for that barbecue in Hurricane. Few understand how hungry runners are after a race. We had found the perfect place to restore, eat heartily, and laugh with our family.

We all rested up since the next day we would enter Zion National Park. As we drove to the visitor center, I felt like this my life's meaning, still euphoric after a great run the previous day. The trails awaiting our family promised adventures ahead. It was suggested we leave our SUV and take the free shuttle bus for stops at destinations like Zion Lodge, Angels Landing, Emerald Pools, West Rim Trail, and the Narrows. We went all the way out to the farthest stop and got off at the Narrows.

The Narrows is the narrowest place in Zion Canyon. It is on a riverbed of the Virgin River and upstream from the main canyon. The Narrows is one of the premier hikes in the park and on the Colorado Plateau. It is pretty much hiking in a river up to your knees. As we got ready for the hike, Logan was smiling from cheek to cheek as he had never walked in a river this deep. Liz and I each grabbed one of his hands, and he laughed and screamed with joy as the initial plunge, waist deep for him, was chilly. We all got used to the temperature and had an hour of fun on this river hike. We again took an ageless photo of us swinging Logan in the air. Water spewing from his shoes and the biggest smile a two-year-old could have. Priceless. His hair was now down to his neck, and it was blown by the wind in every direction he wanted to go. Most people complimented us on what a nice girl we had. We didn't argue with them. As for congestion and pace, this had to be the most populated hike we had done in a national park. The excitement and chill, however, made it feel like a solo trek.

The Narrows hike is arguably the quintessential Zion experience. Water levels change as the seasons do. At times it is knee deep, at times waist deep, and at some points a full-on swim. Be careful in the summer as thunderstorms cause the Narrows to flash flood. This excitement brought us back to Earth as we returned to our bus.

The prominent feature of Zion is the fifteen miles into Zion Canyon. The canyon walls are reddish and tan-colored Navajo Sandstone eroded by the North Fork of the Virgin River. Imagine Earth turning, eroding, and smoldering, coloring the canyon in earthy tones.

Zion includes mountains (up to 8,726 feet above sea level), canyons, buttes, mesas, monoliths, rivers, slot canyons, waterfalls, and natural arches. It could be named many things. Perhaps Falling Canyonlands? But what gave Zion its name?

Zion comes from the Bible from Mount Zion in ancient Israel. Around 1860 Mormon settlers gave it the name Zion. Isaac Behunin, a Mormon pioneer, said of the area, "A man can worship God among these great cathedrals as well as he can in any man-made church; this is Zion."

Mormon settlers named the area Kolob, which in Mormon scripture is the heavenly place nearest the residence of God. If there ever was a place that is so heavenly, this would be it. My God, have you seen this place? Make sure you hike this place, as there is one road, and it's hard to get to the heart of this park without a hike or two.

The history of this park is much like the others here in the Southwest. Humans were in this place around eight thousand years ago. Small Native American families who were Basket Maker Anasazi and Virgin Anasazi, as well as the Parowan Fremont groups, developed as Basket Makers and settled in permanent communities. These groups moved away by 1300 and were replaced by the Parrusits and several other Southern Paiute subtribes.

Mormons came into the area around 1860. In 1909 President William Howard Taft named the area Mukuntuweap National Monument to protect the canyon. On November 19, 1919, Congress redesignated the monument as Zion National Park, and the act was signed by President Woodrow Wilson. The park is approximately 147,000 acres, and there were around 3.5 million visitors in 2020, even during the coronavirus pandemic.

Travel to Zion was not a thing before it became a national park due to its remote location and lack of roads. Touring cars could reach Zion Canyon by the summer of 1917. Work on the Zion-Mount Carmel Highway started in 1927 to enable reliable access between Springdale, Utah, and the east side of the park. The road opened in 1930, and tourism exploded. The most famous feature of the Zion-Mount Carmel Highway is its 1.1-mile tunnel, which has six large windows cut through the massive sandstone cliff. We drove through this tunnel, and it is spectacular.

Our travel to Zion was by bus back to the visitor center, and we would return tomorrow to the stops we missed. We took the bus the next day to the Weeping Rock stop. Weeping Rock looks like a fragile undercut into Zion Canyon with water that has been dripping through the rock for more than a thousand years. Talk about a long time to get a glass of water! This rock is constantly weeping. It looks more like a mountain when you are within it. Its trail is very short but very steep and takes about ten minutes. I remember carrying Logan most of the way. The tunnels and inlets to the canyon make this hike very windy. I remember seeing Logan struggle with his long hair and knowing we would need to cut it soon. I was weeping inside, knowing our son—whom many thought was a girl—was changing . . . He was turning from a baby into a boy. At the last park he turned into a toddler, and now he was turning into a boy. He was talking the language of Mother Nature. These parks were changing him. These rocks really did weep on us.

It was an easy hike with a two-year-old. The next day we would hike a few different trails, take in a few shops, lunch at a fancy restaurant, and buy Logan a small national park SUV toy at the visitor center.

What a way to see Utah for the first time and to worship the creator in a creative, spiritual way. Thank you, Zion! You changed all of us.

The Narrows

MESA VERDE NATIONAL PARK

Our visit to Mesa Verde National Park is the reason I wrote this book. It was on an early morning run, while Liz and Logan slept, that I left our park accommodations and set out on a simple four-to-five-mile jog. It turned into a major inspiration. Halfway through my run, I realized all the parks we'd been to as a family totaled sixteen parks in the first three years of my son's life. He would turn three the next month. As I kept jogging, thinking, and running, I told myself, *You can write a book about this adventure! You can do it. It may take a decade or two, but there's no rush. Every chapter will be a new national park we visit, or a few, and this will be my new passion. I'll have a book to share with my family and the world.*

I got back to the room with my head running a hundred miles a minute, imagining what I would write for my book up to this point in time. This was September 2018.

Liz and Logan were just waking up. There was no TV in our room. This was ideal. I don't know the last time I lived without a television. As a senior in college, I had too much going on, so I threw my TV away, and man was I productive!

Logan was waking up. I wasn't distracted by the morning news. I was writing my book in my head. I was stretching. I opened the balcony door to listen to the ravens swooping by.

I got my son's attention. The smell of piñon and juniper were as familiar as our backyard in Santa Fe, filled with the same trees. It's a hint of nutty evergreen and pollen from the bees. I started to dance for joy as I had my mind on the creation of my first book. Logan was now mesmerized by my movements. I got a bit tangled in my own thoughts and movements as I flipped my University of San Diego running cap in the air. As I tried to catch it with my head, I hit the lampshade, and the volcanic eruption of my son's laughter was seared into my memory. In about three years of his life, I had never heard him laugh as happily as this. His dad was being goofy. I was goofy with my newfound excitement for the book and the love I would put into writing it. I promised myself I would do it.

Our lodging at Mesa Verde National Park was in the park itself at the Far View Lodge. This is how the National Park Service describes their hotel on their website:

> Far View Lodge sits on a high shoulder of Mesa Verde near mile marker 15 on the main park road, offering panoramic vistas into three states. It's simple here, quiet enough to hear the ravens fly by. No TVs. Nothing fancy. Absolutely beautiful. Peaceful. A place to linger and appreciate why people lived here for seven centuries.

That may be the best description for roughing it. While my son was cracking up as my head swayed back and forth from hitting the lampshade, I suddenly realized that roughing it was the best family time. Now I had my wife laughing at me. I had entertained them with such silliness often, at home or in other hotel rooms. However, the rooms had distractions. The television, the phones, the noise. This time, without all that, it was ideal. This was a home I remembered. This is how it used to be before technology. It was like the 1980s. It was like "before" time.

The people who originally lived here later settled in the foothills of the Sangre de Cristo Mountains. That's where my ancestors settled. I could feel my roots here. I thought, *Of course I will write to make sense of it all.*

Mesa Verde means "green table" in Spanish. This national park is a green table in the sky. It was meant to be La Mesa Verde de Montana, or "the green mesa mountain." The land itself goes straight up to flat mesas. Mile marker 15 next to our lodge did not indicate a straight road up to the mesa, but it was more like the switchbacks one drives up to ski basins in the Southern Rocky Mountain resorts.

As a child I had heard about this place. My next-door neighbor and best friend came here with his family once. Even though he told me this was where the Native Americans were from, I couldn't conceptualize there were towns in the mountains built thousands of years ago. I believed my grandparents were the oldest people ever. No one could be older than they were.

History often repeats itself. I hope when people read this book, they understand our one common denominator with the national parks. They were the most beautiful places in our land, and that meant the original people lived in them. Perhaps they chose these places for access to game, vegetation, and water, but I believe it was also because of their beauty. As a human, thinking from the perspective of humans ten thousand years ago, there may be one language: yes, math, but more important, beauty.

Who doesn't like a good sunrise at the top of a mountain or a sunset into the ocean? Beauty is the common denominator for human life in these parks. Mesa Verde was no different.

Mesa Verde National Park is well known for protecting some of the most unique Ancestral Puebloan archaeological sites in the United States and the world. Many museums across the world have artifacts from Mesa Verde.

The park is approximately 52,500 acres and was established as a national park in 1906 strictly on its cultural significance. In 2018 there were approximately half a million visitors. It is in the Four Corners region of the United States, which is where the four states of Utah,

Colorado, New Mexico, and Arizona meet. This is the only place in the US where four states meet. This is the cultural roundabout of the American Southwest. These are the Native Americans closest to my heart. These Native Americans are who we are. They are us.

Around 7500 BC Mesa Verde was seasonally inhabited by a group of nomadic Paleo-Indians known as the Foothills Mountain Complex. Eighty percent of my life I have lived at the foothills of mountains. Wow, mind blown! The complexity of these humans' projectile points, the arrowheads and spearpoints found here, indicate they came from the Great Basin, the San Juan Basin, and the Rio Grande Valley. In and around 1000 BC, the Basket Maker culture emerged, and quickly thereafter, in and around 750 AD the Ancestral Puebloans developed from the Basket Maker culture. Was history repeating itself in my life? Was this sixteenth national park visit a trace back in time? Perhaps. The Mesa Verdeans survived by hunting, gathering, and eating what we grew up eating called *calabacitas*, or "little squash." These peoples farmed the three ingredients in calabacitas crops of corn, beans, and squash. If you have never had this dish and find yourself at a restaurant with it on the menu, specifically as a side dish, make sure you order it and tell me how it is. I'd like to find this restaurant.

The people built the mesa's first pueblos sometime after 650 and towns in these mountains by the end of the twelfth century. These "towns in the sky," as many conquistadores, cowboys, and girls would say, are massive cliff dwellings for which the park is best known and the reason for its preservation efforts and national park structure in 1906. Around 1300, following a period of social and environmental instability driven by a series of severe and prolonged droughts, these people abandoned their cities in the sky and moved south. They moved to locations in Arizona and New Mexico. They went on to claim the Rio Chama, the Albuquerque Basin, the Pajarito Plateau, and the foot of the Sangre de Cristo Mountains as their origin. At the height of the population in Mesa Verde, more than twenty-two thousand people lived here. That must have been the Denver, Colorado, of the Four Corners then. I'm sure they loved their beautiful terrain as the people of Denver keep it so close to their heart. This may have been the most sophisticated sky city in the ancient world. It was like a fancy hotel built right into the mountain.

One of the most famous of these cities in the sky is the Balcony House. After we got ready for the day, we went to the local national park cafeteria and gift shop, just a four-minute walk from our lodge. We drove up the road to a trailhead where we could see the Balcony House. You can take a tour of the area with reservations. With a two-year-old it was recommended that we didn't because of the ladders connecting the rooms.

Our hike took us past other home dwellings, and the trails were fun to walk. The Balcony House is set on a high ledge facing east. Its forty-five rooms and two kivas from faraway look like a mansion in the sky. Visitors on ranger-guided tours enter by climbing a thirty-two-foot ladder and crawling through a small twelve-foot tunnel.

Another famous dwelling is the Cliff Palace. This many storied ruin is perhaps the most famous, often photographed. Cliff Palace is in the largest alcove in the center of the Great Mesa. Many of the rooms were once brightly painted and housed around 125 people. It was likely an important cultural meeting place for a larger community of sixty nearby pueblos, which housed a combined six hundred or more people. With twenty-three kivas and 150 rooms, Cliff Palace is the largest cliff dwelling in Mesa Verde National Park.

In 1776 Spanish Mexican missionaries and explorers seeking a route from Santa Fe to California recorded Mesa Verde, named it, but never saw the cliff dwellings. They, however, were the first Europeans to travel the route through much of the Colorado Plateau into Utah and back through Arizona and New Mexico.

The Utes were the modern Native American peoples in this area, and the US created an 1868 treaty with them recognizing Ute ownership of all Colorado land west of the Continental Divide. Land in Colorado became an interest to many, and a new treaty in 1873 left the Ute with a small strip of land in Southwest Colorado between the border with New Mexico and fifteen miles north. Most of Mesa Verde is in this strip of land. The Ute wintered in the warm, deep canyons and found their sanctuary in Mesa Verde and the high plateaus of the park. Believing the cliff dwellings to be sacred ancestral sites, they did not live in the ancient rooms.

Throughout the 1800s many ventured into and out of Mesa Verde. Some such explorers would take some of the artifacts from the park and either sell them for profit or ethically place them in museums across the world. A lot of these explorers were from Europe. This generated an effort to protect this sacred land forever. In 1889 a part of Mesa Verde was the first pre-Columbian archaeological site to gain federal protection. It makes me wonder if people just didn't believe in history in our country before this time, or perhaps since our US history is so young. It didn't occur to us that there was a history at all. By the end of the nineteenth century, it became clear that Mesa Verde needed to be protected from people who collected and sold their own collection of artifacts from the area.

In 1906 President Teddy Roosevelt approved creation of the Mesa Verde National Park and the Federal Antiquities Act of 1906. The park was a law to "preserve the works of man" and was the first national park created to protect a location of cultural significance.

After hiking for one day and seeing the amazing cities in the sky, we enjoyed our dinner at the cafeteria and a lot of ice cream. It felt like home. We were alone. Not lonely, but a family as one.

I woke up and thought about the mountain of writing I had before me. Could I go back on my personal promise to the writing gods? I had made a promise in this sacred ground. I had not yet met that promise. Was I about to let that promise pass by? I had to do it. The petroglyphs on the mountain walls above told me to.

It would be a lot of work. It would be fun. This writing adventure would be all about our family travel. Who doesn't learn more about themselves, their family, and culture with travel? I'd get to know my country and its people. I'd discover more about my son, my wife, and myself. But more importantly, I'd get to worship the outdoors and

Mother Nature. My run that morning was slower and shorter. I had things to accomplish.

Mesa Verde has many unique stops on its one road to take pictures and hike. We stopped at a few of these that day. Some of my most memorable photos of parks are the Mesa Verde Park itself. Not necessarily the cliff dwellings, but the land itself. In black and white and in color they are all beautiful. It makes sense that people created the first metropolitan hubs and avenues of the American Southwest nearby in this region. Phoenix, Denver, Salt Lake City, and Albuquerque can't compare to the beauty here and the way it makes you feel inside. From atop the green Mesa mountain, one can see farms stretching out below. This valley in Colorado looks to be a great starting point for dreams of farming.

This is perhaps where many of our ancestral Southwestern forebears are from. This is where our DNA was shaped. This, as a Southwestern person, is perhaps where our roots lie. Some of us eventually could be all of us. We are all from the land. As an American, I'm from here. It was the perfect starting point for my book.

A hike to see cities in the sky

Cliff Palace

MAMMOTH CAVE NATIONAL PARK

In November 2018 my family rented a car in St. Louis and drove to Mammoth Cave National Park. I was at a work conference for a few days prior. We drove past the Arch in St. Louis, which would later become a national park. As the city traffic lessened, I had no idea I'd be crossing into a few states to get to our next national park. My wife had made most of the plans, and I was just the driver.

There are a lot of rivers in this part of our country. I had to pay close attention on many bridges. I was not used to this. We drove from the busy state of Missouri into a moderately paced Illinois, and slowed to a speed limit of around forty-five to fifty-five on the back roads of Kentucky. The windy roads of Kentucky reminded me of being a horse. The roads were hilly and grassy, lined with the white fences of the horse farms.

It took about five-and-a-half hours for us to get to our destination. The drive was around three hundred miles. To me, it was scenic, as I'd never driven in this part of the country. Diversity of topography really stretched mile after mile. We started in the Midwest and ended in the South. Mammoth Cave is always referenced as an East Coast national park in many books, but to me it is in the South.

Our destination was a hotel in the park. We checked into The Lodge at Mammoth Cave around sundown into a small cottage that looked rustic on the outside but resembled any hotel inside. Our window looked out on the wilderness, with deer in the large field nearby. I could immediately tell this park was going to be a bit different. We meandered to the Green River Grill for a good down-to-earth meal. We watched an old movie from at least a decade ago and fell asleep not knowing what would present itself tomorrow. We had one agenda. Tomorrow we would take a ranger-led tour into the cave.

The cave here in little ole Kentucky is the world's largest. The second largest cave in Mexico doesn't even come close. Mammoth Cave is named after it being a MAMMOTH. It is monstrous. This cave is more than 425 miles in length. That's approximately 125 more miles than the drive from St. Louis to this national park. Every year a few more miles are discovered underneath Mammoth Cave, and some geologists believe there may be six hundred miles in all to this cavern.

Rise and shine in this park the next day was more like rise and overcast. As I got on one of the many hiking trails just in our backyard, I realized a lot of the sunshine did not come through either because of clouds or the tree canopy. There are more than eighty miles of hiking trails in this park. As for my four-mile run, I saw a few deer, a few people, and could sense that there was a river somewhere close by. I got a bit lost on the way back and ended up running a bit longer. My family was wide awake and ready to go to breakfast when I finally returned. I hurried through a shower, and we ate in a hurry. We all had reservations for the first tour in the morning.

Our tour started with each of the fifteen or so of us placing our shoes in a small container. The container had a towel dampened with disinfectant on it so we wouldn't track in our germs and harm the wildlife of the cave. The wildlife we encountered right away were the many cave crickets. They scurried back and forth to avoid the light from the ranger's large lantern. This cave was very different from Carlsbad Caverns. This was more like a straight-line walking cave on our tour. It was led by a park ranger as it could be dangerous, and she didn't want anyone to hurt themselves.

As we all ventured into the underworld, it was dark. Very dark. Suddenly, our park ranger turned off the light. Our son almost screamed, but instead called our names. "MOM! DAD!" Our park ranger told everyone to be calm and demonstrated the power of the light. She lit a single match. Within a few seconds, we could all see each other. Then she turned on her light. We all started talking to each other. Amazing how you forget something you take for granted. We take for granted the light we have.

These caves are not lit well on purpose. That purpose is to protect the insects and others that make it home.

As the ranger explained the history, I thought about how big our planet Earth really is. Imagine all the tunnels in the world. Wow, how could we forget that just under our toes lies a whole new world.

The world of Mammoth Cave has a tremendous history. We got to a large room in the cave where names and dates—one was 1843—were painted on the wall. Many who had come here would pay top dollar to graffiti the cave. Those early visitors had been here with fire or ash, and now all of it was preserved. These names and dates were like modern-day petroglyphs. A church had even been created in this underworld. Imagine talking about God underground. It may put a different perspective on religion. I could tell that many among us were foreigners to this land. We all had an eerie yet ominous connection to this land underground. From our point of view, we now looked at life above in a different way.

As we returned to outside life, I realized yet again how wonderful this land is.

After the tour, on our own, we took a hike down to the amazing Green River. The Green River winds twenty-five miles through the park. It is at the bottom of all the hiking trails. My son at the time had a favorite stuffed animal, a spotted dog named Ruff-Ruff. He held onto Ruff-Ruff for dear life in the cave. Now Ruff-Ruff was so happy to be outside that he jumped for joy. It was as if Logan and Ruff-Ruff had a new appreciation for the light, the air, and the sky. We could see how life was when we realized there was a different, tougher life below.

We took many pictures of Logan and his pet here in this wild land next to the Green River that looked more like the chocolate river in Willy Wonka's factory. It was tough to get any pictures in the cave, nor would they resemble life itself. This park was just as beautiful outside as the imagination allowed one to envision the more than four hundred miles underground.

MAMMOTH CAVE NATIONAL PARK IS APPROXIMATELY FIFTY-three thousand acres. As a marathon runner, this may be the park to do a Sunday long run among the oak trees, wilderness, hilly landscape, and wildlife. If you are a hiker, make sure you plan one full day just to hike. On our hike back to civilization, I got to thinking about the history of this park. Native American remains have been found and date back to around five thousand years ago. Many explorers from slaves to Europeans introduced the cave system to us in the 1700 and 1800s. The land containing Mammoth was first surveyed and registered in 1798. According to certain records, an owner of the land, John Houchin, was bear hunting, and a bear turned and chased John down the hilly terrain. When John found the cave entrance, he ducked into the cave for protection from the charging bear. Imagine hiking the trails outside Mammoth and being chased by a bear you were trying to turn into stew. Yikes!

The complexion of the cave changed drastically during the War of 1812 against the British, again. Tensions originated in long-standing differences over territorial expansion in North America and British support for Native American tribes who opposed US colonial settlement in the Northwest Territory. In 1812, after two thousand years of anonymity, Mammoth's underground caverns were being mined. Remnants of Native Americans who worked in the mines early on turned up shell scrapers and limestone hammerstones.

During the War of 1812, the British blocked trade of America's gunpowder supplies in the East. For the American Army, Mammoth Cave and its surrounding areas had large deposits of calcium nitrate, which was eventually converted into gunpowder. Long before it was named a national park, the cave played a vital role in a war hundreds of miles away. Because of this reputation, the caves became a tourist destination around 1816. By 1920 tens of thousands of tourists visited Mammoth Cave annually. This created a craze for many landowners to increasingly advertise by the roadside that they too had a cave to see. They just wanted a yummy piece of the tourism pie. One day a pioneer and explorer of the cave, Floyd Collins, got stuck in the cave. His foot was pegged by a falling rock. After seventeen days of exposure and failed rescue attempts, Collins died. It was a mass media frenzy on the radio. Did the caves get a bad reputation? It was up for debate, and this increased attention started the effort to make this land a national park.

Many wealthy elites in Kentucky wanted to make the park a national one. However, there were many landowners. Donated funds were used to purchase some farmsteads in the region, but acquiring many required the use of eminent domain. Eminent domain is the power of the government to take private property for public use, in this case to create a national park. Therefore, thousands of people were forcibly relocated in the process of forming Mammoth Cave National Park.

Often it is said the eminent domain proceedings for this Kentucky land were bitter, with landowners paid inadequate sums of money for their property. This feeling is still in the air and resonates within the region. Around six hundred parcels of land were purchased in this manner. We had stepped into this land seventy-seven years after eminent domain, and one could still feel this park was a bit controversial.

On July 1, 1941, Mammoth Cave became a national park. In 2018 there were around 533,000 visitors to this park. We were three of those visitors.

That night for dinner we drove our rental car to the Cracker Barrel restaurant in Cave City, Kentucky. It was a ten-mile drive. As we sat down, I could tell we were in very unfamiliar territory. The people were locals and different from those at the park.

A couple next to us in their late sixties or early seventies started a friendly conversation. They were driving east, stopping for a meal and not for the caves. We shared our impressions of the park and our plans to see more national parks. Logan was his usual smiling self, and they told us how smart our son was. This was the first time on vacation that a stranger said this to us. I took note. Thank God we were putting $500 per month into his 529 college savings account. He had just turned three.

The restaurant was nonstop busy, with a party vibe unlike the restaurant outside the park we visited in Arizona. We told our waitress we were here for the caves. She smiled as if she had seen many like us before. My assumption was the caves brought some money to town, but it was self sufficient on the park grounds. Was this a restaurant catering to tourists or more a lively community meeting place?

The cave entrance was ten miles away. It could have been a world away.

These parks can take us past our comfort level. This one surely did, where the absence of a beautiful landscape was not only its own beauty, but helped us appreciate aboveground even more.

After our visit we drove to Nashville for the first time, stayed in an Airbnb next to Vanderbilt University, and took in some country music culture before we flew back home. If it weren't for Mammoth, who knows if I'd ever have gone to Kentucky or Tennessee. This park turned my head, upending my understanding of the landscape and our culture. Mammoth Cave sure did a number on seeing life from a different perspective. Exploring under the earth, in the dark, discovering nature in a completely different setting, it was remarkable.

Ruff Ruff at Green River

Walking on Golden leaves

OLYMPIC NATIONAL PARK

OLYMPIC NATIONAL PARK IN WASHINGTON STATE IS NAMED after Mount Olympus. President Theodore Roosevelt made it Mount Olympus National Monument on March 2, 1909. The monument was later ratified as a national park by Congress and President FDR in 1938. Mount Olympus, at just under eight thousand feet above sea level, sits in the park's center. It was named by English explorer Captain John Meares in 1788 when he viewed the mighty mountain from afar and felt it was worthy of a place the Greek gods would live in America. This may have been a place for the gods, but for more than one hundred years, it was relatively left untouched, traveled, or mapped. To this day, this region of Western Washington State in the Pacific Northwest of the United States remains with nature. When we visited in December 2018, it felt like we were the only mortals among the divine nature gods.

Mortality was something I really had to contemplate while walking the trails of this divine national park. Back home, my mother, Pauline, was rapidly dying of ALS (amyotrophic lateral sclerosis, also known as Lou Gehrig's disease). My parents had time-share points they could not use under the circumstances, so we used their points for a hotel.

The resort they reserved for us was about an hour's drive to Olympic National Park.

My father took a sabbatical from his work as an urgent care physician to take on the full-time care of our mother. We wanted them to go with us to Olympic National Park, but it was too tough for my mother in her condition. In the past we had gone with them to New Orleans, Louisiana, before Logan was born and to Oceanside, California, in 2015 when Logan was a month old for a Thanksgiving reunion with my immediate family of twelve.

Those shared trips were the best days, and now my mom was dying. ALS is a nervous system disease that weakens muscles and overwhelms most physical functions. Around 95 percent of ALS cases have no known cause, and at this time, no cure. It was heartbreaking to see this previously very healthy woman suffer.

Mortality is a fragile thing when you know someone you love will soon die. My mother did not cope well with her condition. Liz, Logan, and I had a weekly routine to go to my parents' home every Sunday and take a meal or make a meal for lunchtime. My mom would soon be on a feeding tube, as she could no longer swallow food, and the meals were accompanied by long talks.

One miraculous day, a large brown bear visited us. We watched as the bear went through the large plastic trash can outside. My mom may have sensed that this would be the last wild animal she would see, so she got up and started a joyous scream at the animal outside. I personally had never seen a bear in the wild. I couldn't believe it occurred just outside my parents' home in Santa Fe.

Growing up, my mother was my kindergarten teacher, my best friend, and my savior. Her lesson plans revolved around teaching every kindergarten child to read, regardless of aptitude. She had one lesson plan on dinosaurs, and we took a field trip in 1986 to the newly opened New Mexico Museum of Natural History & Science in my hometown of Albuquerque.

Today, as I write this story, I'm the president of the museum's foundation board, and my son is going to the museum on a field trip next week to see the planetarium with his kindergarten class, as it was in his lesson plan last month. I always think of my mother when I volunteer and help the museum in any way I can. Her legacy may be the many children she taught to read. Many of the children I grew up with still remember my mother as their kindergarten teacher. I can still recall going to our local grocery store in Albuquerque every week and some grandmother or mother would stop her and say, "Thanks, Mrs. Lopez! You taught Luke how to read." They would share proudly that their kindergartener was now a teacher, doctor, lawyer, secretary, actor, or a business owner. She had a huge impact on literacy in the communities around Albuquerque, New Mexico. Whenever someone asked me, or may still ask me, who my favorite teacher was, I always say it was my mother. She set a very high bar.

Nowadays, it may be very difficult to have one of your parents as your teacher due to school policy. I'm glad I had that year with my mother. Growing up with her was a gift. She always made great food, planned wonderful family vacations, and was the cornerstone of my family of five and a few pets along the way. She was alive and well for seventy years. At seventy-one she was dying of Lou Gehrig's disease. I still wish she could be with us on every park adventure. What a time to be alive. I would have a long time to think of my mother on this Earth for the last national park I visited while she was on this planet. Soon she would be visiting the gods above and still around us in spirit.

The suite my parents reserved for us for our first stop in Seattle had two bedrooms, a kitchen, and a living room. My wife's parents accompanied us on the vacation. Antonio, Liz, Logan, Joe, and Josie flew into Seattle on December 1, 2018.

The first thing we did when we landed in Seattle was rent an SUV. We drove to our favorite fish place, one of the best on the entire planet. The restaurant is Shuckers in the Fairmont Olympic hotel in Downtown Seattle. The special that day was steelhead trout. It sounded delicious, but they had run out. We thought we would come across steelhead trout somewhere else on this vacation. We searched for it high and low. It wouldn't be until the summer of 2020 that I found steelhead trout in a grocery store while visiting the Grand Teton and grilled it. And yes, it was delicious.

Every time I see the mention of trout, I think of this trip and my mom. This was the beginning of thinking of my mom not here with us on this planet, and boy, was it tough. We were so alike, but just in different generations. I was already working on grieving her loss.

We walked to Pike Place Market and the first ever Starbucks. My son loved the sounds, smells, and flying fish at Pike Place Market. He was now three years old and catching on to walking everywhere holding our hands.

The drive from Downtown Seattle to the quiet beach town of Ocean Shores, Washington, would be around three hours. The drive was scenic and very diverse. We passed bustling city neighborhoods and corporate headquarters such as Boeing, Microsoft, Amazon, and Netflix. We passed right by Tacoma and Mount Rainier National Park. We also passed by industrial towns like Aberdeen, Washington, once known as the "Lumber Capital of the World," now seen as the gateway to the Olympic Peninsula. All along the way the views were green and lush, unlike the browns at home, and the rivers were wide and beautiful blue, unlike the Rio Grande in New Mexico. Once again, we had arrived on a different planet.

Travel changes you, especially travel to our national parks. As we strolled into Ocean Shores at night, deer were everywhere. We had to slow down to make sure we didn't hit a deer eating a local's well-cut grass. It was time to relax and settle into our resort on the ocean.

The views were to die for. The next morning Liz and I went for a run on the beach. It felt like there were millions of birds all around us. We were all a bit tired, so we stayed in and around Ocean Shores, happy to be alive and well.

As we hit the road on December 3, 2018, we had a goal in mind. That goal was to hike in the Quinault area of Olympic National Park. We first stopped at the Quinault Rain Forest Ranger Station. In December in Santa Fe, we would be wearing heavy jackets and caps, but it was warmer here. We took a few hiking maps from the ranger station, as the trails began across the street. The first trail across the street was the Maple Glade Rain Forest Trailhead. We entered a world of mossy trees as high as skyscrapers. The big-leaf maples of the Quinault Rain Forest were amazing to roam around. We could hear the hurry of squirrel feet everywhere, and the warbling and chatter of many birds above. This Quinault valley receives an average of twelve feet of rain per year and is a temperate rain forest ecosystem. This nearly two-mile hike was a great introduction to the lush, dense forest growth in this section of Olympic National Park. The trail itself was very soggy, thus providing moisture for all the lush plants around. With life so rich and abundant all around, I could not help but think of my mom at home in her last days.

Logan was bundled up in a bright red winter jacket and a monster face winter cap, an unforgettable image to savor. As I smiled at my three-year-old son taking his first strides and leaps on a trail, all his days ahead of him, I could see the circle of life.

We finished our first hike in this park and went to the tallest spruce in the world. This was the Quinault giant Sitka spruce. My son looked up at it, as if it would pick him up and start talking. This giant tree is said to have 883 points and considered to be the largest Sitka spruce in the world. It's estimated to be a thousand years old and stands around two hundred feet tall. It was hard to imagine my mom was dying at seventy and this tree had lived for nearly a thousand years. Life has a very interesting way of illustrating itself in times of mortality. My beliefs are varied and diverse, but one thing I do believe is that our soul or energy goes on to some place. Perhaps one day my mom would catch up to this spruce tree. Imagine if you could have a conversation with a thousand-year-old tree?

Longevity shows itself for us in a national park. It tells us that life keeps going on far from our homes, workplaces, and routines. Out here in the wild, life continues. It might even last longer than a thousand years for some of its residents.

THERE ARE MANY RESIDENTS OF OLYMPIC NATIONAL PARK. The park has four distinct regions: the Pacific coastline, alpine areas, the west-side temperate rainforest (that we just hiked), and the forests of the drier east side. There are approximately 922,000 acres in Olympic, and in 2020, during the pandemic, there were approximately 2.5 million visitors. We didn't run into a single person on our first hike. Perhaps December was a good time to visit. As for wild residents, the park provides a habitat for many species, like the Roosevelt elk that are native only to the Pacific Northwest coast. There are others, including populations of black bears, black-tailed deer, cougars, mountain goats, and the millions of species that are both coastal and forest dwelling. This is truly a place for the gods. As they are divine, they are surely talking to all the animals and plants in this quiet, sacred place.

Before heading back to our hotel, we stopped at the Lake Quinault Lodge. This beautiful structure was built in 1926 and resembled an old log cabin mansion. The views from the large backyard deck were lovely.

We hiked a bit of the Quinault Loop Trail, which connected campgrounds, trails, the lodge, and the Quinault Indian Nation who own the lake. Natives have been in this area for centuries.

Before the influx of European settlers in the Olympics, Native Americans used the area to hunt and fish. I can only imagine the abundance of game. Recently there has been evidence that Natives lived and occupied the subalpine meadows and thrived for hundreds of years. Almost all the Pacific Northwest Indigenous cultures were adversely affected by European diseases, and at times their populations were nearly decimated. This was well before ethnographers, business operations, and settlers arrived in the region, and thus the history is not well established in this park. When settlers arrived in the area, timber was the main industry. Logging became a way of life. Public anger for this industry began to take hold in the 1920s, when people got their first glimpses of the devastation of clear-cut hillsides. This gave rise to the Olympic National Monument in 1909 and Olympic National Park in 1938. The park is not in one straight line or a circular area. The park consists of seventy-three miles of coastline and a larger inland area. In between is Native land, federal lands, and small towns. This land is one of the most visited in the national park system, and one of the most remote.

As we returned from our hike to the Lake Quinault Lodge, we held Logan up into a yeti cutout. His head peeped out of the face. He was now Bigfoot. Smiling from ear to ear, this memory will go down among my favorite park experiences forever. One day he might actually be as tall as this yeti.

We passed by some beautiful trees labeled "Large Japanese Cedar." I had never seen these trees, and their enormous, gnarled trunks are unforgettable. This lake, the lodge, the rainforest, and our experiences that day will be remembered as a toddler's walk in the woods. The image of green, lush woods embedded in my memory is still vivid today.

We drove back to our hotel and rested up for our next adventure the following day.

That day might not come for my mother. She was hit so hard by ALS. My mother was the backbone of our family, tough as nails, and never backed down to a challenge. It was such a tragedy that my mother fell victim to a disease that had no cure in 2018. No one knows when a cure may come. ALS was made infamous when Yankee baseball great Lou Gehrig got the disease in 1939 that ultimately led to his death two years later. The longevity of life when diagnosed is around two to four years, and most cases start around age sixty, or fifty in inherited cases. As none of my relatives suffered from cancer or ALS, this was a new arena of human acceptance. We all accepted that my mom would pass away sooner rather than later. I just had no idea it would be so soon. She still had so much to give. I wanted her to see my son grow up. She could teach him to read. She could show him the world as she had shown it to me.

A lot was going through my head in Washington. I was wondering how much longer my mom would be around. This was our last national park with her still alive. She would later die, just under three months from our stay in Olympic, on February 24, 2019.

My last memories of her still on this Earth were on the trails, roads, and beaches of Olympic National Park. I couldn't think of a better place to think about her last living days. Although she couldn't be with us, she had wanted us to go. She told us to remember her when she was her healthy self. I tried hard to remember her healthy self, and that's just what I did over the next few days. These next three days, with memories of the greatest mother who ever lived, brought so much emotion to the surface. It was her desire for us to get away and think of her here rather than to watch her die at home. My emergency plan was to fly back from Seattle if she took a turn for the worse. She did not, and her grace followed us. And at times it carried us.

On December 4, 2018, we drove a little longer than three hours to get to Port Angeles, Washington, from Ocean Shores. This is where the Olympic National Park headquarters are located. We took in the visitor center, which housed one of the mightiest stuffed elk I have set my eyes on. It was the enormous Roosevelt elk. This animal is the primary reason for conservation of this land. By 1909 these elk herds had shrunk drastically and were hitting critical levels for survival. President Teddy Roosevelt, using the Antiquities Act, redesignated 615,000 acres of Olympic Forest Reserve as Mount Olympus National Monument to not only preserve the land but, more importantly, keep the elk from extinction. The elk was thus named the Roosevelt elk as they were eventually saved by this effort. Today the largest unmanaged herd of Roosevelt elk live in this spot on the map.

Since it was December, and the weather could change at any moment, the road up the mountain from the visitor center was closed. We hiked for a moment around the visitor center. We then drove to Ruby Beach on the shore. On the way there we stopped a few times to see all the bald eagles that were flying above and stopping at many locations. Other than Alaska, I hadn't seen this many bald eagles in their natural habitat.

On the way to Ruby Beach, we stopped in Forks, Washington. There was something in the air, something about this town. The grocery store had turned into the hardware store, and that store turned into the movie rental place. Immediately I realized Forks is where the writer Stephenie Meyer chose as the primary setting for her *Twilight* series. In the story, Native peoples with wolf spirit and adaptations are held by powerful outsider vampire humans who live forever. Wow, talk about a weird place to be thinking of mortality and ALS. If only my mother were a vampire, she could beat this disease. That thought went past me as fast as the sun was going down, and we had to make it to the beach before sunset. Lopez means "wolf," and I had to tap into these instincts to get there in time.

We got to perhaps the most iconic place in Olympic National Park, Ruby Beach, at 4:36 p.m. on December 4, 2018. We hiked the trail to the beach, and let me tell you, this is not a thirty-foot walkway to the ocean you'd see in Southern California; this is a real hike. This is where the mountains meet the ocean. The sun was going down, and we were going to capture this beauty. We didn't have time! We all stumbled to the beach. The beach was like an obstacle course of tree limbs, rocks, sand, and slivers of water inlets.

Ruby Beach is the northernmost of the southern beaches in the coastal part of Olympic National Park. It is located on Highway 101 twenty-seven miles south of the town of Forks. Out in the ocean, mini mountains rise up out of the water, making this perhaps the most picturesque place not widely known by the masses. The driftwood was incredible on this beach, and the many ruby-like crystals in the beach sand shone at sunset as if we were in a crystal ball. This crystal ball slightly rotates at sunset. If you ever buy or rent a national park book from the library, you may see a beach-scape picture at sunset with mountains in the ocean. This is that place, and it might be the most beautiful place on Earth. For vacation in the twenty-first century, many Americans decide on the beach or the mountains. This is both! You can have it all right here.

Wait, the sun was going down. We needed to take hundreds of pictures while we could. Time was running out. We took as many as we could before time did run out. Our day came to an end, and now it was pitch dark. The stars led us into a beach littered with driftwood all around. We used the lights on our phones to lead us to the trail. How far was Ocean Shores from here? Really, ninety minutes.

All I could think about was my wish that my mom would live forever. In my heart, soul, and this book, she will. Everything comes to an end, but I wished I could stay at Ruby Beach forever and keep my mom's memory going, perhaps with her health restored.

We drove back to our nest as a few tears ran down my cheek. It was for my mom's smile and how she would be grinning from this adventure to Ruby Beach. Knowing her, I'm sure she would say something that would make all of us laugh, including her three-year-old grandson.

If you can only visit five places in your life, this must be one of them. We have a picture printed on wood hanging on our wall of the three of us at Ruby Beach. I picture my mother in the picture with us every time I pass it as I go from one room to another.

The next day we rested.

Our last stops along this vast park were Rialto Beach and the Hoh Rain Forest. Before we went to Rialto we had lunch at the Quileute Tribe town of La Push, Washington. We ate at a place called the River's Edge restaurant, and the view was divine. During the overcast brunch hour, the window table allowed us to see the mighty Pacific Ocean meeting the land and the river coming out of this divine Native American reservation. As we left the restaurant, we saw the coast guard doing drills by backing up their boats in the ocean. Seagulls and bald eagles were looking for food to either catch or steal from other animals.

I wondered if our national parks are similar in nature to the Native populations that once thrived in these areas. Suddenly, I heard a blast of child cacophony, or what they call "recess." Across the street from where we were taking family pictures was the local tribe's elementary school. I immediately thought to myself, *This is the most scenic school this side of the Mississippi.* The kids were now on the playgrounds, running and screaming. This was their ancestral land. Their ancestors had been here for thousands of years. We were just visitors today.

The contrast of the commerce at the restaurant, the government coast guard protecting us, the most beautiful views of the Pacific, and the Native children enjoying their land and free time played with my perspective. I thought of my son going to school. It would be here sooner than later.

Soon we were off to Rialto Beach in Olympic National Park. As this park encompasses so much, you may find yourself in multiple spheres of thinking. One moment you may be on a mountain hiking, the next at the beach, and in between, a town known for its fictional wolves, vampires, or in reality the most scenic school you've ever seen.

La Push, Washington, to Rialto Beach was a seventeen-minute drive, or around eleven miles. In those eleven miles we went from a Native American reservation town to a national park. The difference from some points of view may be vast and politically motivated, but on this special day I was happy to be here to experience all of its beauty.

Rialto Beach is a public beach located adjacent to Mora River and is composed of an ocean beach and coastal forest. The miles of seaside topography gave us views of many sea stacks of rock formations in the Pacific Ocean. The beach was named by the famous magician Claude Alexander Conlin after the Rialto Theater chain. Conlin lived close by in Mora, overlooking the beach and ocean, until the home burned in the 1930s. As of 1967, there was no trace of it. The striking abundance of fallen trees on the ocean beach makes it a tree graveyard, with hundreds of tree trunks floating in the surf or deposited on the beach by storms. If Ruby Beach were calm and soothing, Rialto was rough and deadly. If you got caught between a few of these floating tree trunks while the tide was violent, you likely would not survive.

We were all shocked at the violent nature of this beach. We took Logan's hand and at times took turns with him while the other two or three of us went on five- or ten-minute walks up the beach and nearby trails. At times we were concerned for our own safety with the slippery logs in unstable piles. A lot of our pictures and memories are from a distance. In some of the photos I see Liz, Josie, and Logan clumped in a circle and Joe walking in the distance, not necessarily sure-footed. We didn't want the tree graveyard to be ours, so we hopped, skipped, and jumped our way out of this place in a hurry. There were still a few people camping, or at least trying to.

On a hot sunny summer day, I bet you could spend a week maneuvering your way up the Pacific Coast shore one beach at a time. Rialto was our northern beach stop. If I had a choice, I'd pick the southern beaches like Ruby, but Rialto would be wonderous when our son grew up.

The drive from Rialto Beach to the Hoh Rain Forest in Olympic National Park was about forty-five minutes. We were going from one of the loudest places in the park, from the ocean constantly slapping the tree graveyard, to the quietest place in the lower forty-eight states. We parked at the Hoh Rainforest Visitor Center, pronounced "hoe" from what many believe is the native Quinault word for "fast moving water." We hiked the Hall of Mosses Trail first. On this one-mile circular hike I saw some of the most miraculous moss specimens I'd seen in my life. The moss encompassed the land, trees, fallen trees, and by God, my imagination. I think we need to send all our artists on this one-mile hike, not just because of the moss, but because this is the quietest place in the United States. There is a place on this trail called "One Square Inch." This is what the One Square Inch website says:

> One Square Inch of Silence is very possibly the quietest place in the United States. It is an independent research project located in the Hoh Rain Forest of Olympic National Park, which is one of the most pristine, untouched, and ecologically diverse environments . . . Close your

> eyes and listen for only a few seconds to the world you live in, and you will hear this lack of true quiet, of silence . . . By listening to natural silence, we feel connected to the land, to our evolutionary past, and to ourselves. One Square Inch of Silence is in danger, unprotected by policies of the National Park Service, or supported by adequate laws. Our hope is that by listening to natural silence, it will help people to become true listeners to their environment, and help us protect one of the most important and endangered resources on the planet, silence.

They have a point, and our hike consisted of seeing only three other people on this day in December. There was a sign to show where the silence was tested, and this certainly is one of the quietest places in the lower forty-eight states. If you include Hawaii, perhaps Alaska may be one of the only places in our country that has a few more quiet places. I agree with these sentiments, but as you see, there will always be a need for more protection. From Rialto Beach, I felt like we were in one of the safest and quietest places on Earth. I was just scared at Rialto that my son, family, and I would end up being sandwiched between two large dead, floating trees.

Here, in the silence, I could hear my mom's voice. She was saying that it's okay to be confused. It's okay to be scared. She was whispering that death was okay. It was okay to not know how much government laws protect or hinder our lands. It's okay to listen to your thoughts. My thoughts slowed, and the silence was golden. Liz looked thoughtful, and even Logan was still, a rare moment for this active boy. In this golden state we continued to the nearby Spruce Nature Trail.

The Spruce Nature Trail led us to the Hoh River. A few small waterfalls made the water sound like an ocean coming from the quiet Hall of Mosses Trail. Nature was abundant in December. I wondered how loud it was here in July with more people and perhaps the constant buzz of bees and insects.

Timing may have been perfect to be in the quietest place on Earth at a time I truly needed silence.

Maple Glade Rain Forest Trailhead in the Quinault Rain Forest

Ruby Beach

BLACK CANYON OF THE GUNNISON NATIONAL PARK

We went to the Black Canyon of the Gunnison National Park in April 2019. My mother passed away on February 24, 2019, and I was still grieving her departure but was happy she wasn't suffering from the pain and disability that ALS brought her. Our agenda was packed as usual. I had just attended a conference in Denver, and before we drove to the quaint town of Montrose, Colorado, and rented our Airbnb home, we visited my ninety-eight-year-old grandmother in the suburb of Littleton. She was a delight to be around to see us after my intense two-day conference. She lived at a gracious assisted living facility, where she was in good health. We were told she brightened up everyone's day at the facility. My grandmother cried when she saw the bright spring flowers we brought for her, but it was our three-and-a-half-year-old Logan who lit her up with joy.

Her memory was not what it once was, and I didn't bring up that my mother had just passed. The contrast of my mom passing at the age of seventy-one while my grandmother lived to ninety-eight was a sad juxtaposition of how life can be. Don't take your loved ones for granted, no matter what their age.

My grandmother would die in her sleep just three months later, on July 18, 2019.

My life in 2019 was a roller coaster of emotions. It was the year I lost both my mother and grandmother. Gunnison National Park was the only park we visited that year. At times 2019 was filled with grief, at other times with joy. We went to Europe for my brother-in-law's wedding in Amsterdam, extending our trip for a month.

As a father to a three-year-old, life was always in motion. Movement is how things come about, how change comes about.

The marble-like walls of the Black Canyon of the Gunnison National Park in Colorado were carved out by the Gunnison River. Two billion years of the movement of water since the Precambrian era, the oldest era of the Earth. Estimates are that Earth is around 4.5 billion years old, so, the way I figure, the Painted Wall of the Black Canyon, which rises 2,250 feet, slowly but surely cut into the earth at a rate of about one inch every one hundred years. In my grandmother's life of almost a hundred years, the river had dropped by one inch due to erosion.

I compared my grandmother's age of ninety-eight and my son's age of three, the oldest and youngest of my family at the time. I saw a world of difference in their experiences. I couldn't help but consider all the movement through my grandmother's life, all the changes she had seen and experienced. My son has a lifetime of movement and changes ahead of him. What would he see?

We drove fifteen miles from Montrose, Colorado, to the south entrance of the Black Canyon of the Gunnison National Park. This national park is to some a flyby. You can literally fly by this park, take a ten-minute walk, and see the majority of it. Nothing has changed there for centuries.

The name makes you think the canyon walls might be black.

Instead, it gets its name from the lack of sunlight in the canyon in the narrow space between high vertical walls. There are certain parts of the gorge in the canyon that only get thirty-three minutes of sunshine per day. On April 20, 2019, these thirty-three minutes fell around 11:36 a.m. Mountain Standard Time.

The Ute Native Americans had known the canyon's existence for many centuries before the Europeans saw it. It was then, as it has been for billions of years, too dangerous to inhabit. This national park has a vast geological history, but no known trace of human inhabitants. In the 1700s a few Spanish expeditions had passed by Black Canyon, and in the 1800s numerous fur trappers searched the area for beaver pelts. The first official log was in 1853 by John Williams Gunnison, who led an expedition to find a route from St. Louis to San Francisco. He noted that this was the roughest land he had ever seen and skirted the canyon to present-day Montrose. Following his untimely death at the hands of the Ute Natives, Captain Gunnison had called the river "grand," and later it was named after him: Gunnison River.

Black Canyon of the Gunnison was named a national monument on March 2, 1933, and a national park by Congress and President Bill Clinton on October 21, 1999. The park consists of twelve miles of the forty-eight-mile-long Black Canyon of the Gunnison River. This part of the river is the deepest and most dramatic section in the canyon. There are approximately thirty thousand acres in this park, and in 2018 there were just over three hundred thousand visitors.

We visited on April 19 and 20, 2019.

The road through the park has twelve outlooks with short hiking paths to view the canyon. On our first day we drove past all of the first eleven outlooks, which we could view from the car. We stopped at the last stop called High Point and Warner Point Trail. This trail does not look into the canyon but shows the opposite side of the other eleven viewpoints. You can see the town of Montrose and the Uncompahgre Valley; its beauty is so different from the sheer scare of the inner canyon. We hiked a handful of minutes. It was overcast, windy, and there was a sprinkle in the air. We all looked at each other and realized we were walking zombies. We got to the car and decided to tackle the other eleven trails the next day. It was time to grab dinner in town and take it to our rental home.

Going to national parks is a way to see the unique towns you stay in along the way. Montrose was off the beaten path, an oasis of sorts. In the age of renting from a homeowner instead of from a corporation, we booked a lovely home. It offered the many amenities of life anywhere, so we lived in comfort just a few miles from the national park. It's lovely to be able to get up and go, and even better to be able to enjoy a town you've never stayed in.

The morning and evening runs in Montrose were spectacular. Views of the mountains south of town were amazing. I had never seen the still snow-capped mountains in and around Telluride from this vantage point. I wouldn't be surprised if one day Montrose is a bustling town with million-dollar homes. We enjoyed the comfort and hospitality of Montrose in town as much as the park itself. We slept in and all felt like new the next day. We hit the road to the canyon just after breakfast and spent most of the day in the canyon.

The other eleven stops on the canyon rim were spectacular. How does one explain the distinct multiple layers of charcoal gray, white, and the veins of pink on the canyon walls? Black-and-white photos from any of these spots turn into vivid lifetime keepsakes as the walls scream beauty. Every step on the 134-yard walk from the car to the Pulpit Rock Overlook took our breath away.

We viewed the canyon from the perspective of the Gunnison River. We were placed in the middle. If one tends toward vertigo, this may be the worst point in all the national parks, unless you are an adrenaline junkie. Or this could be the overlook to do your morning yoga or sip a hot cup of tea enjoying the view. From this point of view, you can see the greens of the trees in the canyon below. On the top end of the canyon grows a thick forest of Gambel oak and serviceberry, which can canopy mule deer or bear. Meanwhile, farther down in the canyon, Douglas Firs, cottonwoods, and box elders lie closer to the river itself.

We were invigorated by the sights and all started talking very fast. Even Logan surprised us, chattering with a velocity we recognized as our own. Perhaps that's why it's called Pulpit Rock. He found his voice. His voice was of the canyon. Billions of years swept into my son's lungs, and he began to echo the canyon's rhythms.

Logan's hair had once again grown to his shoulders since Zion National Park, exactly one year ago. His hair joined forces with the wind, whipping into his face and high in the air. By now he was able to take the handful of hours hiking. At three and a half, he was a "parker." That's the toddler version of "park enthusiast" and "hiker." His parking was 80 percent on his own two feet and 20 percent begging to be put on my shoulders.

The trails were rocky, uneven, and treacherous—definitely not the park to take selfies. One wrong step and there goes your upcoming 10K from a sprained ankle. We could not let Logan hike without holding our hands, in case he got a foot stuck between the rocks. At one point a nice couple took a few family pictures for us.

From Pulpit Rock, the river was a color I'd never seen. It was the color of turquoise moving into teal. At that perfect moment when the sun hit the river, perhaps for just half an hour a day, the river's secret was this extraordinary color. When the sun shone out of a patch of clouds into the deep canyon and into the river, the color it cast was one we will likely see again only in our dreams.

We hiked to most of the twelve viewpoints. The most memorable was the Painted Wall. It's about a two-hundred-yard hike from where we could park the car. Wow, talk about a roller-coaster experience. The wind and 2,250-foot drop into the canyon made us feel off our feet, crazy and bended. It's called Painted Wall for a reason. Imagine this wall being created by the river for more than 2.25 billion years. It looks as if Logan might have taken a handful of paint brushes and painted white stripes across a vast smoke-gray room. Leave him running in the room for an hour or two, the lines of white cutting across the gray would resemble this 225-story-tall natural skyscraper stretching skyward above us.

Imagine two Empire State Buildings, one on top of the other. That's the distance to the river below from this viewpoint. Picture the chiseled walls of the canyon, with their marbled gneiss and schist running nearly horizontally the length of Manhattan in this amazing metropolis-like canyon.

We are always amazed at what humans can build: the pyramids in Egypt, the Eiffel Tower in Paris, and the Burj Khalifa in Dubai. Of the tallest buildings in the world, only the Burj Kalifa at 2,717 feet is taller than Painted Wall; the next tallest building, Merdeka in Kuala Lumpur, comes in at 2,227-feet tall. But Mother nature and some 2.3 billion years, with the help of the teal-turquoise Gunnison River, created a masterpiece here far superior to what man can build.

One day we may get to those great buildings, but if we never make it, I'm glad I took my family to this canyon. This visit has made me a man more closely linked to nature. Nature one day may take me to those man-made tall buildings. But for now, I am awestruck to see how this canyon's beauty takes time. This idea has become part of me. Time measures many things, including the places we choose to visit and observe.

Into the Canyon

Chasm View

Pulpit Rock Overlook

ARCHES, CANYONLANDS, CAPITOL REEF, BRYCE CANYON, AND ZION NATIONAL PARKS

UTAH'S MIGHTY FIVE: IN 2020 LIFE FOR THE WORLD'S population changed on a dime. We entered the COVID-19 worldwide pandemic. Millions of people would die, and millions more would get the virus and suffer both short-term and long-term health consequences. In March 2020 everyone in the United States quarantined at home. Healthcare workers faced the virus and its devastating effects all day, every day. Most other frontline workers, like those in grocery stores, big box stores, and pharmacies, still worked while the rest of us shifted to working from our kitchen tables. Schools shut down to attempt to limit the spread of the virus. Tens of millions of those in industries like tourism and food service lost their jobs. There was a concurrent financial slowdown.

Working from home was at first easygoing, but the lack of human interactions was difficult for many. We lost something as a connected society. We lost the ability to interact with each other.

What we gained was the ability to pivot and think outside the box. For my family that meant finding a way to go to more national parks while everyone else stayed home. We knew we could respect the efforts to distance from others in public, and we knew open outdoor spaces and fewer crowds would be an advantage.

In June 2020, three months into the global pandemic, we took the risk and adventured to all five national parks in our neighboring state.

Utah is one of the most amazing states. It may be seen from afar as a skiing mecca, but the drive and stay in all the national parks leads me to believe this Western state in the US may be one of our best kept secrets. Even so, this secret has been getting out for decades. The marketing campaigns for the "Mighty Five" national parks in Utah have produced tens of millions of visitors every year, from around the country and world.

As we drove from Santa Fe to Moab, Utah, it became clear the world had definitely changed. Many places were like ghost towns. Everyone was rightfully scared of everyone else. So soon into the pandemic, we knew little about how the virus was transmitted, and even less about how to protect ourselves. It was as if our family was traveling and vacationing in a post-apocalyptic age. In my life the only similar feeling was the few weeks and months after September 11, 2001.

This virus, which the world still says originated out of China, was more deadly than any terrorist plot and attack. The only historical events we could research were the Black Plague in the 1300s that killed seventy-five to two hundred million people and the Spanish flu in 1918 that lasted more than three years and killed approximately fifty million people. Since no one was alive from the 1300s in 2020, and one would have to be ninety-nine to 102 to even be alive during the Spanish flu, it was as if no one on Earth knew exactly what to do. I felt like time was divided by "before" and "after." There was the time before the pandemic took hold, and now we were in the middle of its ongoing aftermath.

In our defense, my family was restless, scratching at our home walls to do something. We believed in the science and took all precautions, yet we had this goal. Traveling by car was less dangerous than by plane. We took to the road to visit the Mighty Five parks of Utah.

Not only was our son's preschool canceled, it felt like work and life itself was canceled. If this was the end of the world, as they say, where would you go? We wanted to go to the parks.

The drive to Moab, Utah, was around six hours. We packed a lunch and ate in Colorado by a river. Our son was fascinated by the mighty rushing river, as if it didn't get the message that the world was suffering. I followed him around like a hawk to keep him safe from contact with other people. We wore masks indoors and sometimes outdoors, but the world was a bit crazy that year. Whether you were wearing masks or not, everyone was angry. They were angry because they had lost their jobs, or because of their inability to cross borders and see family, or because of a death in the family, all due to the virus.

So here, in the Four Corners, where four different states meet, I followed my son closely not just due to my fear of the virus, but because people would scream at each other for either wearing masks or not. The political views were varied and, at this point in our country, explosive.

Luckily, everyone we ran into was nice, cordial, and not hostile. Perhaps that's the more natural way. Perhaps that's the way for those of us wanting to see the natural world. Perhaps it was different for modern urban travelers. We heard news reports of extreme violence in airplanes, crowded streets, and the stresses in city spaces.

As we entered Utah from Colorado, we took photos at the welcome sign. This sign near Monticello, Utah, had an enormous modern painting of Arches National Park as its cornerstone. A similar picture of Delicate Arch is on the famous Utah license plate. We were on our way . . . "Delicately."

On June 2, 2020, we were entering a hot place at a hot time. Temperatures would be more than ninety every day in Moab. This was our summer vacation in the strangest time of our lives. It was a world that would become the new normal for our son.

We stayed at the Hyatt Place Moab. It opened in 2018 and felt brand new. The large outdoor pool was excellent for our now almost five-year-old son. Logan was exactly four years and eight months old.

Liz was now forty, and I would be forty in just over a month. Where did our youth go?

The pool had a large area that was only a foot or two deep, so Logan loved it, as he could walk around—with me close by, of course. Not only was I there to make sure he didn't drown, but there because the virus might be among us. We ate dinner in our room and spent the later evening hours swim-walking in the pool. We got a good night's sleep. It would be interesting to see what our dreams were now in this pandemic state of mind.

The next morning, we would be on our way to Arches National Park.

We drove into Arches National Park early on a cool morning. There were no lines, and the winding road to enter the park was like the world's current roller coaster of emotions in its pandemic state. As we drove to the top, the world opened. The vast landscape filled with brownish-red wet clay, so vast a space that it made us question what our eyes were seeing. This was one of the most cross-eyed moments of my life, and I had to grab hold of the wheel, just in case. The arches around us were of a different dimension. Did dinosaurs sculpt these? Was this the playground of extraterrestrials?

No, it was science, and the natural world was more than millions, if not billions, of years working at it. Most of us at the time may have thought the pandemic would last forever. For us, this land was there to tell us on this hot summer morning that we would be okay. We just needed time.

Can you believe that some three hundred million years ago this land was the sea? Can you also believe that the sea in this part of Earth evaporated and was refilled nearly thirty times? The evaporations left behind salt beds thousands of feet thick.

The soft red sandstone formations at Arches are not shy. They scream at you to stare. They may be the supermodels of all the parks, perched on tall stilettos with arches stretching for days. Think of the tallest athletes or slender supermodels. Fragile yet elegant. Sandstone was deposited 150 million years ago. Thereafter, water dissolved most of the salt deposits. Many of the formations in this area were created as the water dissolved and erosion played its game. I believe the hand of God and this Earth joined to be called Mother Earth.

Mother Earth gave us her beauty and a caution. She demanded we respect her, and for these days we all did. We all knew we were in a global pandemic. We knew to keep space between each other. We and many others wore masks. We were all in the same boat now, trying to trust that everything would be okay. To be out in all of Mother Nature's beauty made us feel safe and grateful.

Our first stop was at Balanced Rock. Think of the world's largest boulder balancing on smaller rocks that you might be able to push off a cliff. There, you got it! We wouldn't, of course, but seeing this huge rock seemingly balanced precariously was a remarkable sight.

Maybe it was fear, but walking my family around this national treasure was as if this very moment would be the time in history the balanced rock fell. Not only would it fall, but it would pulverize us. The wind, with its incense of juniper and pine—a mint of the desert—whistled in my ears. Was the wind going to blow the rock off its foundation? No, Balanced Rock will still be there when I'm gone. It will be there for all of us until the sandstone supporting it wears away many, many years in the future.

In his book, *Desert Solitaire,* the late, famous environmentalist Edward Abbey states, "The extreme clarity of the desert light is equaled by the extreme individuation of desert life forms. Love flowers best in openness and freedom."

Abbey was a seasonal park ranger at Arches, and the book is about his experiences in and around the park. The hike around Balanced Rock reminded me of this cosmic reason why we can see things in nature for their extreme clarity. Leaving them there makes them the lifeblood of the open desert and its freedom to exist at this moment *and* into the future.

Abbey was on to something. *Desert Solitaire* perhaps reminded me about life in the pandemic: "The fear of death follows from the fear of life. A man who lives fully is prepared to die at any time."

Perhaps our own need for the national parks eased for us the fear of death by reminding us to live fully in the moment.

Our decision to make these stops in the national parks put a lot into perspective. So did a hot, cranky child. He was ready to get into the shade, the air-conditioned SUV, or into the hotel pool. Luckily it wasn't quite ninety degrees yet, and we had many more stops in this park. By the time we were finished, we would all be ready to jump into the pool.

Delicate Arch was our next stop. It had been a few months since the shutdown limited human interaction, and this was our first stop among other people. Yes, we may have gone to the grocery store once or twice, but now we were in with a lot of other people. This is the most visited stop in Arches National Park. I'd say by the time we drove away, there were around thirty people in and around the hiking path.

A few weeks before, we had watched *Indiana Jones and the Last Crusade* on TV. The scenes of 1912 filmed in Utah with River Phoenix as the young Indy are perhaps the most vivid movie scenes of America's desert ever. Arches National Park was the backdrop, and those scenes gave me the courage to follow its trails, even during the pandemic shutdown. I think a lot of us out there on the trail felt like Jones with his spectacular way of juggling risk and reward. We were all putting our lives in danger to treasure life at its most beautiful.

Life is meant to be spent moving. Interacting. Juggling. But while staying at home, we only did those things with the family. After a while, we all got on each other's nerves. Laugh out loud, we all loved each other, but the Indy in all of us called for adventure.

The treasure of Delicate Arch was of pure joy. The thing soars above your presence. At fifty-two-feet tall, Delicate Arch makes those fifty-two feet feel like so much more. This arch is the most widely recognized landmark in Arches National Park, maybe in Utah, and perhaps of all the national parks. It may be the image foreigners have in their minds of the American Southwest when they think of us here. Popularized by movies like *Indiana Jones* and the famous

Utah license plate, Delicate Arch should not be missed. Many would say there are much better arches around many other parks. There may be, but please don't miss this one if you get the chance to see it.

Around and under this arch, I saw people stand transfixed, drop to their knees, or cry with joy. Perhaps the pandemic had something to do with it. Overall, many of us in this moment had a very religious experience.

In 2002, some eighteen years prior to our visit, the Olympic torch relay went through this arch for the 2002 Winter Olympics in Salt Lake City, Utah. In this moment we were all passing our torches for positivity on Earth at this fragile moment in time. We were in World War III with a virus. We were all hoping to live another day. Under the Earth's arch, we would listen to her. We would help more. We would keep her in our memory.

With masks on I took pictures of a family who had been hiking nearby. They took off their masks, then put them back on. They took our family photo. We took our masks off and then on. We all thanked each other, perhaps with a tear in our eyes. The new world order would stop for a few more minutes. Wasn't it nice to take a few more minutes?

We drove around the park in close to one hundred degrees. We took pictures from our Jeep. An hour or two went by, and we hiked a few more trails. Our son was napping. We thanked God. My wife kissed me. The small things now made even more sense.

In all the other parks we took such small moments for granted. Not anymore. Our time together was the treasure. Our treasure at one degree or a hundred was this moment in the park.

By 4:47 p.m. we were back in the comfort of our new hotel, and Logan was taking his longest nap of 2020 in his plush bed. His dreams were now of a miraculous desert and not just the new words in his vocabulary like "COVID," "hand sanitizer," and "pandemic." Hopefully one day, when someone asks him what he remembers of the pandemic, he will say going to our national parks.

ARCHES NATIONAL PARK IS A UNIQUE PARK. THERE ARE more than two thousand sandstone arches located in the park, the greatest number of natural arches in the world. Although small at around seventy-seven thousand acres, it had more than 1.2 million visitors in 2020 during the pandemic and more than 1.6 million visitors in 2018. Arches is only four miles north of Moab, Utah. If you travel in search of Arches, you may come back wanting more of Moab. Or perhaps if you go for Moab, you will certainly come back wanting more of Arches.

The park was named a national monument on April 12, 1929, and later a national park under Congress and President Richard Nixon on November 12, 1971.

Humans have been in and around Arches since the last ice age, or around ten thousand years ago. Fremont people and Ancestral Puebloans lived here more than seven hundred years ago. Spanish missionaries encountered Ute and Paiute tribes in the area around 1775. The Mormon Elk Mountain Mission settled in around 1885 but soon thereafter abandoned the area. Ranchers, farmers, and prospectors later settled Moab in the riverine valley in the 1870s.

To me, Moab felt like a bustling town about to become a major city. It's testosterone Jeep tour outlets and outdoor tourism made it feel like a desert boomtown. The food and hospitality felt like the best in towns next to national parks. And, once again, we took our eight-year-old Jack Russel mix pup Krug. This was a vacation town that welcomed not only our families, but our four-legged friends as well.

THE NEXT DAY WE TOOK OUR FAMILY AND, THIS TIME, Krug to both Dead Horse Point State Park and Canyonlands National Park. We got to Dead Horse Point State Park around 10:00 a.m. on June 4, 2020. This Utah state park features a dramatic overlook and viewpoint above the Colorado River. The park is around fifty-three hundred acres and sits at fifty-nine hundred feet above sea level. The park charges a fee to enter, and at first I thought the charge was outrageous. But then, when I stood on the overlook, I understood. I was in heaven. They could have charged an arm or a leg for this view.

Why is it called Dead Horse? According to legend, this is the place cowboys in the nineteenth century used as a natural corral to trap wild horses. Some would die of exhaustion or thirst; some would leap to their deaths. The park sits above Canyonlands National Park, and its austere parking lots do not hint at what we could see below. As we took our toddler out and put our dog Krug on a leash, we had no idea of the upcoming view. The trail was also unremarkable. As we strode along joking in the morning, we suddenly came to the edge.

The edge was like looking into the Grand Canyon from halfway down. Seeing the green and brown hues of the Colorado River bend around a gray and red mesa rising two hundred feet in the sky looked like a balanced cathedral. The flowing river dissected Earth's history with sweeping cuts and turns into the mesa. We took pictures of this unique overlook. A family photo with the dog. Then me holding the dog atop a bench made from large sandstone rocks. More photos of the Earth and sky. We wanted to save this moment.

Many movies have been shot at Dead Horse, including the amazing opening scene for the 2000 movie *Mission: Impossible* 2. What's funny is that we saw this movie in our hotel this very week. What a coincidence. What's no coincidence is this amazing state park right next to the even more amazing Canyonlands National Park.

To compare: Dead Horse had around 560,000 visitors in 2017 with around fifty-three hundred acres. Canyonlands had around 733,000 visitors in 2019 with just over 337,000 acres. I have a feeling many people like us combine both when they enter the "Island in the Sky" district of Canyonlands. Driving Moab to Dead Horse is around forty minutes. What an amazing appetizer for the upcoming Canyonlands.

We started exploring Canyonlands around 11:30 a.m. The desert heat was rising. This hostile land was courageously telling all of us, including my dog, to keep going.

Canyonlands National Park is divided into four districts. They are the Island in the Sky, the Needles, the Maze, and the combined rivers —the Green and Colorado—which carved two large canyons into the Colorado Plateau.

This park was finally established as a national park on September 12, 1964, after many failures of Congress to pass it under President Lyndon Johnson.

Edward Abbey was a frequent visitor to Canyonlands and described it as "the most weird, wonderful, magical place on Earth; there is nothing else like it anywhere." When we stopped at Mesa Arch, I could tell this park dabbled in something weird, wonderful, magical, and different.

Mesa Arch is ten, twenty, maybe thirty feet above you. Just be careful, because if you take a wrong step, it may be your last as you tumble below into the Canyonlands.

How can I explain the Canyonlands? It's as if millions of smaller canyons have formed between the Colorado and Green Rivers. A magician shows up and casts the most magical browns, reds, whites, greens, and grays all around. This land makes you feel as if you are in the belly of the Grand Canyon. The proximity to the bottom makes you feel like a god in this desert land, but the heat in June takes you back to reality. You want your air conditioning back in your car. How could anyone live here in the summer?

Life here began around ten thousand years ago. Geology and art meet at places like Horseshoe Canyon, where pictographs and petroglyphs are etched into the walls all around. Although people have been here that long, the canyons took millions of years to form from geologic events, such as uplifts, volcanic activity causing the area to rise more than five thousand feet above sea level. This allowed the Colorado and Green Rivers to do their thing. That thing was again more magic, revealing horizontal bands of rock in the spires and canyon walls. Red is formed from the rich deposits of iron carried here by rivers from nearby mountains. The white crust on top is mostly beach sand left behind from a shallow sea that covered the park millions of years ago.

We stopped at the end of the road at the Island in the Sky district. My son was taking a nap, and it was around one hundred degrees by 2:00 p.m. Liz waved me off to take the hike by myself. It was one of the only hikes I've taken alone in the parks. Most times, I'm with my tribe. At others, just my wife, son, or both—and at the very least my dog. In the past we would just strap our son on our backs, and he'd sleep.

Today it was simply too hot. On the half-mile hike, I passed a family of four and a few others. Where were we all going? Luckily there were some shaded areas as the deep roots of the junipers and pinyon pines found a water source somewhere underground.

Wow, the view at Upheaval Dome looked like a bomb went off. From afar it looks like any earth indentation, such as Canyonlands, the Grand Canyon, or from a perch above Death Valley. But up close it is much different. It is a round crater approximately 6.2 miles in diameter, a runner's 10K, and is known to be almost 170 million years old. Scientists will be debating this unusual formation forever. To this day, some believe it was formed by a meteorite, while others contend a giant salt bubble, known as a "salt dome," is responsible for the abnormality. For me this is where the dinosaurs lived and where my own roots started. Here is where they might have seen their last flash. I think perhaps their extinction was a combination of events, with this place as one part.

I trotted back to the car deep in my own thoughts of dinosaurs, a testament to seeing the park on my own as I hiked. I was glad to be back with my family. The end of the Jurassic period may have been right here, just below. Who knows what lies even farther below that surface?

That last lonely hike would have been a bit crowded if it had not been during the lockdown, and I'm sure we would have managed, masked or unmasked.

On the way back to Moab, my wife checked online for dinner. We picked up Thai food and ate under trees for an impromptu family picnic.

I asked my wife one question: "Do I have enough time to become the next foundation board president of the New Mexico Museum of Natural History & Science starting July of 2022?" As we debated my time, the idea started to fly. These parks, the canyons, the arches, they've stood the test of time. Will we? Will we as a couple, family, region, country, or world? I'm sure we will. Could I do something to make sure?

The museum had called me the day before and asked if I'd take the leadership role. I told them immediately that I was probably too busy, but I'd check with my wife. After my hike, I started to reconsider. If I didn't do it, who would? Would I do a good job in this volunteer role? Giving back is something I love to do. I had been on this nonprofit foundation board for about three years and had been on more than ten other boards in the past. My late mother always had a dinosaur lesson plan for her kindergarten class, and the end of that plan came with a field trip to this exact museum asking for my support.

Liz and I said yes. I called the incoming president from where we sat under those trees and told her I would commit. In celebration we packed the car and went to Moab Giants. This open-air museum has a dinosaur park with a desert trail dotted with life-size models of T. rex and other prehistoric beasts. Like I said, it's hard to beat Moab. Logan loved Dead Horse, Canyonlands, and the dinosaur trail we led him on that day. We all got our minds off the pandemic, and we took a step onto a new path. It was a good day. It was a good life.

The next morning, I was up well before my family. I slipped out of the hotel room without them hearing me leave. Again, I was on my own. I had read that there were public trails around Moab with dinosaur tracks. I drove the fifteen minutes to the Poison Spider Dinosaur Tracksite, a handful of parking spots on a cliff overlooking the highway next to the Colorado River. I was the only one there. Again, it was a worldwide pandemic. I was not sharing the view with a single soul. I was talking to the Earth.

I did a quick four-mile run on the path made of Navajo Sandstone slickrock. It was slippery. On the way back to my car, I read the few descriptions of the dinosaur tracks and walked them—walked the actual footprints of previous giants. These were quite small dinos. Here is what one of the informational signs said:

> PROWLING PREDATORS – Tracks of theropod dinosaurs are relatively common in the early Jurassic rocks of the Navajo Sandstone and occur in several places around the Moab area. The tracks from this site represent up to 10 different individual animals. The rocks containing the tracks fell from the cliffs above, splitting along the bedding plane where they were preserved. Both the original tracks and the layer that filled them are present on the slabs. From these larger tracks, called Eubrontes, we can tell that the animal was just over 5.6 feet tall at the hip. There are several small tracks preserved on these two slabs as well, which are named Grallator. Some of the animals leaving them behind would have been as small as a modern-day turkey, just 1.5 feet tall at the hip. We can tell that these small animals were moving at a speed of 3 miles per hour. How many tracks can you find?

I found around five tracks. It was fun, and I wanted to bring my family back to see these tracks. I knew they would want to see.

First we had another national park to go to on this fine, hot summer day. The drive from Moab to Capitol Reef National Park was around two hours. As we got closer to the park, the earth formations on the side of the road got as magical and bizarre as I've seen in my life. This area is known as the Waterpocket Fold, a wrinkle in the landscape that stretches on for nearly a hundred miles. It's called a monocline with one side much higher than the other. This unique geology is its magic even before you enter the park, and one of many of Capitol Reef's sought-after features.

Capitol Reef National Park is approximately 242,000 acres and had around 1.2 million visitors in 2018. The park encompasses the Waterpocket Fold, some sixty-five million years old, which probably caused the colliding continental plates that created the Rocky Mountains. If you like hiking, skiing, or seeing the Rocky Mountains, this is the birthplace of such memories. This place has been weathered, eroded, and glistened over millennia to expose layers of rock, fossils, and colored sandstone cliffs. The gleaming white domes and cliffs of Navajo Sandstone give the name Capitol to match the color of the United States Capitol Building. You would think that the word "reef" would refer to the former oceans here, but the park's reefs refer to their abundant canyons, colorful monoliths, obtrusive buttes, and gigantic white domes. They say the view from above is as spectacular from the land below.

We first stopped in the visitor center. This amazing visitor center had a scaled version of the park on display and allowed us to see the geology from above. We got a few souvenirs from the bookstore and asked a ranger where to hike, as we had packed a lunch. The ranger suggested the hike around the visitor center was one of the best in the park. We took the ranger's advice and stepped foot onto the trail.

This trail was on Sulphur Creek, and some of the trail was in the shade, as the large cliff above blocked out the sun's rays. We walked here until we realized sand or rocks could easily slip off and hit us. So we changed our walking from time to time with the knowledge of the danger from above. The hike was rather slow, as the creek had mostly soft sand, and the views from the creek encompassed canyons, mountains, and plains we had not yet seen on our adventures. A few families passed us by.

The rock formations from the visitor center looked like Castle Mountains and are actually known as "the Castle." It was as if the magic of Disney's castle was built to mimic this rock formation. We got hungry, ate our lunch in the shade, and stared at the Castle rising up into the sky. As we started to move again, we noticed Sulphur Creek was flowing with more water now. The ranger suggested we take our shoes off to dip our feet in. We did just that. It cooled our toes and our souls. The temperature again was approaching a hundred on this fifth day of June. As we hiked and jogged in the water, we were all laughing and splashing, having the time of our lives.

Our pictures atop a three-foot rock in the middle of the mostly sandy creek with water flowing in the shade captured this memorable moment. We raised our hands to celebrate the hot hike we had just accomplished and scrambled over the sandstone to jump into our car. We drove to the town known as Fruita to visit the Gifford Homestead, which lies within Capitol Reef National Park.

The human history of Capitol Reef National Park started around the year 1000, with the Fremont culture Native Americans living close to today's visitor center on the Fremont River. They irrigated crops of corn and squash and stored their grain in stone granaries made from the black basalt boulders that are all around. In the thirteenth century most, if not all, the Natives moved, possibly due to severe drought. Everything was abandoned until Paiutes moved into the area.

Later, following the American Civil War, officials of The Church of Jesus Christ of Latter-day Saints in Salt Lake City sought to establish missions here. In 1866 a quasi-military expedition of Mormons in pursuit of Natives penetrated the high valleys to the west. The town of Fruita was established around 1880 by a group of Mormons. Fruita was named The Eden of Wayne County for its large orchards.

We stopped in the orchards of Fruita. As we stepped outside, deer were grazing among the fruit trees, families were picnicking, and the famous Gifford Homestead was selling fruit pies. We bought three small cherry pies. Probably the best homemade pies we'd ever eaten. We saw Farm-Opoly, the farm version of the Monopoly game we had at home. Our Monopoly at home was a battered hand-me-down from my mom. Logan wanted us to buy Farm-Opoly. We got the pies and the board game. Under a very tall cottonwood tree in Fruita, close to the old, famous barn, we ate our pie and all played Farm-Opoly. People passing by chuckled at the sight of Logan playing so passionately. Our son was well ahead of us by the time his attention span gave out an hour later. We declared him the winner.

Who thought a national park would be a farm with cherry pies? Who knew it would be Capitol Reef? If my son ever becomes a farmer, this will be his origin story. He might think to himself, *I became a farmer the day my parents took me to Capitol Reef. There we ate pie, hiked, and learned about the dynamics of farming on the board game Farm-Opoly. I knew one day I'd become a farmer.*

As I wandered into the Gifford Homestead to clean up, I saw there was a live emergency. Two workers at the Gifford Homestead, maybe teens or girls in their twenties, had just been notified by a ranger on the CB radio that a hiker had just had a heart attack in this near hundred-degree heat.

"What can I do to help?" I asked.

They snapped out of their initial shock and thanked me. Thank goodness they told me they had everything under control.

The reality of this situation hit me as I stepped outside and looked at the amazing Pendleton Barn and its acres of peach and cherry tree orchards where deer grazed peacefully. Nearby was a packed camping site. It was as if the pandemic was not among us.

My family, oblivious to the emergency, were chasing each other among the fruit trees. I briefly mentioned the emergency to my wife as we got into the car, and we silently thought of the hiker and wished him a swift recovery.

Capitol Reef National Park in Utah took a while to be established. There in Fruita, all the farmland around us was once private. During the 1960s, the National Park Service purchased the private land parcels at Fruita and Pleasant Creek. By 1970 Capitol Reef National Monument comprised 254,000 acres, but the actions of the park were controversial to locals who saw this place as home. Some saw the staffing at the park as inadequate to properly manage all the land. It wasn't until December 18, 1971, that Congress and President Richard Nixon made Capitol Reef a national park.

As we exited the park my son was in the mood for ice cream. I pulled into a dusty grocery store parking lot for the Bull Mountain Market. He chose a Push-Up orange pop that took me right back to my childhood. I scanned the store and saw a local art co-op section. The checkout clerk said the store paid the artists when any of the pieces sold. One of the paintings was a small abstract piece that looked like a brontosaurus. I couldn't believe this animal roamed here once. When I brought this cool piece up to check out, the cashier said he was the artist. His four canvases on the wall here were composed of paint he combined at hot temperatures and moved around. He said they didn't have any specific forms, but people had said they looked like space or a dinosaur. I paid for the Push-Up pop, water, some sodas, and his painting. He signed it with a Sharpie, his big smile telling me I had made his day. I had also made my son's day with the orange ice cream now dripping down his chin.

I would later frame the art and think of all the ways the dinosaur has changed my life. From my mom's lesson plans to running around their feet that morning and thinking of Capitol Reef and the how land that created the Rocky Mountains was home to such prehistoric creatures. Now an abstract painting from this land and the local artist would grace my walls to remind me that dinosaurs still had something to say, even if it was just in our imagination.

Again and again, this beautiful land brought that imagination to life.

We imagined a life as a family with joy. We were accomplishing that even through the global pandemic.

The next morning we checked out of our hotel in Moab. I wanted to show my family the dinosaur tracks at Poison Spider Dinosaur Tracksite. As we got on the road, the air was dense with moisture. The high in Moab was going to be seventy-five instead of ninety-five degrees Fahrenheit that day. Finally, an overcast day with moisture and we were leaving. Just our luck. Even so, I felt we received what we needed from this trip, even if it wasn't what we thought we wanted.

As we were about three quarters of the way to the dinosaur track trails, a black and gray cloud enveloped the canyon. We were driving next to the Colorado River and a few campgrounds when a *tap, tap, tap* on the window turned into a thunder of earthshaking, quarter-size hail.

Bryce Canyon National Park, our next destination, was more important than a cracked windshield. I asked everyone if we should turn around and heard a resounding, "Yes!" come simultaneously from my wife and son's shouts as the thunder, lightning, and hail shook in all eight of our eardrums, including those of our dog. Krug crawled his way under the blanket he was sitting on, shaking. He was ready for anything. As we got out of the canyon and onto the highway, departing both the great Moab area and Arches National Park, we saw the storm cell had just passed by. The roads were moist and steaming, looking a lot less sun drenched. The quick-moving monsoon made the desert floor look and feel different. The air was cooler, and curtains of rain showed in the distance.

All along the highways to Bryce Canyon were incredible rest stops with magnificent viewpoints. We stopped at the San Rafael, Black Dragon, and Salt Wash view areas. There we refreshed ourselves, had lunch, and looked out at the views. It was a microcosm of the national parks we had just visited. I'm amazed at how the state of Utah, and perhaps their Department of Transportation, took pride in these stops. Everything was designed for showcasing the beauty of the state and to be family friendly. Kudos to you, Utah!

We stayed at Ruby's Inn, about two miles from the entrance of Bryce Canyon National Park. Ruby's was more like a resort and perhaps a local institution. We were not only staying in their Deer Lodge hotel area, but there was a general store that tripled as a grocery store, souvenir shop, and the closest thing this area had to a small big-box store.

In 1916 Reuben (Ruby) Syrett established his family ranch at this location. Ruby's family was so impressed by the beauty of the nearby park that they got permission in 1919 to build a lodge and host the tourists of America and the world visiting this area. The rest is history.

During the next two days, we lived, ate, shopped, and devoured the unique hospitality this resort offered, just steps to one of the most beautiful parks we had laid eyes on. One evening I left my family and went into their general store to look for a park cowboy hat. I looked among hundreds of options, and yes, this was the best selection of hats any ranger may grab to go to work, and my choice was an olive-green "Outback" cowboy hat that would be my go-to hat when hiking, sightseeing, or enjoying parks over the years. It's dubbed as the Southwestern Aussie hat. With time and the sun's wicked display of power, the olive green has faded to a greenish brown, a paint color by BEHR paints called "Kilimanjaro." We painted our backyard deck Kilimanjaro in honor of the aged hat's color. We have a funny way of embedding the memory of our parks' beauty in what we collect on our journeys.

There was nothing special about our hotel room, but we weren't going to spend much time in it anyway. Perhaps we could have upgraded to the better rooms, but it was the pandemic, and everyone around was on pins and needles. In addition, this was the start of no room service or cleaning. Booking hotel rooms during the pandemic was all about buyer beware. For that time, in the not-too-distant past, amenities like room cleaning did not occur. It didn't matter. We were not there for the housing; we were there for the park. Ruby's not only had the best location, but they had many things to see and do nearby. Just before sunset on June 6, 2020, we drove the scenic eighteen-mile one-way-in-and-one-way-out road to the end of this majestic park. The views were stunning. Luckily, we were here for more than two days and could take our sweet time. We had just spent the last five hours slowly sightseeing Utah from Moab to Bryce Canyon.

As the sun was setting, we got to the last stop on the road, called Rainbow Point. We felt the crisp air as we rushed to get out of our

Jeep. The cold air hit us as Bryce's elevation ranges from approximately seven thousand to nine thousand feet above sea level (compared to the four-thousand-foot elevation in Moab). It was probably close to fifty degrees Fahrenheit, but it felt even cooler. We quickly grabbed our spring coats, and on this June evening, we watched the most stunning and elegant sunset of our family's life. The peach and sea-salt pink spires that rose from the floor below were known as "hoodoos." Hoodoos? I'd never seen this word. Logan chanted, laughing, locking the word as his own.

At the edge of Rainbow Point, I took an ageless photo of Liz and Logan on a wooden bench looking at the hoodoos some two thousand feet below as the sun grazed its trajectory out West. I can't say this is my favorite photo from our park adventures, but I can't deny that every time I see this amazing photo, I almost lose it and cry. It represents the ability to get out of the car, our everyday routine, take a risk, and see how beautiful our planet is.

Bryce Canyon National Park is quite small, just about thirty-six thousand acres, but one of the most visited, with some 2.7 million visitors in 2018. In 2020, the year we visited Bryce Canyon, it was the fifteenth most visited national park of the total sixty-three, with approximately 1.5 million visitors. However, we never had the feeling of the masses in Bryce Canyon like the numbers seem on paper. The many stops and flow of the park made it feel as if we had her all to ourselves.

The spirit of Bryce Canyon perhaps speaks for all time. Although there is little known about the early human history of this park, it is believed that some ten thousand years ago people began to live here. Archaeologists have found Basket Maker Anasazi artifacts that date several thousand years old. Some other artifacts from the Pueblo-period Anasazi and the Fremont culture date to the mid-twelfth century. Around this time the Paiute Native Americans lived and hunted in this area. The Paiute developed a culture around the hoodoos. They created stories, or a mythology, about a wise, tricky coyote. This story became legend and grew about the original formation of the peculiar rock formations all around the park. The story says there were spirits around this park long ago, a group of animal-like creatures that could transform into people. However, they were bad spirits, so Coyote, being so tricky, turned them into rocks of various configurations. These colorful rock-like people now stand along the Paunsaugunt Plateau. Geologically speaking, it has taken millions of years for water to carve these colorful hoodoos. Water may split the rocks as it freezes, expands, cracks, and forms—sometimes hundreds of times a year. This was the most spectacular erosion I've seen.

It wasn't until the eighteenth and early nineteenth century that the first European Americans explored Bryce Canyon. Mormon scouts looked at the area in the 1850s to see if their cattle could graze the area. In 1873 the Kanarra Cattle Company used the area for cattle grazing. The Church of Jesus Christ of Latter-day Saints sent Scottish immigrant Ebenezer and Mary Bryce into the area because of Bryce's carpentry skill set. He might be useful in this unusual land. The Bryces set up their homestead right in the middle of the hoodoos next to the Bryce Amphitheater—the main collection of hoodoos in the park. Hoodoos by the hundreds stand high, like a crowd of ghosts, gaps between them creating a maze of hidden places. Ebenezer famously said, "This is a helluva place to lose a cow." I can only imagine the tricky Coyote persuading the cattle to move in the wrong direction and the hoodoos and their legend annoying Ebenezer and his inability to find all his livestock.

This would be a tough place to lose anything. What I lost here was my sense of reality. This is a place that makes you feel like you are in a movie, a book, or a dream.

Other settlers in the area, because of the Bryce legend, called this dreamlike area "Bryce's Canyon," which was later formalized into Bryce Canyon.

In 1923 a road was built on the plateau to provide the hundreds of millions of visitors access to its beauty over the next century. Eventually, the government bought the private land. President Warren Harding and Congress made Bryce Canyon a national monument on June 8, 1923, and on June 7, 1924, Congress passed a bill to establish Utah National Park, when all the land within the monument was acquired, and the name was restored to Bryce Canyon.

On February 25, 1928, Bryce Canyon officially became a national park. This was the nineteenth national park to be created by the United States government, not quite twenty parks, yet a teenage park system. This park did make me think I was in my teens.

This was the park where I fell in love with my family even more. Love, a strange thing, can take over your vision. We were a single unit. We could accomplish anything. Love would allow us to travel together even as the world and its leaders were saying we were dying. The pandemic, on the news and in the paper, was killing everything. Thank God our national parks were still open. Some of them eventually closed, but on this day Bryce was open. Like Ebenezer Bryce's crazy cows, if we had to be at home for a few years, we might be turned into hoodoos.

Who do you love? I love my family. Now I love them more. Travel brought me to this realization. Bryce Canyon brought this to us.

When we visited Bryce Canyon National Park, it was open twenty-four hours a day. As I woke up early the next day, I drove the one road into the park around 6:00 a.m. while my family was still sleeping. I felt like the only person alive in the world. Have you ever had that feeling or seen a single person, alone, looking out on an endless horizon? I felt like that person. Not only was the pandemic shutting down nearly all activity, but here no one was up driving into the park at 6:00 a.m. The parking lot was dark. As I drove the road, the sun started to stretch its rays toward eternity. I stopped in a parking area above Swamp Canyon. I stood on the opposite side of the road of the parking lot and looked out on the canyon for about twenty minutes, watching the sunrise.

The lush area had every color of green as I looked below. The middle portion, consisting of hoodoos that had a tricolor of peach, pink, and white, glowed, illuminated by the sun's golden hue. Below my viewpoint, two tiny creeks and a spring provided enough water to sustain more lush vegetation like grasses and willows. As it was the most silent moment in my pandemic years, the sound of breaking branches jolted me out of my thoughts. I saw a herd of deer in Swamp Canyon. I'm sure that the moment they saw me as I took in the sunrise, they started to move. Their movement was a symphony of breaking branches. They weren't scared of me; they were just on the move. They must have been grazing on grass and sipping the cool water below. Early risers like me, and this was their breakfast.

As I got used to the sounds, and the sun had risen, that thirty minutes of peace allowed me to have a different perspective for the day.

I walked across the road to my Jeep, and the same herd of deer was waiting for me, grazing just feet from my car. They stopped their breakfast and scattered in many directions. If a cow gets lost in this area, it might be hell to find them. These deer were in their forever home. They were like the land disguised, and perhaps like trickster Coyote and the evil hoodoos, in their own place. We didn't see deer the rest of our stay. Their early hour was for my eyes only.

As I walked toward the deer, I stumbled on brush, bark, and branches. If I had been their natural predator, they would have had to be swift on their hooves. My morning run was now in the spirit of the deer, who by now were half a mile away. They had disappeared.

By the time I returned, my family had showered, eaten breakfast, and were ready to be on the trails by 9:00 a.m. We hit Fairyland Point and hiked the rim trail for a fresh moment of clarity. This point in the park also has the famous hoodoos but a different sort of landscape as it passes through gently sloped badlands with denser tree cover. Out of nowhere, an evergreen, possibly a cousin to the pine, jutted out of the cliff above the level where we were walking. We looked above us to its exposed roots, a sight we would never otherwise see. The softer green of the tree contrasting the colors of the land below was amazing. Expect the unexpected in this fairyland.

We drove on to the Bryce Canyon Visitor Center close by. We heard from informative rangers, kept our distance from other visitors because of the pandemic, and picked up a few things from the store. We rushed out as we had a date with a photographer for family photos.

Our photographer had shot many family masterpieces in this park, and we met him at Bryce Point, sitting at around eighty-three hundred feet above sea level. We walked to five different locations on the rim trail as he took our pictures. These were the first family photos with my new hat, in its fairest green for Bryce Point. I wasn't sure if these would be our last family photos. The pandemic worried me. How would our world look in years to come? Would our species survive? I paid our photographer, and he promised to return the photos to us in a day or two. That quick forty five minute family photo shoot was divine.

On this trail we stopped at not only Bryce Point, but also Inspiration Point, Sunset Point, and Sunrise Point. I kept looking for the morning deer I encountered four hours before. Did they turn into the hoodoos?

We got back to Ruby's for a late lunch. As we walked the surrounding area, across the street was Bryce Canyon Wildlife Adventure. They had a candy store, fun, games, and Ruby's Horseback Adventures. A real cowboy eating his lunch at a rustic table welcomed us. Logan was too young to go horseback riding, but the cowboy put him up on a horse anyway, with Liz holding his hand. At the age of almost five Logan was up on a horse for an impromptu horseback ride, a gentle walk around their oval stable. This cowboy was so kind.

The next few nights when we ate dinner, we saw him walk in with his cowboy boots and spurs and waved a hello and "thank you, sir."

Liz had read about a great hike off the beaten path near a town called Tropic. The Mossy Cave Trail had a waterfall about ten feet high at the end for people to jump in. A National Park Services U.S. Department of the Interior sign read:

> Hike the Hoodoos – Mossy Cave – The trail splits here, with each side leading to water that is crucial for life in a dry land. To the left, a natural spring seeps from a rocky cliff, watering plants as it has for untold time. To the right, Water Canyon is fed by the Tropic Ditch—an irrigation canal dug by Mormon pioneers in the late 1880s. Historically, this was flowed only during periods of melting snow or heavy rain. Today, irrigation water flows May to October, bringing life to valley crops and orchards.

We went to the left to see Mossy Cave. The trail was an immediate uphill struggle. We were high above the water canyon and tropic ditch in mere minutes. We looked down to see people playing in the waterfall. It was amazing to see this water bring to life the hoodoos above and in the distance. In the shelter of the hoodoo walls, this hidden space was green and cool, and we could hear the water splashing long before seeing it. We had seen the hoodoos from two thousand feet above on the rim trail; now we were down among them. Hands down, this was our favorite hike of the day. The cave was amazing and different, not as mossy as Olympic National Park last year.

We quickly came down to the sign in the road and went right, heading for the waterfall itself. As we passed those eight or ten people we had seen before, we waved and kept our distance. The three of us had the waterfall and ditch to ourselves. We were not brave enough on this day to jump in, as the water was quite violent and fast. If Logan had been ten or so, he may have jumped in. Liz and I just didn't bring a change of clothes. Liz put her hands in the air next to the powerful waterfall. We were all grateful we had planned this great hike.

Back at the hotel we booked a dinner with a concert. We didn't know what to expect. Around 7:00 p.m. we went across the street to Ruby's modern barn for entertainment. The Bryce Canyon Wranglers band was playing daily at Ebenezer's Barn and Grill. We got there first.

We sat down in a barn and grill that probably maxed out at 250 people. A few workers greeted us and took our tickets. We grabbed soda from the fountain, and a few others started to show up. A long-haired gentleman greeted us. As we talked, he explained that he produced the band and was one of the musicians. Just prior to the pandemic he had moved his family of four, kids similar in age to Logan, from Manhattan to Tropic, where we had just hiked. He bought a home with an acre or so and was expecting great attendance at this nightly show, his first concert. I, too, moved west from Manhattan to Santa Fe in 2005 and experienced a similar change. I can only imagine a change where the pandemic and possibly one's business model is challenged completely. The band played mostly country, great by the way, and around eight or twelve people attended. As he came to thank us afterward, I saw a glimmer in his eyes that everything was going to be okay. He loved Logan and realized all of us were breaking some sort of pandemic rules from where most of us came from. I said a silent prayer in this sacred place that his family, band, and Ruby's would be safe from the virus and survive. Survival is very Darwinian.

We checked out of our hotel the next morning. It was freezing. We got our winter Patagonia and North Face jackets out. We had saved the best hike for last. On this freezing morning we would hike from the top to somewhere below. We hiked the Navajo Loop, which at 1.3 miles packed a massive spectacle of colors within hoodoos, dirt, and people. Our dog stayed in the car, as he was shivering from the cold. His loss.

From the hike we saw a hoodoo that looked like Thor's hammer and passed under doors called Wall Street. Logan had fun on this hike, and many strangers, including a newly minted park ranger, congratulated him. This trail was known as an expert trail, and many warnings were posted. We added the Queens Garden Trail, which made the hike around three miles. If a queen had a desert garden of sand, dust, and rocks, this would be it.

Elizabeth, my wife, was my queen. As I look at the captured videos of this hike, I hear, "Hello, we're on Queens Trail in Bryce Canyon National Park. We're right in the hoodoos."

This is the trail to make a family feel, yes, they are in and part of the hoodoos. It's not easy, but it's worth it. I assume the feeling of being a movie star on the set of a neighboring planet may be like this hike. Their strange world, not ours.

As we maneuvered past one area and under a man-made tunnel, underneath a hoodoo, we ventured into a new area full of bursting pink, peach, and white hoodoos. I put my son on my shoulders and started to run to get warm. He screamed with joy and erupted with laughter. Now he was with me on my happiness scale.

The hike back up was arduous, tough with a four-year-old, but well worth it. We had enough of a moment in the freezing cold, and now it was best to depart. Even so, I'm glad we hiked. On the way out we took pictures at the park entrance sign: "Bryce Canyon National Park."

As I gassed up to head to Zion, a cold wind blew. It took me right back to February in Santa Fe. Suddenly it started to snow. Liz was on a work call, and Logan was on his iPad. It was not a normal snow, but one with a winter's intensity. Winter was coming, if not just for a day. This park was intense in so many ways. This park had become our favorite in Utah. One day we hope to be back.

On the drive to Zion National Park to accomplish the Mighty Five, we stopped at the Coral Pink Sand Dunes State Park in Utah. The drive was about ninety minutes. This state park, at around thirty-seven hundred acres, was sitting at about six thousand feet above sea level. The pinkish dunes were formed over ten thousand to fifteen thousand years from the erosion of pink-colored Navajo Sandstone surrounding the park. It was a smaller, more colorful version of the Great Sand Dunes National Park in Colorado or White Sands National Park in New Mexico. Sandboarding was popular here, and one could rent such boards. We decided to walk the mountainous dunes and jog back down.

At the peak we took some time to reflect on what we had accomplished this vacation and realized we were exhausted. We needed a vacation from our vacation. Our plan was to drive to Zion, stay a day, and drive through again before we went home. Home sweet home! Luckily, we had already visited Zion, and this would be the first national park our family would visit twice. It was only fitting, as it's such a beautiful place. Logan took his sandals off to walk down the pink sand dunes. When his feet got a bit hot, we carried him on our backs or shoulders. How much longer would we be able to do this? He was a growing boy, and a growing boy was getting harder to trek around a park on my shoulders. He was having the time of his life!

We arrived in Zion National Park around 7:00 p.m. on June 8, 2020. We entered the park on the east side along the Utah Scenic Byway-9, also called the Zion-Mount Carmel Highway. The road's third name is the Mt. Carmel Scenic Byway. So many names for such a small highway.

We first stopped at Checkerboard Mesa and were amazed. This iconic mesa is 6,520 feet in elevation and holds pools of rainwater that provide a vital source of water for resident bighorn sheep. The pink, brown, and gray colors of the vertical walls of the mesa split into squares, giving it the look of a checkerboard.

Our next stop was at the Watchman, a mountain standing at 6,545 feet above. Its prominence was dinosaur-like and was said to have been created during the Jurassic era. This red Navajo Sandstone must have been what created the pink coral sand dunes. The Watchman towers some 2,600 feet above the town of Springdale and Zion Canyon, where we were standing. The name was formed as this mountain is a watchman guarding the south entrance to the park. It certainly watched after us in the pandemic, and so did the Mighty Five of Utah.

We drove to our favorite restaurant in the park, the Spotted Dog café, where we ate on our way into the parks. Though the name doesn't represent this fine-dining experience, its hospitality does. Our spotted dog stayed in our car at sunset, took a nap, and enjoyed our doggy bag of treats, leftovers we brought him on our return. This was his vacation of a lifetime too.

We booked an Airbnb in Kanab, Utah, on a whim. We weren't planning to go back to Zion, but as the Mighty Five were in reach, we thought twice. As we left Utah, we had memories and all the wonderful moments of pivoting during the pandemic, taking one step at a time.

Delicate Arch

Balanced Rock

A Hoodoo background

A mom's hug

Mesa Arch

Island in the Sky

The Watchman

YELLOWSTONE AND GRAND TETON NATIONAL PARKS

A MONTH LATER WE WERE ON THE ROAD AGAIN TO VENTURE on another American safari. We got on the road with Joe and Josie, my in-laws, taking two vehicles. Our stop for the night was a motel in Fort Collins, Colorado. Around 6:30 a.m. on June 24, 2020, I got out for a quick run around Colorado State University. What a fabulous campus. A lot of state and publicly funded colleges, community colleges, and universities state they are green, or eco-friendly. This campus truly was! The campus was like a ghost town in the summer pandemic month of July, though that could have been because I was also running at 7:00 a.m. I came across the Annual Flower Trial Garden managed by the horticulture department of the university. Open to everyone was a field of row on row of blooming flowers surrounded by lush lawns in all directions. Wow, this campus knew how to cultivate plants! A field of chilis included new chili variants: FlameThrower Salsa Verde, FlameThrower Habanero, and FlameThrower Cajun Spice. Was this where unique spice flavors originated? *Yes, I'd like my boneless wings with a splash of FlameThrower Cajun Spice.*

Now I understood another reason why people who go to Colorado State absolutely love it. Go Rams!

Casper, Wyoming, was our lunch stop. A little more than three hours later we got to our two-story Cody, Wyoming, Airbnb and settled in comfortably. A roaring river was just a walk away, and running trails wound along the banks of the Shoshone River.

By 10:00 a.m. the next morning, we were at Buffalo Bill State Park near Cody, Wyoming. This park's showcase is its Buffalo Bill Dam. Buffalo Bill Cody was one of the most eccentric and colorful figures of the American Old West, known for the shows he organized with cowboy themes. He once owned a lot of the land that makes up this state park. Upon its completion in 1910, the dam, rising 325 feet from the bottom, was the highest in the world. It's quite the spectacle to see the massive Shoshone River surrounded by a mountain and dam nearly three hundred feet above the dam's floor.

The sight of the massive wall of the dam with water roaring as it flowed from its base scared Logan. I'm sure he wondered if we were going to hike the vertical walls to the bottom, an adventure he definitely didn't want to take. We explained that it was how water was used in the West, like a big faucet. I don't think he got it.

Logan finally relaxed and got the point that we were just tourists today. He warmed up to our Western safari.

Our next stop was the tremendous museum, Buffalo Bill Center of the West. This Buffalo Bill guy was the institution in Cody. I read about him and his traveling show in my history books as a child. Now he was the center of tourism here.

This museum is made up of five museums. The Whitney Western Art Museum showcases classic and modern Western art. The Buffalo Bill Museum and Grave explores stories of cowboy life of the past and present. The Plains Indian Museum shows Plains Indian culture, traditions, and history and an impressive collection of Native American art and artifacts. There was also the Cody Firearms Museum and the Draper Natural History Museum.

These museums connected around a central grand entry in a

seven-acre building, each museum branching off from the center. It's like one city blending into another. Just blink and you are someplace new.

These museums have more than fifty thousand artifacts, and our favorites were, I hate to say, the stuffed bear, bison, and wolf. The preserved grizzly bear at the entrance of this museum says it all: "I'm just looking for food," as the grizzly claws a moose antler. It is as if this bear just gobbled a large moose. We were about to gobble a lot of information in the next hour or so.

If these were the animals we were going to encounter in Yellowstone and Teton, we were in for an American safari of a lifetime during the worldwide pandemic. Crowds were small, and most were masking. The political pull and tug was all around.

As Logan and I got close to a display of preserved wolves in a swamp next to a mural of encroaching mountains, we felt as if we were the ones being hunted. I think I whispered to him, "You know your last name means 'wolf.' You don't have to be scared." He didn't listen, and their glowing eyes scared the bejesus out of both of us.

One of my favorite exhibits in this museum was the contemporary Native American art on canvas. I especially liked the *Future in Our Eyes: Indigenous Apsáalooké Madonnas*, by Ben Pease. Ben said about this artwork, "It's part of my Indigenous Madonna series. The painting talks about the Crows' belief of women as being the most holy beings, the most sacred beings, the closest to creation. If you have a strong need or a strong prayer, if you're really in a hard time, you're supposed to give your prayer and your thoughts to a woman so she can pray for you. Because she can give life, she is sacred."

The painting in india ink and vivid acrylic colors shows a mom with her child in classic Native American dress on a horse holding an umbrella to block the sun's rays. Above both their heads is the sun. This is the modern native mother showing her child her traditions upon a horse. Beautiful.

Outside the museum the sculptures were breathtaking.

As we walked downtown Cody, we ran into a street theater of an

Old West shoot-out. Actors, both men and women, reenacted a common Western scene of two cowboys dueling to the death. Perhaps they had an argument inside the restaurant/bar at the corner where we were standing. We watched, and as it ended, we got on our way to the rodeo. Yes, Cody, Wyoming, has a nightly rodeo in the summer. This is the ecosystem of our national parks in the West.

Our family was together here in the middle of a pandemic, and we had no idea what to expect. As an extended family, we met a few times in the last four months. As the pandemic ripped through everyday life, the core of family was also disturbed. Who had the new flu? "Coronavirus" was a new word we said daily. There wasn't any family in the world who was not affected. One solution was to isolate from everyone and avoid being part of a crowd. Another solution was to wear a mask and hope for the best.

We masked up and entered the rodeo as sunset hit the mountains. I paid a man from Australia twenty dollars to take pictures of me on top of a live bull. I posted those pictures on social media with little applause. I think people thought I was crazy to be at a rodeo in Wyoming on a bull, looking happy to be sitting on a wild animal. At times I thought we were all crazy for hitting the road and going places with a surge in illness and death. Maybe it was a way to mask the era, a way to avoid the worry and heal untapped wounds.

The rodeo was spectacular, attendance was minimal, and we ate a few hot dogs and saw the heroic cowboys and cowgirls of the West put on a show. The bull riders rode, fell, and got up again for more. We left thinking to ourselves, *This may be the end.* Would there be a rodeo tomorrow? According to the announcer, the world may shut them down any minute, but they'd keep truckin'. This wasn't our first rodeo, but the athletes at this one were outstanding. I wouldn't be surprised if these were the best rodeo athletes in the country, especially on this day.

Tomorrow we would enter the first national park this nation created. We would step into Yellowstone.

Standing by the Yellowstone National Park sign with Liz and Logan was a dream come true. I had no idea we would be there on June 26, 2020. This park had always been on my mind, and I envisioned visiting in a perfect world. The world was not in a perfect place, but summer solstice had just passed, and we would have the delight of a sunny, long, warm, perfect day with family, sights of a lifetime, and thousands of wild animals.

We entered the park through the East Entrance at approximately seven thousand feet above sea level. Our first stop a half hour later was a pullout off the East Entrance Road next to Yellowstone Lake. The Earth's thermal current was creating steam from below the land. We got back on the road, and about ten minutes later we stopped at the Fishing Bridge General Store. This was the largest cabin-constructed accessory store I'd been in at a national park. We walked across the street, and the Fishing Bridge Visitor Center and Trailside Museum, which normally would have been open, were already closed due to the pandemic.

There wasn't a soul around. We hopped, skipped, and jumped to the lake's sandy beach. Yellowstone Lake is the largest body of water in Yellowstone National Park and largest freshwater lake above seven thousand feet (7,732 feet above sea level) in North America. It has an amazing shoreline of 110 miles. We all dipped our toes in the chilly lake and looked toward the mountains in the distance. The lake took on a life of its own, something out of a seascape or ocean topography. This lake was life itself. This is what I'd been missing my whole life. No one ever told me I'd dip my toes in Yellowstone in one of the largest lakes I've ever encountered. The shallow waves off the sandy beach were from a nearby wind current. This place was WILD. Logan started skipping to his own beat, picking up sticks, and smiling from ear to ear.

On the road again, twenty minutes later, we encountered our first herd of bison. The American bison on this American safari was not a water buffalo as in the African safari. When I hear people say "Buffalo," I don't tell them they are wrong. We think Buffalo Bill or the team in New York, yet we're wrong. I was wrong for more than thirty-nine years. Bison has a nice ring to it. I can use that.

The bison herd we ran into may have totaled hundreds, if not thousands, of bison. They were weaving themselves between Mount Washburn and Yellowstone Lake. The topography turned into their habitat. Just when we thought we saw them all, a group, or maybe just a single dude, was strutting his stuff walking his land. From afar they looked like ants on the land, but as we approached so slowly in our vehicle, they became massive beasts.

I'd seen specials on these beasts, astonished that they know how to survive the frigid winters of this park. It was summer, and they were feasting on the lush grasses of the prairie. This American bison may have been our most unique character on this safari. The bison herd in Yellowstone is probably the oldest and largest public bison herd in the United States, estimated in 2020 to be more than forty-eight hundred bison. They are an American bison of the Plains bison subspecies. Yellowstone bison may be the only bison in America that were never extirpated since they continued to exist in the wild and never needed to be reintroduced. It has been estimated there were around sixty million bison in the US around 1800. The genocide of these cultural and creative creatures may be one of the harshest wrongs in our history, as by 1900 their numbers had fallen to just around three hundred, mostly in this area. That means more than fifty million may have been murdered in a hundred years' time after surviving for thousands of years unthreatened. Someone upstairs is not happy about this.

Over my lifetime the bison has become a great symbol of the West. I'm proud of that as an American. I'd be even more proud if we had a goal to go from five thousand Bison in Yellowstone to fifty thousand in the next hundred years. What can we really achieve in a century? I'm sure with time the bison may become the symbol of our country. What will that symbol represent for our land, people, and culture? Will we be able to be resilient, to right a wrong?

In honor of this magical beast, I slowed down to a standstill to watch one out-of-place beast right on the shoulder of the road. The creature, a thousand pounds in weight, had a goatee about two feet in length, fur everywhere. It was shedding its light-brown upper coat from winter. Its summer coat, three shades of dark brown and black made this hooved bison look like the largest sea lion ever discovered. Horns protruded in an oval, three-foot upward arc from its head. Any move made me jolt. There were tire marks a few feet from this animal from a car that may have dodged the beast and sped away. Had they come too close, the car and its passengers would have had hell to pay. This is how close the bison get to you here. They are the alpha to our omega. They rule this land. They are king and queen in this Yellowstone adventure.

We came to the Grand Canyon of Yellowstone shortly after our bison safari. We all stopped at a grand inspiration lookout point. This canyon encompasses the Yellowstone River, creates the Yellowstone Falls, and runs for approximately twenty-four miles. Think slightly less than a marathon, 26.2 miles, but as fast as a sprint.

This power is God-like. From the viewpoints we were far away from the river and waterfall. This is the most amazing waterfall we may see in nature. The lower falls drop more than three hundred feet, which is almost three times higher than Niagara Falls. On this day, we had the sight almost to ourselves. On guard, of course, should a herd of bison wander too close. Bright greens of bison-manicured lawns in the distance, splashed with the most evergreen forests, blended with the palette of greens, blues, and whites of the splashing waterfalls and the eroded browns of the canyon made me think we were visitors in an ecosystem all its own.

It was that feeling I have when I'm snorkeling somewhere special, and I realize I'm the only human among hundreds of living creatures. It's a distant land of life. Maybe we shouldn't be in it, and at this point during our safari, hearing the roar of the water and the rip of the wind, I realized it was not hospitable to humans. It was a perfect day outside, but nature was warning us it was fierce. Should I fall to the bottom or encounter a determined bison, death might be certain.

We were off. We drove past a herd of elk grazing atop a mountain slope. Who knew what was in the evergreens above them?

We had packed our belongings, and our next stay was in a comfortable home, another Airbnb, in Gardiner, Montana, close to the North Entrance to Yellowstone. We swiftly passed by a handful of stops we'd see the next day. It's that feeling when I see a movie, and there are posters and the name of other showings I want to see. The one I saw today was great, Grand Canyon of the Yellowstone, but I was really eager to see Obsidian Cliff and Sheepeater Cliff.

Our new digs were atop the Yellowstone River, and our neighborhood had deer wandering casually around the yards. On our street was a burger joint, open late, with the most classic shakes, perfect after a long walk in the woods—on top of the world of parks.

Yellowstone National Park lies mostly in the northwest corner of Wyoming and extends into Montana and Idaho. It encompasses more than 2.2 million acres, and in 2020, the year we visited, there were slightly more than 3.8 million visitors. In 2019 there were more than four million visitors, making Yellowstone one of the most visited national parks in the country. In 2021 Yellowstone would be the third most visited national park, with around five million visitors, and in the month of September there were 920,000 visitors to Yellowstone, setting a monthly record of pent-up pandemic travelers just like we had been fourteen months before.

Yellowstone may have been the epicenter of social distancing during the pandemic.

Yellowstone National Park is actually the epicenter of conservation and has possibly the largest underground thermal volcano in the world. If there is a true end of the world, many speculate the world will explode here in this place.

Yellowstone was the first national park in the United States and is also widely held to be the first national park in the world. It was established by Congress and signed into law by President Ulysses S. Grant on March 1, 1872. A military man by the Civil War, a president by choice, President Grant became the grandfather of the national parks that Teddy Roosevelt would come to love.

As I stood in the park that Grant established, I remembered that at one point in my life, while residing in New York City, I'd go on a long run with my friends only to end at Grant's Tomb in the Morningside Heights neighborhood of Upper Manhattan. Fittingly, the National Park Service oversees this final resting place for President Grant and his wife Julia. Grant, who wished to be buried in New York City, got his wish, and today this classic mausoleum is one of the largest in North America. The tomb was completed in 1897, and the National Park Service has managed it since 1958, possibly because of his contribution to creating Yellowstone. After a period of neglect, it has been restored and rededicated.

Imagine a world if President Grant didn't go out on a limb and create Yellowstone. Would this wonderful safari land run into a century of neglect only to be taken care of starting in 1958?

Here it was, 2020, and I realized it was our species that spread the disease. It was also our species that killed fifty million bison. In fact, if we had been left unchecked, we would have probably destroyed this precious land, more animals, and its resources. The next time I run to Grant's Tomb in New York City, I'll think of our Yellowstone.

NATIVE AMERICANS HAVE LIVED IN AND AROUND Yellowstone for approximately eleven thousand years. These Paleo-Indians of the Clovis culture used obsidian found in the park to create cutting tools and weapons such as arrowheads that have over time made their way to the Mississippi Valley. This suggests a regular obsidian trade existed between local tribes and tribes much farther east. Think of the game that these Natives hunted in abundance and saw as sacred. They saw the land, and especially the bison, as sacred, unlike us who came next.

On this safari, I came to see the land and animals as sacred thanks to conservation efforts more than 150 years ago—and America's first ever national park.

Europeans finally came to the area around the early 1800s. The famous American expedition of Lewis and Clark recorded an endless land of abundance in their 1805 journaling of the area. Fur trappers had already named the place Roche Jaune, or "Yellow Rock River," for the yellow sandstones found along the riverbanks. This is where the yellow in "Yellowstone" comes from, not the idea of the yellow coloring caused by rhyolite lava seen at the Grand Canyon of the Yellowstone.

The American Civil War stopped a lot of exploration into Yellowstone. In 1871, eleven years after his failed attempt to explore the region, Ferdinand V. Hayden, a famous geologist, brought a larger safari for exploration. Thus, their tenacity and lucid talks convinced President Grant to withdraw this region from public auction. The area was our first national park by the Act of Dedication. The act states:

> The Act of Dedication – An Act to set apart a certain tract of land lying near the headwaters of the Yellowstone River as a public park. Be it enacted by the Senate and House of Representatives of the United States of America in Congress assembled, that the tract of land in the territories of Montana and Wyoming . . . is hereby reserved and withdrawn from settlement, occupancy, or sale under the laws of the United States, and dedicated and set apart as a public park or pleasuring ground for the benefit and enjoyment of the people; and all persons who shall locate, or settle upon, or occupy the same or any part thereof, except as hereinafter provided, shall be considered trespassers and removed there from . . .
>
> Approved March 1, 1872
>
> Signed by:
>
> Ulysses S. Grant, President of the United States
>
> Schuyler Colfax, Vice President of the United States and President of the Senate
>
> James G. Blaine, Speaker of the House

This law was another core inspiration for writing this book. Without it, we wouldn't be on this American safari. I'm sure someone, or some family much wealthier than I, would have ranchland here. It has been 150 years since this law, and I dream this place will be as sacred as it was from the beginning in another 150 million more years.

The next afternoon, not too far from the North Entrance and Gardiner, Montana, we ran into our first bear sighting on Grand Loop Road. The brown bear, black from afar, was in a ravine below chopping at the vegetation. Small compared to the grizzly bear at the Buffalo Bill Museum, it was perhaps in its first, second, or third summer on its own. A few years ago it was only a cub following a hungry mama bear with a sibling or two. We watched the bear for a good twenty minutes, thinking this may be our only bear sighting. Ten minutes up the road we ran into the most elegant, well-fed antelope that I had ever seen in the wild. They were so large that I mistook them for deer or elk.

All the wildlife was accustomed to tourists like our family whizzing by in their gas-guzzling vehicles. We got out of our vehicles to stretch our legs around Soda Butte Creek. As I walked ever so slowly to the creek, I noticed a bobbing mass in the water. It was . . . it was a massive bison! From where I was to the car was about a quarter mile, but the bison was very close. He moved his head and torso ever so slightly. A jolt of adrenaline shot through my brain and body. In high school I had run the four hundred meters in many four-by-four races and had my best split of 52.5 seconds for a quarter of a mile, not so bad for a marathon long-distance freak.

The bison had spoken to me with one gesture to move away. I bolted at my top speed, looked back, and lucky for me he hadn't moved and was in the same place. If only they had a mask on; then I would have felt much more comfortable. I had read months back that a lion in a zoo in the US had tested positive for coronavirus. I wonder if any wild animals in Yellowstone got the bug? They let you know how to keep your distance. I listened.

Two hours later, way up the road, we ran into around twenty stopped vehicles and forty people out and about. A circus of phones out and expensive camo-enveloped cameras trying to shoot a few bears. A gentleman told us as we drove by at around three miles per hour, "Two brown bears in there," pointing to the wilderness below a mountain. This was bear season. We didn't see the bears and kept driving.

We came to our destination for the afternoon at Tower Fall. This is what the sign read:

> Tower Fall is the story of two rocks: easily eroded rocks and rocks that are resistant to erosion. Rock at the brink and underlying the waterfall is a hard volcanic rock. Erosion at the base of the fall causes the upstream migration of the fall. Look for the soft and hard rocks in the towers and pinnacles that line Tower Creek. Over the centuries, wind and water eroded soft rock, leaving fantastic shapes of hard rock.

This waterfall, mighty at 132 feet, gives off a sense of elegance. There, in the middle of the woods, out streams a river of sorts. This part of Yellowstone looks and feels like a mini Yosemite. I'm glad I got both those park names in one sentence. The magic and elegance of the place makes you stare into the waterfall as if you, too, have the powers of the animals that call this place home.

Before we crossed into the North Entrance of the park, we stopped in what looked like a small town. This town houses rangers, the Mammoth Hot Springs Hotel, Mammoth Hotel Dining Room, cabins, and our destination, the Yellowstone General Store. In the distance we could see many people hiking up to Mammoth Hot Springs, where it has been bubbling and misting for thousands of years.

My son was more interested in ice cream. We got him some at the general store, and I picked up a unique semi-large green, blue, white, black, and brown coffee mug. I don't think I've ever bought myself a coffee mug while on vacation. This would be my first. I still drink my best coffee at home from this mug, which not only has this famous park's name on it, but a few bison and Old Faithful.

We had come to a point where we gave into our moods. By golly, I didn't want to buy this mug, but I'm glad I did. Whenever you see someone with a national park mug, hat, or shirt, ask them about it. Hopefully they don't hand you a book like I will, but I'm sure they'll have a story or two. What would I tell someone about Yellowstone in a few short moments? Here it goes. I'd tell them, "It's the most original, wild place on the planet."

While looking at my new mug on a park bench and hearing my son tell the world how good his ice cream was, a handful of the largest elk I've ever seen came, ate, and lay down for a nap just feet away. Wow, this place was wild! Wild as any African safari.

I got up before everyone the next morning, and instead of running, I drove to the Gallatin National Forest and a place called Jardine, Montana, a few minutes and miles from Gardiner. It was a small village in a large forest. A fairy-tale-like drive into some viewpoints unlike any others I've seen. At around 8:00 a.m. on June 28, 2020, I took a video on my phone of this magical place, cautiously checking over my shoulder, as the river next to me was called Bear Creek. Campgrounds were plentiful, as I'm sure this was a local favorite. When I come back, this may be a family camping destination. As a few minutes turned into an hour, I realized I better drive back down the road to civilization.

By noon we were all at Old Faithful.

Old Faithful may be the most famous geyser in the world. It was named in 1870 and is a highly predictable geothermal feature of the park. It has erupted regularly and repeatedly between every forty-four minutes to two hours since the year 2000. This may be the showcase feature of all national parks. It was like Disneyland when we got there. There was moisture in the air, and the excitement of the huge Disneyland-style parking lot made us forget our umbrellas. We didn't want to miss the next eruption. We had to park in the thirty-third row of about a hundred rows of parking.

This place is known as the Old Faithful Historic District with a huge wooden cabin, Old Faithful Inn and restaurant. The inn was closed due to the pandemic, but we were very hungry, and the restaurant was only serving lunches to go. The to-go was pretty good, and my son loved the hot dog served in a paper school bus. We talked about kindergarten, wondering if it would have in-person classes come 2021. School for his best friend who had just entered kindergarten was all online during 2020, that first year of the pandemic.

In the distance we could hear hundreds of people hooting and hollering about the geyser. It would be our turn to get closer to the geyser in about an hour. Hopefully the clouds, looking dark and very threatening, would not pour down rain.

Old Faithful is a cone geyser and spits thermal waters one hundred to two hundred feet into the air, about the height of a twenty- to twenty-five-story building. There are no buildings that tall in Santa Fe, so we had nothing to compare it to.

The park service and their rangers created a great observation deck for this spectacle. The deck allows you to stroll for a little more than a mile around the geyser. As I was concerned about the rain, and Logan wasn't acting like a model citizen, I decided to stick close by. My father-in-law Joe walked away. We lost him in the masses. At one point I lost my wife and mother-in-law too. When Logan and I saw Mom a few minutes later, the geyser started its classic hissing and sputtering. The eruption every hour lasts between two and five minutes.

Wouldn't you know, it started to rain. The drips turned into a torrential downpour. We got soaked, and by the end of the three-to-four-minute show, with hundreds of people around, the crowds started to scramble for shelter. I asked Liz what she wanted to do. We couldn't find her parents. We started running to the Old Faithful General Store. Puddles of water and jogging people made the mess even worse. Laughing, but drenched, we joined the masses in the store. I quickly went to the men's apparel and found some sweatpants that read "Yellowstone National Park 1872." Luckily my wife and son hand-packed a change of clothes in the car. I, on the other hand, had not.

The line to the cashier to check out was at least twenty people back. Everyone had umbrellas, ponchos, other clothes, and items to purchase as they dripped or shook off the rain. When I got to the front, the lady laughed. My shivering hands holding dripping jeans told her where I'd been. She rang the tag in my hand, knowing I was wearing what I bought. I had the feeling she was thinking to herself, *What an amateur.* That's exactly what my father-in-law told us as he came walking through the door, wearing waterproof everything. His mile walk around Old Faithful was productive, and with crowds avoiding the rain, he had room to spare. Everyone laughed at me in my fancy collared shirt and sweatpants.

Old Faithful was an amazing sight, quite the dramatic wait, and I'll never forget the wet experience.

Clad in sweatpants, with my tail between my legs, I drove the family on in the overcast, rainy conditions. Over the next few months, we would take an umbrella with us everywhere, especially after that day.

Our next stop was the Grand Prismatic Spring, the largest hot spring in the United States and third largest in the world. The spring is located about five miles from Old Faithful in the Midway Geyser Basin, yet a lot of people don't even stop to see it. The spring is a wide, almost circular steaming pool of water, its edges rings of color: green, yellow, orange. The colors are from specially evolved bacteria called thermophilic microorganisms and cyanobacteria, thriving in the highly acidic and very, very hot waters of the spring.

Warning signs tell us to stay on the boardwalk as the surface near the spring is a very thin crust, ready to break and dump an unsuspecting tourist into acidic water as hot as 180 degrees Fahrenheit. Yellowstone National Park, even with its beauty, is another park that can be dangerous.

The magical, bright, vivid colors in the spring are the result of trillions of microbial mats around the edges of the mineral-rich water. These colors, like we learned in grade school, are rainbow in nature—ROYGBIV: red, orange, yellow, green, blue, indigo, and violet. The center of the pool is crystalline blue, as the extreme heat makes this area in the middle sterile. This place is an extreme boiling lake with what looks like a rainbow eye. The wooden boards post clear cautions: "Don't get in the water, or you will die."

As we walked in the rain, we realized it felt like winter. Logan was freezing, and we hurried back to the car without stopping to enjoy the views.

We stopped at a few more boiling pools along the way. Logan opted to stay cozy in the car with Nana, his grandmother. This time out, with a sprinkle in the air, I wore a warmer jacket and hat. We stopped at the Black Opal Pool. In this cold environment it was tempting to want to dip a foot in the steaming water. More scary signs reminded us to avoid it:

Use Caution in Hydrothermal Areas

- Stay on boardwalks and designated trails.
- Hydrothermal water can severely burn you.
- Never run, push, or shove
- Supervise children at all times.
- Do not scratch hydrothermal mats.

You are responsible for your safety.

Think safety, act safely. Yellowstone is a dangerous place.

It's been rumored that every so often someone goes in and never comes out. Imagine a time when there weren't warnings. I bet a lot of people lost their lives, or a toe or two.

As we got on our way, the weather changed; it started to snow on this late June afternoon, and the temperatures rapidly dropped to the low thirties. Quickly the pines along the road were dusted white and snowcapped along the boughs. While listening to the Red Hot Chili Peppers on the radio as we drove, their Southern California sound vibrating, we knew we were worlds away.

Our vehicles already packed for our next destination, it was time to get out of Yellowstone and head south to enter Grand Teton National Park. We drove through the South Entrance in Yellowstone, briefly through the John D. Rockefeller Jr. Memorial Parkway, and stopped at the Grand Teton National Park sign. Significantly different from other more humble national park signs, this one had an expensive resort look. We were some seventy minutes south of the fresh snow in Yellowstone, ready for our next set of park entry photos. It was still cold but not snowing. Recreational vehicles passed by like they were the state vehicle here in Wyoming, and they blew past us every minute. We clung to the wonderful times in Yellowstone, not believing Grand Teton could be as good.

As we drove, an unimaginably beautiful landscape started to emerge. We wondered if this road was the most beautiful drive in America. For me, it was—and still is. The two-hour drive from Yellowstone National Park through Grand Teton National Park to our destination in Jackson, Wyoming, took us past the most amazing geysers, forests, lakes, and mountain ranges I'd seen in my life. If just for this drive, Grand Teton had lived up to its name.

Funny to discover that Teton is French for "nipples." Some French fur traders and trappers named it the "Grand Tits" as they probably hadn't seen a woman in months or years up here in this neck of the woods and thought the emblematic Grand Teton peak, sitting at 13,770 feet above sea level, reminded them of a nipple. This name was bestowed on this place sometime around the 1870s and stuck.

We all have places in our environment where locals say they look like tits. In Santa Fe we have the Sun and Moon Mountains. This place had the audacity to stick with Big Nipple National Park. Hats off to you, Wyoming.

In 2020, while popular trends often opted for politically correct labels, more than likely "Grand Teton" would have experienced a name change if it had been in its English translation. Luckily, it's in French. Oh, those French. First, they come up with their kiss, and now they name our most beautiful place after nipples—and it sticks!

While driving past the nipples, I got a cosmic sense that we had entered a new phase in our lives, one that could last a lifetime. Logan was growing up so fast. It was time to slow down, to stop and smell the roses. Life was about new adventures, places, and experiences.

Grand Teton Park was about to go down as the absolute favorite national park we visited in Logan's young life. We visit our first thirty-one national parks in this book. Of those thirty-one, this park is my clear favorite. We hope to get to all sixty-three-plus one day, but based on this day, sign the tits up for number one!

At around 4:00 p.m. on June 29, 2020, I drove through the spectacular downtown area of Jackson, Wyoming, like I owned the place. When I entered the town, I felt like I had come from a ranching family rooted here for generations. In the driver's seat of my Jeep, I said out loud, "I'm a fifth-generation rancher from Teton. No, wait, I'm a sixth-generation rancher from Grand Teton."

A few miles from the plaza and steps to the Snow King Mountain Resort, we unpacked everything we had been lugging along the entire country into our two-story townhome. Then reality set in. This townhome was beautiful. When we visited in 2020, it would probably go for $600,000. We were staying for less than a week. Rancher in us or not, we saw that our host put two cans of bear spray on the kitchen table. The cans were holstered on a belt we could wear to keep them within reach at all times. A note warned us to take them with us on all trails, walks, and runs—or else. Or else what? Did we just step into *The Twilight Zone*? It had been the most beautiful two-hour drive ever, among million-dollar homes in a classic Western town with a ski basin, and now we must worry about hungry bears everywhere we went. It was like pieces to a board game of Clue. To make things even stranger, our townhome community was named Pitchfork Townhomes. If this was the end, this might be the exact place to be. I turned on the nightly news, and yep, it was the end of the world. The pandemic had gone global.

Quickly I turned off the tube, and we hit the road to see the park before sunset.

The lights were on in the Million Dollar Cowboy Bar in downtown Jackson, Wyoming, as we passed by. Ten minutes later we were in Grand Teton National Park. We parked close to the main Highway 189 in the park and Sagebrush Drive. We walked into the sagebrush with violet-crested lupine flowers carpeting everywhere underfoot. The purple colors of these wildflowers made the sunset glimmer. The majestic Tetons in the distance, circled by low-hanging clouds, still had their tops dusted with summer snow. Was that snow from the winter, spring, or yesterday? It was probably from all three. The top of the Grand Teton mesmerized me.

Grand Teton, at just under fourteen thousand feet, is the highest point of the Teton Range and the second highest peak in Wyoming after Gannett Peak. The mountain is surrounded by the Snake River basin, with the river of the same name that weaves in and out of its reach. It is as if Zeus sits atop the nipple and has an ever-present snake of water and life below.

The Tetons are a part of the Rocky Mountain range. These Teton mountains are said to be some of the youngest mountains in the Rockies, just nine million years young. From my perspective these were the mightiest mountains I'd laid eyes on, and also the youngest we'd seen on our journey, from the most Southern Rockies in Northern New Mexico to these subranges of the Rocky Mountains. Nature again was playing tricks on me.

"Here you go, Antonio! The young will be mighty." The mountains were calling me. Having lived in Southern California for my undergraduate days, I always have the poetic bumper sticker, "Open Mountains, Open Minds," stuck in the back burner of my mind. It was originally a reference to opening the ski slopes to allow snowboarders. The saying stuck with me.

My mind had continuously expanded over the decades since that bumper sticker. The road that we just drove was the way for people to see this majestic mountain. I could feel my mind open to the idea that life from now on would be different. I was brought up in the city of Albuquerque, went to college in San Diego, experienced life in the Big

Apple, and had my family years in Santa Fe, but Grand Teton changed me forever. I'm a mountain man. No sunset in Tucson, Arizona, surf in the ocean, or ski atop a mountain changed me more than this Grand Teton. From this moment forward I'd be chasing this moment, the first moment I saw the Tetons and took time for them. How many humans had seen this or had felt this?

Human history here dates back some eleven thousand years when the climate of Grand Teton was much more freezing cold during the winters. The Paleo-Indian culture had a presence in the area, hunting and gathering in the summer months. Then the Clovis culture had a presence in and around Jackson Lake, where firepits, tools, and fishing weights have been found. From eleven thousand to five hundred years ago, no evidence has indicated any permanent human settlement in this area. My assumption was there would be a long line of descendants in this remote area, which was flooded with abundance. I was wrong. Better to assume it was the unworldly, difficult winters that forced people away and left behind only today's very small population. In 2020 the regular population of Jackson, Wyoming, was eleven thousand, but on this day in the summer, the local population shot up to fifty-one thousand with visitors like the five of us. In 1900 the population in Jackson was fifty-nine; the census in 2010 was 9,577 people. The warm summer months bring thousands of visitors, while few of the resident population stay all year.

I bet the locals hate us. Some famous local favorites are actors Harrison Ford, Sandra Bullock, Brad Pitt, Uma Thurman, Matthew McConaughey, royalty Pippa Middleton, and the tiger athlete himself, Tiger Woods. Do they really live there in the winter?

When those fifty-nine first colonists entered the area in 1900, they were met with the Shoshone tribe who had moved from Yellowstone. Several upper slopes of Grand Teton are thought to have been used by Shoshone people during their vision quests. A vision quest is a rite of passage in some Native American cultures when a boy enters adulthood. Sign me up for that vision quest. Wait, this is exactly what I was doing on the side of the road looking up at these mountains.

You could say all the national parks were my adult vision quest. During this quest, the young person prays and cries out to the spirits to give them a vision, one that will help them find their purpose in life and their role in the community where they can serve and help their people. I realized this amazing scene could be the backdrop to my book. My real quest only started at the Teton, the mountain that brought this vision to me.

Start again on your book, Antonio, it said.

I wanted to write as soon as I got back to our Pitchforks townhome. I found myself sorting through this vision quest. The quest, the journey, is the experience of taking my family to the parks. The experience builds the thoughts and enhances my understanding. Those thoughts then simmer into ideas, and finally those ideas make their way to my computer and into words on the page. Teton got me started. It's that simple. This connection is hard to beat.

The hundreds or so Jackson Hole residents were opposed to making their place a national park but were in favor of the establishment of a separate national park, which would include the Teton Range and six lakes at the base of the mountains.

On a freezing day on February 26, 1929, during the Great Depression, President Calvin Coolidge signed the executive order establishing the ninety-six-thousand-acre Grand Teton National Park. Today the park is approximately three hundred thousand acres. How did it grow? One of the richest families to walk this planet, John D. Rockefeller Jr's, saw this magical place in the late 1920s and went on a spending spree to buy as much land as possible to grant it over to the park system. As the Great Depression took its toll, I'm sure Rockefeller's money was a windfall for many. What hard-working farming and ranching Wyoming family wouldn't want to become rich in the most difficult economic time in our country's history? I wonder how those places looked in 1929. This place, the Teton, looks the same. That's the beauty of it.

Rockefeller made the land deal of the century for many of us who visit, live, and love Grand Teton. We always hear how the US bought

Alaska from Russia and are amazed that in 1867 we bought Alaska for two cents per acre, right? With inflation, that's thirty-seven cents per acre in 2022. Add another century and it's probably a dollar. Wow!

Rockefeller's purchase of farms and ranches totaled approximately thirty-two thousand acres that he would donate, though it was like pulling teeth to get the Park Service to accept it. He said donating the land was harder than buying it.

That makes no sense, but it made a lot of sense at the same time. "I'm rich; let me buy your land. Here, America, I'm a philanthropist; let me give you land. What? Here, America, please for God sake's, take my land," I imagine him saying.

By 1942, thirteen years later, Rockefeller had become increasingly impatient that his purchased property might never be added to the park and wrote to the Secretary of the Interior Harold L. Ickes that his family was going to possibly sell the land to another party for a large profit. Immediately, Secretary Ickes shouted to President Franklin Roosevelt, whom I'm assuming had World War II to worry about. With power from the Antiquities Act, which permitted presidents to set aside land for protection without the approval of Congress, he not only took the Rockefeller thirty-two thousand acres, but also Jackson Hole National Monument in 1943, and donated land from the Snake River Land Company and the Teton National Forest to incorporate another approximate 221,000 acres into Grand Teton National Park.

The Rockefeller family–owned JY Dude Ranch in the park was donated on June 21, 2008, during the financial crisis. Their family transferred ownership of the ranch to the park for the establishment of the Laurance S. Rockefeller Preserve.

Our vacations turned into vision quests, inspired by the beauty of the natural world. The Rockefeller family may have donated their ranch as part of their own vision of a better world. As a philanthropist it must be the top of the mountain to donate such stunning, life-changing places to the people. I'm sure we'll see more donations, as ecotourism is on the rise. The Rockefellers gave parks; the Waltons give art. What will the Bezoses and Musks do?

We didn't go to bed until around midnight because Logan was talking our ears off. At five years and eight months he had rarely talked in full paragraphs. Now he was spitting off a novel an hour. We couldn't contain our excitement. It was like the night before running a marathon. We want to go to sleep, but we can't. We need the energy for tomorrow, but there's that adrenaline circulating in and around our brains. Logan inspired me. I just wanted to write my book and jump to this point, this moment where he finally had the words to spill out everything in his mind. I was probably only a few chapters in, and I didn't even bring my personal laptop. As midnight turned to 2:00 a.m., I realized I wasn't going to sleep. I thought about going out, but that's too crazy. What trail would I walk alone in the wildest place we have? A grizzly would get me.

I finally settled into a few hours of sleep and woke as if something was calling me. I quietly was out of bed, clothed, and on the road by five-ish. The forty-five minutes I drove as the sun came up felt like five hours. This rejuvenated my life. How had I never heard of this and never been to this place? I had heard of Jackson Hole, where some major financial and communication sector conferences are held every year, but not Grand Teton National Park.

I had shared our plan to visit every national park with hundreds of people. A select few pulled me aside. Something in their eyes changed. It was as if they had baby-blue eyes one moment, and when they said Grand Teton, their eyes turned hazel, like the mountain forests. I had seen a few of those: eyes that saw the Grand Teton against blue sky. But this was different. I could not have understood until I was driving fifty-five miles an hour at 5:00 a.m. to see this park by myself.

I first stopped at a large parking area off Teton Park Road to take sunrise pictures. Truly a spectacle. A short while later I was at it again, driving the speed limit, or above it, trying to take in everything. A sign on the road pointed to Signal Mountain. I hardly noticed I was forty miles from our temporary home. The mountain road was like any on the way to the top. It felt as if around any of the hundred or so switchbacks I'd run into a moose or family of grizzly bears. I was alert like during any marathon at the midway point, or at the end of a half-marathon, garnering perhaps the most adrenaline I'd carry. Adrenaline on this road was at a peak. I had seen only one car on the road in the last hour.

Near the peak, I stepped out of my car onto a trail that was moist from a shower an hour before. Not a human soul for miles. At 7,727 feet above sea level, Signal Mountain had a sunrise like no other. If this was my last sunrise, it was worth it.

Suddenly, a wicked flapping came through the evergreens and landed on the road. Was it a bird? Was it a plane? Was it Superman? I jumped. Luckily the lone ruffed grouse was more like a wild turkey I'd walked past many times. She was curious to see a human up here at this hour. I looked down on the valley, with its hot springs shining like lakes. Every shade of green was moist from the passing showery white clouds. Then the clouds shifted. It was the first time the sun came out that morning. Driving before sunrise, I didn't realize the sun had already risen and was behind overcast skies. Like a baby seeing her mother for the first time, it was like the first time I'd seen the sun come out of the clouds. From this height on the mountain, I was looking straight into the early sun, neither above me nor below.

I felt a presence. It was my mom. She put me at ease for a brief moment before illustrating the facts: "Be careful, Antonio, there could be bears."

Oh shit, I had forgotten the bear spray on the table when I left the kitchen in the dark an hour ago. That fear would have to wait a few moments. My mom was with me, so I'd be okay. As the sun came through, like the grand prismatic spring in Yellowstone, suddenly there was a cascade of all the colors imaginable. The sun brought a violence of yellows, reds, and oranges. The forests brought proud greens, olives, and darks. And the sky, clouds, and water in the valley brought the calms of whites, blues, violets, and blues. I felt immersed in this onslaught of color.

As I got back to my car, the turkey thing was gone, thank God. I had no idea I'd parked next to the largest, most robust radio and cell-phone tower I'd seen in a national park. It's hard to imagine all who had dialed from far and wide to reach this signal. Who had called and reached this tower for emergencies, family, and friends? This truly was a Signal Mountain. I bet out of the many calls that had come through here, there were many calls to a loved one to exclaim that this was the greatest place on Earth. Not only could I see panoramic views of Jackson Hole and the Teton Range from here, but also wide-open sky for miles.

I vowed to call my dad and tell him today!

Luckily, I didn't encounter any bears on Signal Mountain. I returned safely, and by nine Liz and I were on our way out for our morning run in civilization, bear spray firmly attached to my belt. Logan was left behind, happily conversing with his grandparents. We took the wet trails from our townhome and ended up in a campground a few miles away. We passed a horse ranch and a few eager tourists in their Subarus ready to seize the day. We got back, showered, ate, and stopped by the local Jackson Visitor Center to pick up some literature before our caravan was back in the park.

Today would be our first walk in and around Jenny Lake. That was our goal.

Just after the noon hour, on an overcast summer day, Logan, Liz, Joe, Josie, and I were in for a walk through the woods. Jenny Lake was formed more than twelve thousand years ago by glaciers and the force they impacted throughout this land. These glaciers pushed rock debris, which carved Cascade Canyon in Grand Teton National Park. This created the terminal moraine, sometimes referred to as glacial till, which now impounds the lake. This is the perfect center point to the Grand Tetons. There are many hiking trails, scenic boat rides, and quick access to the major climbing routes onto the tallest peaks of the Teton Range. Today we would hike from the northwestern part of Jenny Lake starting at the Jenny Lake Overlook, venture over to String Lake, and end up in the southern part of Leigh Lake and back. Our total mileage would be around six miles, or ten kilometers. The tranquility of water on an overcast day among deer, large boulders, and tall evergreens was a slow way to welcome the afternoon. As we hiked the southern rim of Leigh Lake, we reached a handful of steps. In the lake stood Boulder Island, a magical-looking island with huge glacial boulders as its foundation. The wake in the lake was slow, the wind bringing us chills, and from this vantage point we could see the magnitude of Leigh Lake's 2.4-mile width and its 2.8-mile length from north to south. The surface area of Leigh Lake is 1,792 acres, and it is approximately 250 feet deep. There are two islands in this lake. Strung in between Jenny and Leigh is String Lake. We didn't notice it was a different lake. What Josie noticed was a creature in the water. Swimming along beside us was a beaver. We said out loud, "Look at that beaver!" Another family of three adults followed us with every step on the way to the lake.

Our minds were not on our anxiety over coronavirus; our attention was on taking a grand picture of a swimming beaver in String Lake. Eight of us ignored the demand to stay six feet apart; we were so eager for photos of that beaver.

Guess what? It was a log floating in the lake, not a beaver. We were all tricked and laughed all the way back to Jenny Lake where our vehicles were waiting.

After a quick lunch we were all about downtown Jackson, Wyoming. Some stores had taxidermy bears, bison, and wolves for sale. I almost wished I had a reason to buy one. Sometimes these unique stores felt like a natural history museum.

Soon we came across the store MADE that I wrote about in my first chapter of this book. This store sold the national park poster we have at home where we stick an evergreen on the parks we have visited. It was open, and in we went. The contemporary, chic New York City vibe was nothing new in this posh town. How could such a small place have created the mecca of my book's beginning? I bought a simple ring that had the Teton Range on it and four matching glass coasters that had a bison, bear, cowboy, and Teton Range on them. I told the checkout clerk our story about how this place started our family adventures five years ago.

They were busy, but she smiled and said, "That's amazing," before we went on our way.

We stopped in an Albertsons mega grocery store, an enormous store too huge to be serving a small town like this. Guess what? There in the fish section I found Idaho farm-raised cutthroat trout. This was the fish we couldn't find anywhere in and around the Olympic National Forest in 2018, where days earlier it had been sold-out on the menu in Seattle. Immediately I bought a wrapped two-pound portion. Things happen for a reason.

On these grocery runs, the four of us usually go our separate ways with a handful of things on separate lists. When we met up a few moments later, I announced that I had our main course. Everyone shouted for joy that it was the fish of our dreams.

Back at the ranch I turned the outdoor grill on low and placed the cutthroat on the top level for a slow simmer to medium. The day slowed down, and the time passed. On the deck I took in the view of this amazing town, the ski basin blocks away, and the horizon of the most amazing park we'd been to. The aroma of roasting trout got to my nose, and I'm sure by that time a few animals around the area had also smelled it. A squirrel ran past the parking lot, and I kept an eye out for a citified bear. Young children laughed in the playground at the city park across the street. This was the way to live. God had put everything in motion today, and we ended up with the trout we'd been looking for for a couple years. It didn't disappoint. To this day, I haven't run into cutthroat trout on any menu or store again! Dinner was a blessing. We ate, played a few board games, including an hour's long UNO game, and finally I got a good night's sleep. Grand Teton was becoming part of me. I was becoming part of its legacy.

The next day was July 1, 2020. The world had been through a lot this year. We took it easy and went across the street in the morning to play with Logan in the playground. We ran into a summer camp program of some twenty children. Logan didn't want to play with them, even though I was eager to see how he would interact with children his age. It was warm, sunny, and July. Today would be another perfect day in the park.

Our first stop was at the National Museum of Wildlife Art. It sits between Jackson and the Grand Teton overlooking the National Elk Refuge. If you enjoy wildlife art like I do, this is the place to stop.

As we walked in, we were checked with a laser thermometer. It instantaneously read our temperatures. Eventually, most places around the country would have these temperature scanners. This was our first encounter on our pandemic national park tour that did.

Within the museum we saw the most amazing wildlife art we had seen. A 1925 work by Philip R. Goodwin titled *The Surprise* is of a flannelled man who just paddled a canoe taking a picture of two cubs playing in the woods while their mama bear watches, all under the dominance of a cascading mountain range. *This could be us today,* I thought.

Georgia O'Keeffe (1887–1986), who has her own museum in Santa Fe, had an oil on canvas here, *Antelope,* of an Antelope's horns and skull in the desert horizon, resembling her iconic paintings of cow skulls. It was good to feel a little closer to home in Santa Fe.

Finally, we came across the Master of Wildlife art. Carl Rungius is that master of North American Western landscape and wildlife. This museum preserves and exhibits the largest public collection of Carl Rungius's work in the United States. Carl (1869–1959) was born in Germany and studied at the Academy of Arts, Berlin from 1888 to 1890. Carl has said that his wildlife expertise came from his father shooting stray cats and allowing Carl to paint them. Rungius felt this was critical to his artistic development. In 1896 Carl immigrated to the United States. After a few hunting trips, Carl's fascination for the West and the moose was surreal. Some say Carl's real art career on canvas began in Wyoming, not far from the Museum of Wildlife's location. Later, as a resident of New York, Carl spent most of his summers in Banff, Alberta, painting the vast Canadian Rockies and plentiful populations of bighorn sheep, mountain goats, grizzly bears, and moose. At the age of ninety, Carl died in 1959 in New York City.

Rungius had his ashes scattered on Tunnel Mountain in Banff, Alberta, some say for his everlasting love for the view overlooking the town and the Bow Valley.

When I die, can you please spread some of my ashes there?

The National Wildlife Museum had many of Carl Rungius's masterpieces, including my favorite, *Northern King*, a gallant male alpha moose who sits on a mountaintop looking at the artist. The moose appears to be standing in the rubble of a clear-cut forest. What happened here? It's as if you're there with the moose. Scary yet elegant. A king in his patch of wilderness. A king in this museum. This is what a well-done display read at the museum:

> The paintings in this gallery are by Carl Rungius, the premier painter of North American wildlife. German-born Rungius first came to the United States in 1894. During his first decade here, he hunted, sketched, and painted every summer in the Wind River Range near Pinedale, Wyoming. During this period, he also traveled to New Brunswick, famous habitat for moose. In the winters, Rungius lived in New York City, creating finished paintings in his studio. Over the course of his life, Rungius met prominent figures in the conversation world, including Charles Sheldon, William Temple Hornaday, and even Theodore Roosevelt. He built a seasonal home and studio in Banff, Alberta, and created a lasting legacy that echoes to this day, inspiring generations of artists and admirers to go out and experience wildlife and wilderness firsthand . . .

Hopefully I'm doing that same thing with this book.

We were inspired and in awe. My son liked the paintings so much he almost touched one, as it looked so real. It was of an extra-large grizzly bear trekking up a mountainside. We finally took pictures next to Rungius's *Lake O'Hara*. The logs in this large lake are so lifelike it's almost a postcard of a photo. Soon I'd have this exact scene in my phone from a hike around Jenny Lake. Art imitates life, or is it life imitates art?

BOTH.

We met up with Joe and Josie and had a lovely lunch outside on the terrace during this pandemic summer. Every worker masked at this upscale dining experience. The views of National Elk Refuge, Bridger-Teton National Forest, and Gros Ventre Wilderness were a breathtaking backdrop for the delicious lunch. I think this was the most peaceful lunch we have ever had, and during the worldwide pandemic. A herd of seven bison were passing by, but hey, this had been their path forever. These bison were life-size sculptures set just below the restaurant on manicured grass. Between us and the sculptures was a patch of sagebrush, giving it the feel that they were real and we had just a thin barrier between man and wild.

Who knew we would spend so much time in a museum at the footsteps of the wild?

Our next stop was to visit the famous town of Jackson Hole, Wyoming. We got to Teton Village with umbrella in tow, as it looked like it might pour today. Teton Village, with its many resort luxuries, houses the Four Seasons Resort and the world-famous Jackson Hole Mountain Resort ski slopes. We had a quick bite to eat, bought a few things at a large sports store, and Logan found a fountain outside on this summer day. Water spit up periodically from the floor, making it immensely popular with little kids. This water feature was for children to run through. At first he used our umbrella as a shield. The weather had warmed, and it was actually a bit hot. We burst out laughing as Logan placed the umbrella on the grounds for the water to launch it, and up it went. He chased it over and over, and by golly, he was soaked.

In the foreground were the slopes of the ski basin. Maybe one day I'd try. I'm told skiing here can sometimes feel like negative forty on a windy day.

We headed out on the dirt back roads entering Grand Teton and headed for the Laurance S. Rockefeller Preserve. The road was so rough that if I hadn't had my Jeep, I'm sure we would have blown a tire or two. We flew a foot in the air at points, bouncing out of where the puddles turned into tire graves. Luckily, we survived. As others passed us in sedans, I felt for them, I really did.

The Laurance S. Rockefeller Preserve, some thirty-one hundred acres, is the old JY Dude Ranch, located south of Phelps Lake. It is a unique place. It was donated in 2008 and feels like an upscale dude ranch. With its contemporary LSR Preserve Center, another one closed for the pandemic, and unique bathrooms—open, thank goodness—it's a bathroom experience I'll always remember. The doors are probably twenty-five-feet tall and move with gravity. The bathrooms inside are like sleek Manhattan hotel entrances. It made me feel like a Rockefeller. Is this the future of philanthropy? Whatever it was, Logan was very impressed, and so was I. We hiked in and around the preserve and tried to imagine how it might feel to occupy this ranch. Just thirty minutes later we collected our thoughts and drove the rough roads to Phelps Lake.

From Phelps Lake, we were closer to the massive Teton peak looming over us. Phelps Lake is in the southern section of Grand Teton National Park, close to the entrance to Death Canyon. We did the popular 1.8-mile hike around the lake. This natural lake's surface area is around 750 acres and sits at an elevation of around sixty-six hundred feet above sea level. On this very sunny July day, we had spectacular views of multiple mountain ranges, the lake, and a sprawling wilderness as our background. Liz, Logan, and I used this photo as our 2020 Christmas postcard, and it was the kind our friends might want to post on their refrigerators.

A friend in Connecticut whom I hadn't visited in more than a year remarked that I was different from the last time we met. I was. I now had a good growth of facial hair and an Aussie cowboy hat from Bryce Canyon National Park. What did people think when they saw the photo of us here, in the middle of the pandemic, hiking around this miraculous lake with no others in sight?

If you only have an hour to hike in Grand Teton and are staying in Jackson Hole, Wyoming/Teton Village, this is the place to go. Again, if you are short on time, be golden and hike/swim Phelps Lake. Since we were jumping for joy in our family pictures, we took the Lake Creek Trail and hiked over spectacular wooden bridges and again entered what felt like never-seen-before wilderness. I felt like I was an astronaut exploring a new planet. With every sound of deer in the distance breaking branches, we jolted, fearing it might be a bear. We had our bear spray just in case.

We hiked for hours, finally stopping at around 7:00 p.m. without ever running into a single person. This was absolute bliss. Finally, we drove to a place called Moose to try to snap a shot of a wild moose. No luck.

The next morning, we were at it again. This would be our last full day in Grand Teton National Park. We were all rested up and on the road by 9:00 a.m. We first passed many bison on the plains. Just east of Jackson Lake, on the side of John D Rockefeller Jr. Parkway, we came across a few vehicles parked, their passengers looking into the wild. Bears! We got out to get a better look as we saw a very large mama grizzly and her two large cubs far off across a wide field. This was our first experience with grizzlies.

It's true what they say. This is the largest animal on the land in the lower forty-eight states of America. She is queen, and she's teaching her cubs to survive. What were they doing? More cars started to park any which way they stopped to see what we were looking at. Queen Mama Bear and her two cubs, Prince and Princess, were uprooting the turf, hunting for worms and other grub down below. To see their strength was like seeing three excavators turn and churn the land. We watched them put their heads up to sniff the air and then upturn the earth. Their extra power of smell added to the ferocity of this task. I'm assuming there were a lot of nutrients in the grubs they were uncovering. I wish I had them to help me dig for fishing worms. At this point around forty people were watching, and twenty-five vehicles were parked on the side of the road. Park rangers and volunteers started to direct traffic and give instructions for this bear sighting. This really beat waiting in line for an hour for one of the rides at Disneyland.

Since this was our last day, we got on the road. By the time we passed everyone, it looked like there might be more than fifty people out and about watching the bears.

Our last and final hike was again at Jenny Lake. Jenny Leigh was a Shoshone woman who married an Englishman, Richard Leigh. They had six children. The lakes, Jenny and Leigh, are named after her. We parked at the north end of Jenny Lake and hiked the Jenny Lake Loop for several miles to Hidden Falls. Picture postcards of this landscape do not come close to the reality of the experience of hiking here. Logan bounced along singing "The Bare Necessities" while we hiked. So did I.

It was time to leave Mama Bear and Jenny Lake and start a new journey. I snapped lovely photos of Liz and Logan along this amazing hike. The dips and dives of the trail were at times a challenge. At one point I was hiking on my own, Joe and Josie way in front of me, and Liz and Logan way behind me. This is where I found myself. I imagined a beautiful bird, and one moment later it was there, right in front of me. A vivid western tanager with its orange head, yellow body, and black, brown, and white wings flew to a fallen tree steps away. I stopped. Had I conjured this vision, or was I dreaming? I pinched myself. It was reality. The bird looked at me and offered an earful of chirps. I chirped back. Then it flew off to find food or Hidden Falls that we were all searching for.

I looked back, and there was no sign of my family. Twenty-three minutes later I found myself with a handful of strangers at Hidden Falls.

Hidden Falls drops for approximately one hundred feet of stream water from the mountain down a rugged, rocky ledge. It's tucked in a corner of wilderness. Of course it attracts many hikers like us. At first glance I felt like it was fake and man-made, something you'd see in front of a Las Vegas, Nevada, hotel. Even so, Hidden Falls is one of the busiest tourist attractions in Grand Teton National Park, so one does get a Vegas feel from all the commotion. Liz and Logan had not yet caught up. I wanted to get away from the masses of forty or more people, so I climbed up the moist wilderness cliffside. I didn't know

I'd meet local wildlife waiting for me. From under a large mountain face cave, a marmot peeked out, looking curious about this strange-looking human with a hat. He came out and sniffed to greet me. He looked like a squirrel the size of a large house cat and appeared to have been eating well this summer. He had found his niche. As my family wandered into the crowd, I watched as Liz and Logan took in the beauty of the falls, pointing and nodding as they talked. I kept my eye on the marmot and called to them to come see. Logan didn't believe me. As the creature came out, Logan jumped into Liz's arms. Then he began to smile. It was a huge, friendly marmot. Others saw him as they began to picnic in and around the area. This marmot waited calmly, knowing there would be leftovers. A banana here, some bread there, anything left behind it may consume. Although people didn't feed the bears, they did accidentally feed the Hidden Falls marmot.

There's an interesting relationship we have with the wildlife here at Grand Teton. It's a very delicate balance. Some of us, like Carl Rungius, paint. I write, and millions of visitors somehow stay safe, keep their distance, and allow this place to stay wild.

Joe and Josie were going to hike a bit more. Logan, Liz, and I were tired, so we were going to hike back down, catch the park service shuttle boat across Jenny Lake, and hike back from the southern part of Jenny Lake to the northern part where our vehicle was parked. We had lunch packed in our car. The hike from Hidden Falls to the free shuttle boat was only about twenty minutes, and then it was another twenty minutes before the boat arrived. We put on life vests with fifteen others, boarded, and had our first boat ride of the pandemic. The views from the water made the experience of Jenny Lake all that much better.

As we got off the boat, I noticed hundreds, if not thousands, of very large trout under the surface all around the boat. There were a handful of park rangers out and about, so I asked one, "Can you fish here?" She knew this question was coming and probably had already answered it many times today. She replied as if scripted, "You can fish anywhere on Jenny Lake with a permit, except here. This is where the trout spawn, so it's off-limits."

The symbiotic relationship between man and fish was evident. An angler could catch hundreds of these beautiful trout here in a day. But not here. I could see that having the rangers always nearby was a way to keep the ecosystem thriving.

Man, I wish I would have brought my fishing rod, got a permit, and fished somewhere else on this lake, I thought. That could have been the best trout story in the family. But for now, it was time to get our hungry kid back to the car and eat lunch. A few snacks from the little store near the dock would help Logan make the three-mile hike back to the parking lot. The hike was just as beautiful as all the others in this oasis. We passed people hiking, jogging, biking, scuba diving, snorkeling, canoeing, and just having their own wonderful time. We got back, found a friendly park bench, and ate our lunch in this paradise.

Remember Carl Rungius's lake paintings with the magnificent Tetons in the distance? I snapped what might be the most perfect picture postcard shot I've ever taken in my life. I took off my hiking boots, got into the freezing Jenny Lake, and photographed the lake, wilderness, and Teton Range. Mother Nature. When Liz and Logan came around the turn, they wondered why I was up to my knees in the lake. I thought to myself, *This is the picture on the front of my book.* My Family looked at me like I was crazy and nose-dived into their lunch. Hunger, like the bears and marmot, creates motion. Now it was time to return to reality. After lunch I wondered if we would ever see such beauty again.

By this time tomorrow we would be gone.

An ice bath in Jenny Lake & a view of the Teton Range

Running off a boulder

Phelps Lake

Yellowstone Sign

Lower Falls of the Yellowstone River

WHITE SANDS AND BIG BEND NATIONAL PARKS

We rented a recreational vehicle to go to both White Sands National Park and Big Bend National Park in March 2021. The Fleetwood Jamboree Class C RV was large enough to take five humans, one dog, and a kitten across the desert on spring break. Logan was now six years old, and his preschool had been canceled due to the continuing coronavirus pandemic. We packed our belongings and hit the road.

At first I noticed how the winds in the month of March in New Mexico made driving this RV no easy task. The two-lane highways down to our destination, Alamogordo, New Mexico, made it feel like the RV was going to tip over. Winds pushed at the RV at every moment. This must be what truck drivers face every trip. Hats off to all truck drivers around the world.

With my wife, in-laws, and son's life at stake on this windy road, we all were uncertain whether this trip would be a success. White-knuckling it down the highway was tough. Luckily Joe and I split up the driving. Four hours later we were having dinner at a restaurant in Tularosa, New Mexico, near the RV campground.

Joe and Josie Jaramillo had raised their family in this small desert town in Southern New Mexico near the town of Alamogordo. Liz grew up minutes from White Sands National Park, and after she and I first met in 2007, we visited the park a few times. Her parents met at New Mexico State University, and Joe was an educator in Alamogordo for all of Liz's childhood.

During my senior year of high school, my track and field team competed in an Alamogordo meet. I won the mile and two mile, and we stayed overnight. I remember the night before telling the others that I was going to get up around 6:00 a.m. to run the town. I invited anyone from the thirty boys and girls on the teams to join me. One long-distance runner showed up. She and I ran the main street early in the morning. I remember running next to the Alameda Park Zoo, and we could see nearly half of all the animals and exhibits. For a small town they put on a good track meet and had a very interesting zoo.

Alamogordo is one of those places where you can't do much in the summer days because it is over a hundred degrees almost every day. That weather is ideal for growing pistachios.

I had no idea my future wife had grown up here and might have been here as I ran along her main street back in the day.

Our RV was comfortable, and I'm glad we rented one instead of buying one, as I still was not sure I felt safe driving in the wind. The next morning, we walked across the street to one of the largest pistachio farms in New Mexico. They had a great store to buy many assortments of nuts. I've always been a nut for pistachio ice cream, and that flavor is usually my go-to at Baskin-Robbins. We returned to the RV park, threw away the trash, dumped our waste, and were on the road by noon. By 12:30 p.m. on March 14, 2021, we were entering White Sands National Park. It was rather busy for March, and I guess a lot of people like us had the same idea of how to spend this pandemic. We noticed a lot more RVs around us and a handful in line with us to enter the park.

When we first started this adventure, White Sands was a national monument. White Sands became a national monument on January 18, 1933. White Sands became a national park on December 20, 2019.

The park is just under 146,000 acres, and in 2021 there were 782,469 visitors, including the five of us and our two pets. A large part of the Alamogordo economy is the White Sands Missile Range, which surrounds the park.

The park is in the Tularosa Basin and is filled with white sand dunes composed of gypsum crystals. This gypsum dune field is the largest of its kind on Earth. It has an approximate depth of thirty feet, dunes as tall as sixty feet, and around 4.5 billion short tons of gypsum sand, which formed about seven thousand to ten thousand years ago. During the Permian period, many shallow seas covered the area of White Sands. The seas left behind gypsum (calcium sulfate), and many tectonic movements lifted areas of the gypsum-rich seabed to form parts of the San Andres and Sacramento Mountains. Over time, rain dissolved the water-soluble gypsum in the mountains, and rivers carried it to the Tularosa Basin, thus creating the white dunes.

The Tularosa Basin has seen many inhabitants, from Paleo-Indians twelve thousand years ago to modern farmers, ranchers, miners, and my wife's family of four. Paleo-Indians lived in and around Lake Otero hunting mammoths, camels, ground sloths, and bison with their Folsom and Plano points. After Lake Otero dried up, people entered the Tularosa Basin about four thousand years ago because of the cereal-like grass called Indian ricegrass. The first evidence in this land of agriculture is found in the Archaic period. More than seven hundred years ago, bands of Apache followed herds of bison from the Great Plains to the Tularosa Basin. Apache groups, led by Victorio and Geronimo, fought with settlers in the basin and engaged in military battles with the buffalo soldiers. This basin was not really established with humans until the nineteenth century. Hispanic families started farming communities at Tularosa in 1861. At the turn of the twentieth century, the discovery of oil, coal, silver, gold, and other precious mineral deposits inspired many settlers to cover the Tularosa Basin in mining claims. During the 1920s, an Alamogordo businessman named Tom Charles promoted the potential economic benefits of protecting the White Sands formation. He lobbied for a national park but was told a national monument was easier to achieve, and in 1933 President Hoover designated it as such under the Antiquities Act.

Eventually, on December 11, 2019, the U.S. House of Representatives passed the National Defense Authorization Act for fiscal year 2020, which includes legislation redesignating White Sands National Monument as White Sands National Park. The Senate passed the act on December 16, and President Donald Trump signed the bill on December 20, 2019. The act included the transfer of land management both to and from the missile range, as well as the protection of additional land, adding a net of 2,029 acres to the park.

As we entered the park, we drove slowly, looking for an ideal location to sled these massive white sand dunes. About three miles into the drive, we found our spot. The white sands were blinding, and the desert's sun waves reflected right off the beach sand, making it an ideal spot for a tan. Sunglasses are highly recommended. We got our green and red plastic snow sleds and hiked the dunes. At first Logan was a bit apprehensive to barrel down the dunes like we did, so he slowly slid down feet first and enjoyed himself. Then after a while, and some convincing, he would go with Mama. The two laughed and screamed all the way down. We were all like children on the beach without an ocean for the next few hours. We buried Logan in the sand, slid down the sand dunes, chased our dog around, and finally took in some lunch in the shade of our RV. We were in the middle of a frightening pandemic but having family adventures. Just a week before, Joe, Josie, and I had gotten the one-shot Johnson & Johnson COVID-19 vaccine and were feeling a bit better about being out and about. Liz had already gotten her two shots of Pfizer. Logan would have to wait until November, as it was not yet approved for his age group. When we ran into people, we all masked up, as the world was still in panic mode.

We all got out of the RV to take pictures next to the White Sands National Park sign at the entrance/exit of the park. Our rented RV was on the side of the picture like a member of the family. Liz and her parents had been here countless times. This was my third trip and

Logan's first. I'm sure we will be back, as it's just four hours down the road from where we live in Santa Fe.

Big Bend National Park in Texas is said to be the hardest national park to get to in the lower forty-eight states. Having our RV was ideal to get to Big Bend from White Sands. The drive was about six hours from park to park, but we stopped at another RV park in the middle of the night. We jumped on the road the next morning and were at the Big Ben National Park sign by around 1:00 p.m. on Monday, March 15, 2021.

The first place I wanted to hike was Santa Elena Canyon. Big Bend is huge, so anywhere we went might take an hour or two to get to. From the Entrance Station to Santa Elena Canyon, due to road work and our massive RV, it took us more than two hours to get to our destination.

Santa Elena Canyon is the most picturesque part of the park. We saw two countries, the US and Mexico, the Rio Grande River, and Mother Nature. Here at Santa Elena Canyon, I immediately saw the massive canyon walls rising up as much as fifteen hundred feet from the Rio Grande. The canyon made me feel like I was in the Grand Canyon on top of the Colorado River. But here we were in Texas, atop the Rio Grande River. If this type of spellbound land were in or near a major metropolitan locale, I'm sure it would see millions of visitors a year. That perhaps is the beauty of Santa Elena Canyon. There were plenty of park visitors for our visit, but the beauty of this place with minimal visitation made us feel like we were the first people to get a glimpse of this canyon wall.

We walked the Santa Elena Canyon Trail. Over a bend, we could get into the Rio Grande and walk the riverbed. The middle of the river is the exact location where the United States touches Mexico. This is a border of sorts. As I walked the Rio Grande riverbed, I had the interesting feeling I was in two countries at the same time. There were probably ten others doing just the same thing, as I could see about a half mile in each direction. The great canyon walls above made me feel like I was chasing a starfighter in a *Star Wars* film. It had a feeling of its own.

The informational sign read:

> Santa Elena Canyon Trail – 1.6 miles round trip and 80-foot elevation gain. This trail enters between the walls of spectacular Santa Elena Canyon and ends where the cliffs meet the Rio Grande. The walls of this canyon rise 1,500 feet from the banks of the Rio Grande, making this one of the most dramatic and popular places to view the river. The sheer face of this canyon was formed by the Terlingua Fault, which is mostly covered in gravel. Calcite crystals filled in the cracks formed by this fault and can be seen along the trail. The deepest channel of the Rio Grande is the international boundary, with each half of this canyon protected by a national park. The southern side belongs to the Area Protegida del Canon de Santa Elena (Mexico), and the northern side is within Big Bend National Park (USA). During wet times abrupt rises to Terlingua Creek can make this trail impassible. Always watch for distant rainfall that could lead to flash flooding to avoid becoming stranded within the canyon.

We didn't have to worry about any distant showers and for the most part enjoyed every step of the hike. Who can really say they've been in two countries and respective national parks in one day? We could.

We all walked back to our RV, saddled everything up, and made our way back to our RV park, where we'd stay for the next three days. On this national park adventure, our amenities would be in our hotel on wheels.

The sunset that evening was amazing. After dark we watched millions of stars above.

The next day we traveled a few hours to the east side of the park. There we went to the Rio Grande Village Visitor Center. We took a walk around the lush grass RV campgrounds. Too bad it was sold out. Next time I'll have to stay here if we take an RV. Then we took the

Boquillas Canyon Overlook. The few miles of hiking took us to an overlook where the Rio Grande is in a horseshoe. As we ascended down, we got to a part of the park where in March the Rio Grande encompasses both sides of the two countries. I was brave enough to go for a swim in an area where there was a large pool. I swam back and put my toes in the sand. There was tourist activity and general vacation commotion all around. Some people were having lunch, some were swimming in the river, and others were passing by on a hike. As we hiked back up the trail, we took another view from Boquillas Overlook. From here we saw the village of Boquillas, Mexico. In the shade we could see, just next to the Rio Grande, a few horses with a man. My assumption is we could rent the horses. On the trail we passed a few people selling their handmade Mexican art. At every turn there was something to rent or buy.

It's always been interesting how different cultures interact with tourism. Down the road a family of three asked me if I wanted to go in with them to buy a dozen tamales from someone selling them.

"Sure, why not," I said. We each handed the man ten bucks, and he walked across the river, grabbed a dozen tamales, and brought them back to us. We snacked on a couple tamales; they were tasty. Back at the RV we made lunch and had the rest of those homemade Mexican tamales. They weren't hot, but they sure were good.

On the road again we came across a fossil bone exhibit off one of the roads and decided to stop. This was the open-air Fossil Discovery Exhibit of the Big Bend Conservancy. We walked around sculptures of a T. rex head and a large prehistoric alligator head, animals that had once lived here.

We got back to our RV park and called it a day. Driving was half the battle in this park; the other half was the heat. I'm glad we went in March. Temperatures in March have a high of about seventy-five. It felt more like ninety in the sun. Come July temperatures would be well over ninety and probably feel like a hundred in the sun.

We didn't see much wildlife on our walks, but Big Bend protects more than twelve hundred species of plants, more than 450 species of birds, fifty-six species of reptiles, and seventy-five species of mammals.

The Chiso Indians were in and around Big Bend before 1535. They were nomadic hunters and gatherers who probably practiced limited agriculture on a seasonal basis. In the eighteenth century, the Mescalero Apaches invaded the Big Bend region and displaced most of the Chiso Indians. Following the end of the Mexican-American War in 1848, the U.S. Army made military surveys of the uncharted land of Big Bend. In the nineteenth and twentieth centuries, valuable mineral deposits were discovered, and the towns of Boquillas and Terlingua sprang up with economic fervor. By the 1930s those who saw Big Bend as a unique place began to preserve it. In 1933 the Texas legislature passed legislation to establish Texas Canyons State Park. Later that year it became known as Big Bend State Park. In 1935 the U.S. Congress passed legislation that would enable the acquisition of the land for a national park. The state of Texas deeded the land to the federal government, and on June 12, 1944, Big Bend National Park became a reality under President Franklin Roosevelt. The park opened to visitors on July 1, 1944.

As visitors those past two days, we decided our third day would be well spent in the Terlingua Ghost Town. We shopped, hiked, and marveled over the interesting things this true ghost town was. As we had packed all our belongings into our moving hotel, we were on our way back home. The experience of Big Bend National Park would have been much different without the RV. I'm glad we rented it and took the journey to the edges of Texas.

Thumbs up at Santa Elena Canyon

Shall we walk to Mexico?

Boquillas Canyon Overlook

White Sands

Atop a sand dune

HALEAKALA AND HAWAII VOLCANOES NATIONAL PARKS

The American Paradise: Our 2022 summer family vacation took us to an American paradise. On Thursday, May 26, 2022, a day after Logan had his kindergarten promotion ceremony, we left for Hawaii. We drove the hour to Albuquerque International Sunport airport, stopped at LAX for lunch, and five hours after LAX we were in Maui. The time change was four hours earlier. It was midnight back home and only 8:00 p.m. on the island. We would be officially on "island time" during the next few weeks. On our flight in, we saw the diverse landscape of Maui from the Southwest Airlines windows. The flight wasn't full, and Logan and Liz took one window, and I took the other in the opposite row. We flew over mountains, valleys, and scenic ocean resorts.

We rented a brand new 2022 Subaru from an app called Turo that allows you to rent vehicles from owners. We noticed right away that there was a large screw in the rear right tire. The next day we were all planning to get on the road to Haleakala National Park. We were too chicken to risk a flat on our drive to the top of a mountain and decided the next day would be a beach day so the owner of our vehicle could repair the tire in the afternoon.

We drove the Subaru, picked up some fish tacos, and called it a night at the Airbnb we rented for the next week. Bright and early, we walked across the street to Kamaole Beach Park II. The beaches of Maui were amazing. It was like San Diego on steroids. We also heard and saw many roosters and chickens roaming around everywhere.

We were staying in Wailea and took in a few beaches on Friday. Wailea was first a fishing settlement, and its name translates to "water of Lea," the goddess of canoe builders. The legend is she transformed the area into a beautiful forest for birds and would frequently fly above it to appreciate its beauty. In ancient Hawaiian times many natives lived more toward the mountains of Wailea, where they grew sweet potatoes (*uala*) and would venture down to the beach to fish. Now in 2022 the town, with a 2020 population of 6,027, was a tourist mecca. Multimillion-dollar homes were scattered among many exclusive corporate resorts like the Four Seasons.

Our first beach stop was Polo Beach. Public parking was in between two resorts: the Fairmont and Four Seasons. We took beach gear and a few chairs. This smooth beach spot was paradise. We stayed for a few hours and took in the warm Pacific Ocean. Logan played with the sandcastle toys that came with our car rental. Being in paradise was very relaxing. We packed our belongings, got a few fish tacos from a truck on the side of the road, and ventured to Mākena State Park.

Mākena State Park is comprised of 165 acres south of Wailea in Maui. This park contains three separate beaches and a dormant volcanic cinder cone. This beach seemed to go on for miles to the farther end of the island. The waves on this beach were spectacular, but the incoming waters were too violent for swimming. Instead, Logan took my hand, and we ran from one end of the beach to the other.

It was gently raining, and in the distance we could see a rainbow over the little island of Kahoolawe. We made a pit stop back home for the owner's father to take the screw out of their Subaru tire and patch it up for the week. With a little bit of the afternoon left after the tire was fixed, we headed for Lahaina Banyan Court Park. The drive was supposed to be about an hour, but traffic and the hundreds of surfers we saw on the waves on a Friday night dragged it out to more than two hours.

We ignored our jet lag as we made our way to this plaza where one of the largest banyan trees in the world stood. This massive 150-year-old Banyan tree looked like something in the forest where Yoda sits to meditate. Its branches spread wide and drop roots to form new trunks, almost twenty of them! Kids can climb in and out, but Logan was not in the mood to do anything. His regular bedtime of 9:00 or 10:00 p.m. in Santa Fe was happening now at 5:00 p.m. in Maui. We were all tired and jet-lagged.

To memorialize the fiftieth anniversary of the first American Protestant mission in Lahaina, a banyan tree seedling was planted on April 24, 1873, in the courthouse square by Sheriff William Owen Smith, who had received it as a gift from missionaries in India. The banyan, native to India, is one of sixty types of fig trees in the Hawaiian Islands. The seedling was approximately eight feet high when it was planted, but when we visited it was nearly fifty feet tall, had almost twenty trunks, and covered a circumference of about a quarter of a mile around this unique plaza. The plaza itself was just under one acre. The tree is an iconic tourist attraction and much beloved by residents. The banyan tree survived the 2023 Hawaiian wildfires with only partial damage.

Across the street we found the famous fish market, Paia Fish Market, on Front Street. We ordered our dinner, and Logan again was being a little devil. Not only did he not want to eat what he ordered but was getting on Liz's nerves. I took him by the hand and went on a walk with him under the banyan tree in the plaza. We talked it out. I told him we were on vacation, and things were not going to be perfect, but to keep an open mind. On our walk we saw boats unloading hundreds of adventurous tourists who had gone snorkeling. This took his mind off his frustrations, and by the time we got back to the restaurant we were a unit ready for dinner. Liz said she had to fight off wild birds that tried to eat our fish. Others sitting outdoors laughed while she fought off birds and saved our dinner. This was definitely not Kansas. We ate dinner. Then we strolled this famous shop district, got some ice cream, and savored another beautiful family sunset together. The sun changed to different shades of orange, yellow, and pink. Our first full day in paradise echoed memories of the past and promises for adventures in the future. Would we make it to all the national parks? Would I finish this first book?

As I drove back to our home away from home, Liz and Logan sleeping, I was glad we had set this goal of going to all the national parks. In the background were economic challenges with inflation at a forty-year high, the highest I had known in my life. Knowing this, I probably wouldn't have set out on this vacation if it weren't for our goal. Now, being present in Hawaii, this American paradise, I'm glad we made the time to see our beautiful country.

According to archaeological evidence, the earliest habitation of the Hawaiian Islands dates to approximately 1000 to 1200 CE. They were probably Polynesian settlers from the Marquesas Islands. Some archaeologists and historians think it was a later wave of immigrants from Tahiti around 1000 CE who introduced a new line of high chiefs, the kapu system (Hawaiian code of conduct of laws and regulations), the practice of human sacrifice, the building of heiau (Hawaiian temples), and *mo'olelo* (Hawaiian mythology). This lifestyle gave rise to a complex and fascinating culture. Europeans wouldn't arrive until the 1700s.

Our plans changed. We decided that Saturday would be our bay and snorkel day, instead of our first national park day in Maui. We drove to the beautiful Kapalua Bay in an hour and a half. This bay won Condé Nast's title of America's Best Beach in 1991 and 2018. The best resorts in the world are nearby. The beach was packed, but the view and snorkeling were amazing. Liz and I took turns, as Logan could not yet swim, and we saw numerous sea turtles eating algae off lava rocks in the ocean.

We tried to find a burger joint for lunch but ended up at the Burger

Shack on the grounds of a Ritz Carlton resort for incredibly delicious burgers, worth every penny of the—gulp—hundred-dollar bill. We only ordered one shake, and this one was Logan's; it was thirteen dollars. It was the Hula Girl, consisting of pineapple and coconut. The shake was half the size of Logan and came with half an Almond Joy bar, caramelized dried pineapple, and dried coconut. This put the biggest smile on Logan's face we'd ever seen. The fifteen-second video of this moment was the most viewed shot of our vacation shared with friends on Instagram. He was in heaven, our jet lag was gone, and we were ready to find the only place I had as a goal for the day: Honolua Bay.

From the Ritz we drove up a large tropical mountain. The two-lane mountainous jungle road is called the Honoapi'ilani Highway. My assumption was that Honolua Bay was going to be like Mākena State Park beaches with hundreds of parking spots. I was wrong. When our smartphone said we had passed our destination, I knew we were lost. But in paradise the drives are spectacular. We made a U-turn on a hairpin and went back.

Honolua Bay and Mokule'ia Bay comprise the forty-five-acre Conservation District mixed in with local Native lands. In many of the national park books I was researching, this bay is mentioned as the best place to snorkel. The only way to access the bay is to walk through the jungle for about a mile. This was our first family walk in a jungle. We passed banyan, mango, coffee, and other tropical trees. The fallen fruit had a sharp fermented smell that made our nostrils twitch a few times. We expected to see monkeys or jaguars. On the trail I heard some tourists say there were no predators in Hawaii, and that's why it's so peaceful. I thought to myself that just a few feet into the Pacific Ocean there were many predators, like the great white shark.

As we reached the bay, we found it was a bit different from our last resort bay. It felt wilder. The beach was narrow and rocky, but the view was beautiful.

As I began to snorkel near the surface, I could see the ocean floor stretch deeper to the bottom a few stories down. Just below me were a few brilliant fish with wild colors like turquoise, olive, and green. I was in a different world.

As I stumbled on boulders at the beach, Liz asked, "How's the snorkeling?"

"It's okay."

"Should I go in?" she asked, looking at Logan, a signal for me to look after him.

"I don't know. The last place had much more fish and turtles. This one's a bit horrific with its depth."

Ten minutes later I was having a snack, watching Logan balancing on the rocks and dipping into the ocean. Liz went off to join three other divers for her first Maui bay dive. She went out and returned to tighten the snorkel gear. Round two lasted twenty minutes. Liz agreed this wasn't as nice as the last place we went.

Sunday, May 29, 2022, was our day to drive up the mountain for our first of two days in Haleakala National Park. The first thing we realized while we were driving about two hours up the mountain was that Maui is as much a mountain as it is a beach. Then we started to wonder if any people at all came up there. The lush land and estates up the mountain were amazing. As we started to get closer to our destination, we saw signs illustrating to stay clear of the geese: "Nene Crossing." The Hawaiian version of Canadian geese are called "nenes." We didn't come across any on this spring day. I assume they are much more prevalent in the winter.

This crazy road up to the top had more switchbacks than I'd ever seen. I wouldn't want to try that with ice or treacherous weather. We got out of our Subaru to take pictures at the Haleakala National Park sign with what looks like a tropical god parachuting into the mouth of a volcano.

Our entry to the park became a math lesson for Logan. We got to the gates of the park and purchased our national park annual pass for a fee of $79.99. To a first grader, this seemed like a lot until I explained that it would pay for itself just in this trip. Without a pass, every time you enter a national park, it costs thirty dollars. He did the math and agreed.

A national park annual pass may be the best family pass of all time. A month before this trip we all went to LEGOLAND, as I was running a half-marathon in San Diego. The ticket was $99.99 per person per day. With a $79.99 annual park ticket, we could take a vehicle in with the three of us or more all year long to any national park on any day the parks were open.

This park's website says, "Haleakala National Park is open all year round, 7 days a week for 24 hours per day, just so long as the weather is agreeable. Severe weather is the only event that does close the park from time to time. Headquarters Visitor Center is at 7,000 feet above sea level and is open between the hours of 6:30 a.m. and 3:45 p.m."

We got to the visitor center around 10:30 a.m. It was the only place on the islands we saw that required wearing a mask during the pandemic. We wore our masks on the plane, when it got busy, and always had them in our pockets. No problem, we masked up.

As we looked around, I realized how rich the birding was in these jungle settings.

My priority for the day was to do a two-or-so-mile hike on the Keonehe'ehe'e (Sliding Sands) Trail. At that point I zoned into the bird display at the visitor center. It was of the "Rare Winged Wonders, Birds of Haleakala" and read:

> CULTURAL SIGNIFICANCE – Native Hawaiian birds are significant to the Native Hawaiian culture. Birds are depicted in Hawaiian *mo'olelo* (stories), they are seen as *'aumakua* (guardian spirits), and their feathers are used for adornment. One of these birds is the *'apapane* or Hawaiian honeycreeper. Its crimson feathers were prized by Hawaiian nobility and used to make *'ahu 'ula* (feather capes), *mahiole* (helmets), kahili (feather standard), and *na lei hulu* (feather lei). Skilled bird catchers would line the branches of *'ōhi'a lehua* (Metrosideros polymorpha) with the gummy sticky sap of the Hawaiian ulu or breadfruit (Artocarpus altilis) tree. When the 'apapane

> would land on a branch to feed on the nectar of the ʻōhiʻa lehua, it would become stuck. The bird catchers would remove the bird from the branch with delicate care and proceed to remove only 1–3 feathers from the neck, wing, or tail, then release the bird back into the forest.
>
> Exhibited here is a photograph of the ʻahu ʻulu of the Hawaiian chief Kalaniʻōpuʻu. It is estimated that it took approximately 20,000 birds to produce this ʻahu ʻulu.
>
> ARRIVAL – The Hawaiian Islands are only around 5 million years old and were created by volcanic activity. They are also surrounded by over 2,000 miles of water. So how did birds get here? Well one of the birds that we have at Haleakala has a long and interesting history of how it arrived and evolved in this place. The nene (Hawaiian Goose) exhibited is the only living endemic goose to the Hawaiian Islands and is the state bird! This goose is closely related to the Canada goose (Branta canadensis) and is the only species of goose found on islands. It is believed that the nene's ancestors evolved from a Canada goose that took a wrong turn during migration about half a million years ago and ended up here on the Hawaiian Islands. Since arriving here, they have adapted to the volcanic landscape and have become their own species. Sadly by 1952 the population of the nene had dropped to 30 birds in the Hawaiian Islands. With the help of a nene breeding program, Haleakala was able to introduce 500 birds in the 1960s. To help reintroduce the birds, the Boy Scouts helped carry them into the wilderness. Today, the park has an estimate of 280 birds and a statewide population of 3,159.

I guess I was wrong. The nene birds must live here year-round. After a while we just liked saying the word: "Nene!" We wouldn't run into any of the three hundred or so here at this mountaintop.

We drove up the mountain to one of the parking lots. It was our stop for the hike we had been waiting for and our access to the Sliding Sands Trail. We went to the restrooms and then to the park store. In the store there was a half-page congratulatory message for visitors. I stamped it in the middle with the date—May 29, 2022—and around it, it read "Haleakala National Park – Haleakala Summit." The standard read:

> HALEAKALA NATIONAL PARK – House of the Sun – I have survived the 37- mile drive up from sea level to the summit of Haleakala volcano (10,023 feet/3,055 meters) one of the greatest elevation gains in the shortest distance in the world!

As I contemplated this moment, I thought of all the dads and moms who also looked at this message. I'm glad we are all alive.

Haleakala National Park was named after Haleakalā, a dormant volcano within its boundaries. This dormant volcano last erupted sometime between 1480 and 1600 AD. Perhaps the experience to live or walk among the clouds at this elevation may have inspired the Hawaiians to name their volcano Haleakalā, or "House of the Sun." Maui, the Hawaiian god who was said to have raised the Hawaiian Islands with a homemade fishhook and line, knew where the sun resided. One day Maui overheard his mother complain that the days were too short and that there wasn't enough time for her kapa (bark cloth) clothes to dry. So Maui climbed Haleakalā to lasso the sun with his sister's hair. Caught, the sun pled for its life and agreed the days would be longer in summer and shorter in winter. On this vacation, my family wanted the days to last a lifetime. Who wouldn't want to have a few extra hours in paradise? The picture from the park entrance was not of a god parachuting; it was of Maui holding onto his sister's hair, lassoing the sun for longer days into the volcano of Haleakalā. This may be the only myth picture on an entrance sign of a national park. This culture kept getting better every minute we learned about it. It made me want to be Hawaiian.

The park itself is about 33,265 acres. Twenty-five thousand acres are a wilderness area, or about 75 percent of the park. This area is sacred, allowed only by permission to pass, and has no modern societal means like roads, campgrounds, or electricity. This allows for the abundant biodiversity to thrive in this park. More endangered species live in Haleakala than any other national park in the United States, and the park's unique ecosystems make for one of the world's most interesting and studied living laboratories.

In 2018 there were approximately one million visitors to Haleakalā. It was originally part of Hawaii National Park, along with the volcanoes of Mauna Loa and Kilauea on the island of Hawaii, created in 1916. Hawaii Volcanoes National Park was made into a separate national park in 1961 by bill S.3623. President Woodrow Wilson was the US president in 1916 and created the two parks under one name, and the bill in 1961 created two separate parks. The land we were now on was designated a national park in 1976, and its boundaries expanded in 2005. Our hiking trail was the dormant Haleakalā (East Maui) Volcano, which last erupted sometime between 1480 and 1600 AD. The park is divided into two distinct sections. That day we would hike the summit area, and in a few days, we'd hike to a waterfall and see the ocean in the Kipahulu area.

The year I was born, this park was designated an International Biosphere Reserve. A volcanic rock with a copper plaque read:

> By decision of the bureau of the international coordinating council of the program on man and the biosphere, duly authorized to that effect by the council, Haleakala National Park is recognized as part of the international network of Biosphere Reserves. This network of protected samples of the world's major ecosystem types is devoted to conservation of nature and scientific research in the service of man. It provides a standard against which the effect of man's impact on his environment can be measured . . . 20 November 1980.

In my forty-one years of life to this point, I could only think what this summit might have been like without the protection of its national park designation. It may have become a tourist destination with a few horse ranches, a corporate hotel, and many eateries. Looking down into the volcano, I was glad it had been protected since I was born.

Liz, Logan, and I ate a quick packed lunch before we set foot on the Sliding Sands Trail. I love peanut butter and jelly sandwiches. Liz settled on a ham and cheese, and Logan gobbled a few cheese and ham rolls. The grocery store run a few days prior gave us a frugal alternative to the thirty-dollar burgers we had enjoyed, even with inflation also factored into the food we bought. When our stomachs were full, we tucked into our hiking boots. This was the one and only trail we used these suckers on our vacations, as we opted for sandals for most of the hikes. Hiking boots on lava rock: check. We were glad we packed them. The circular turn from our parking spot felt like circumnavigating a lava field. As we reached the top, we could see down into the dormant volcano. The trail was dusty, light brown, almost blond. It stuck to our hiking boots like glue. Our boots resembled the one-year-old golden retriever we got during the pandemic back home. Logan prattled on happily about our pets: our two dogs, cat, and koi in the pond out front.

Even after so many beautiful sights, we are still speechless at the sight of nature's beauty, whether that is the beaches, mountains, or skies. Now the experience expands to include more conversations of wonder and discovery through the eyes of our son. We talk and share as only a family can.

This volcano looked like Mars. My son had studied the solar system in kindergarten, and we talked as if we were the first humans to land on the Red Planet. The red sand all around made us feel as if we were on the Red Planet. Although our hiking boots resembled our golden retriever, the distant landscape showed red, brown, and shades of green and gray. We were also walking among the clouds at about ten thousand feet above sea level. We soared over the jungle like it was an American Machu Picchu, which is only eight thousand feet above sea level.

Five percent of the Earth's volcanoes are called "shield volcanoes" that flow thin lava. All the Hawaiian volcanoes are shields. The thinner lava flows over a larger surface area, often the ocean floor, so the volcano looks like a shield. As I walked on this shield, it was hard to imagine that at ten thousand feet above the sea it once was at sea level.

Walking with my family on this shield volcano was straight out of a dream. From the nearby black volcanic rock top to the interior of this red planet, we measured history in color. Some say this is the Grand Canyon of Hawaii. They aren't wrong. This Sunday hike was one to cherish. The wind made it feel about five degrees cooler, mixed with an occasional cloud that hit my baseball cap. Being on a different planet I forgot about the trials and tribulations our current planet is enduring.

Hiking on this Sunday would not have been allowed back in Santa Fe, as a massive four-hundred-thousand-acre wildfire was burning over a mountain about forty miles away from our home. The wildfire started as a controlled burn and went wild. I prayed for my local communities and the farmers and ranchers back home who lost their livelihood and may never get it back. I stopped to ask Pele, the god of volcanoes and fires, to look after my neighbors and all others suffering.

At one point on the hike, I stopped to worry about the rest of the world: inflation, shootings, fires, and unrest. On the other hand, I looked back and saw my small family hiking in our twenty-seventh national park together and smiled. We had made the right decision to take this vacation.

At noon we got to our mile mark and rested, took a sip of water, pictures, and looked below at another red planet on Earth and decided this was the end of the road for us today. We hiked back out, again passing a few others, periodically chased by the clouds filling the jungle around us. We took way too many pictures on our smartphones of this amazing shield volcano. As we investigated the Haleakalā crater from the summit, we realized the summit itself had once been three thousand to six thousand feet above its current peak. Erosion for centuries caused by wind, rain, ice, and snow made that portion fall into the crater.

Many famous writers have visited this Mars on Earth landscape.

Mark Twain wrote:

> A growing warmth suffused the horizon, and soon the sun emerged and looked out over the cloud-waste, flinging bars of ruddy light across it, staining the folds and billow-caps with blushes, purpling the shaded troughs between . . . It was the sublimest spectacle I ever witnessed, and I think memory of it will remain with me always.

He's right. If there's a word that explains this feeling, it's definitely *sublime*—lofty, grand, or exalted in thought, expression, or manner; of outstanding spiritual intellectual, or moral worth; tending to inspire awe usually because of elevated quality, as of beauty, nobility, or grandeur or transcendent excellence.

We drank about a gallon of water when we got back to our vehicle. Now the parking lot was full, and many cars were circling like predators for their prey—our parking spot!

As I watched the families gather within the park, I had feelings of joy, as many of the kids and their parents interacted with each other for the first time during this pandemic. So many families had been isolated for long periods. Gathering wasn't allowed.

Our next stop was the top of Haleakala National Park. We parked in a not-so-full parking lot at the Pu'u'ula'ula Summit. From afar we could see the Haleakalā Observatory, unfortunately closed to the public during the pandemic. Immediately I told Logan that's where space scientists worked, feeding his awe with a subliminal message that a career path was now reality in motion.

In Logan's kindergarten class each child was asked what they wanted to do for a living. One wanted to be a paleontologist. Logan's was a space scientist. Perhaps it was Mrs. Jamison's lesson plan on our solar system where Logan memorized the planets. Or perhaps it was their first field trip to the New Mexico Museum of Natural History & Science in Albuquerque. Liz and I were two of the four parent chaperones. As the incoming foundation president of the museum, I helped his teacher get the tools to request the trip. She got the budget item of buses for the two classes and off we went for an hour or two in the planetarium and a walk around dinosaurs, a volcano exhibit, and our natural history. A child's introduction to the natural world is important. I can see how it expands Logan's understanding of the world and activates his curiosity. Every child needs those opportunities.

This observatory, also known as the Haleakalā High Altitude Observatory Site, is Hawaii's first astronomical research observatory. It is owned by the Institute for Astronomy of the University of Hawai'i, which owns some of the facilities on the site and leases portions to other organizations like the Air Force Research Laboratory and Las Cumbres Observatory Global Telescope Network.

From this parking lot we ran into a patch of the famous endangered silversword plants. This plant has a triple-spiked line pattern, making it look like its spines are sharp like a cactus, but they're not. It almost looks like a silver coral that should be found on the bottom of the sea.

This is what a brochure at this summit read:

> View the Haleakala *'ahinahina,* or silversword, found here and nowhere else on Earth. This silver-leafed plant can grow for several decades before sending up an enormous stalk of purple flowers, signaling the end of its life cycle. The 'ahinahina relies on native insect pollinators that live among the rocks.

As we made our way to the enclosure for viewing, I got goose bumps all over. The 360-degree vista allowed us to see the clouds all around Maui and, in the distance, our next destination, Kona, the Big Island. I told everyone who could hear that we would soon be there to visit Volcanoes National Park. I was a proud dad.

The two-hour drive down was more treacherous and the opposite of sublime. The afternoon clouds now carried moisture with them. At first we opened all our windows and bragged that we were driving in the clouds. I think Liz shouted, "We're on cloud nine!" We were until some of those clouds started to burst with moisture and rain on us.

Luckily the windshield wipers were new and worked perfectly. However, the many switchbacks were slippery and now better taken at a snail's pace. At every moment I felt like we were in a winter storm coming down from skiing. Luckily that hour, although it felt like ten hours, passed without any tragic event.

Our next stop sign was a large wooden bamboo sign in Haleakala National Park. It stated the crater was twenty-two miles away, there was no gas or food, and reservations were required for entry between 3:00 a.m. and 7:00 a.m. That was for those wanting to see the sunrise.

If only I could warn families about the feeling you get when you can't see two feet in front of you, driving on the curviest switchbacks, with many signs warning of the unseen nene birds. Maybe I can try: white knuckles on the steering wheel, eyes glued to both the road and the edges of the road, aching worry about what might happen to my loved ones. I could hardly take in the sights.

Good luck my adventurers. Just remember to save some energy to make it back to your paradise down below . . . and watch out for the nene birds!

The next morning, we went to the Maui Ocean Center, a lovely aquarium with much to learn, see, and interact with. There was a movie on how the ocean here has been the birthplace over the centuries for tens of thousands of whales every year, specifically in the month of January. It was May 30, so we missed this miraculous migration.

Scientists still don't know why these whales, most migrating thousands of miles away from Alaska, choose Maui. We can agree the warm ocean waters provide an optimal place to give birth. Some believe the shallower waters provide an environment where large predators don't often go after the newborn calves.

The five largest mammals in the world are the great whales, elephants, hippopotamuses, rhinoceros, and polar bears. The humpback whales that make Maui their home in January are so majestic, and so much larger than elephants, the next largest mammal on Earth. It's as if they were sent here from the gods to look after our oceans.

Imagine if your species was able to return to Maui every January. As of this moment, that's my dream.

On the way back from the aquarium, we stopped by the Kealia Pond National Wildlife Refuge. We spotted a few red cardinals, the ones like the birds capped on the St. Louis baseball team's hat. The pond is a coastal salt marsh land and bird sanctuary with 691 acres, home to thirty species of waterfowl, shorebirds, and migratory ducks. We noticed it was showing signs of being in a drought, just like back home. Perhaps there were more birds with more rain.

Kealia Pond was selected as a wildlife refuge in 1953, protecting an initial three hundred acres of land. The refuge joined the National Wildlife Refuge System in 1992. The thirty minutes we were there, we looked for birds, watched the surf steps away, and chatted with the ducks. A family of four nearby enjoyed the solitude too.

Sixteen miles south of the pond was the ʻĀhihi-Kīnaʻu Natural Area Reserve, our next destination on this lovely holiday Monday. It was Memorial Day. On the drive I thought of all who had served in our armed forces. My two biological grandfathers died in World War II. Liz and I have five grandfathers, three grandmothers, and one mother in national cemeteries. I tip my hat to those who gave the greatest sacrifice and those who have served and still do for a cause greater than us all.

The parking at the end of the lava fields for ʻĀhihi-Kīnaʻu Natural Area Reserve was sparse and a bit treacherous. We parked far away, taking care not to pop a tire on the jagged lava rock, and walked in. This preserve consists of 1,238 acres of land and 807 acres of ocean along the coastline a few miles south of the most luxurious resorts on the island—and in the world. The purpose and intent of the reserve is to preserve and protect three unique components: the geologic setting of the most recent lava flow on Maui that happened in 1790, the unique assemblages of nearshore coral reef ecosystems, and the anchialine ponds found there.

What we found unique about this reserve is that this is how Maui really looks in its totally natural state. To the east was the grand mountain we drove up the day before. To the west was a field of lava next to the mighty Pacific Ocean. As at times we tippy-toed on this lava field hike, we noticed hikers waiting at different locations. Then suddenly water spit out of the lava rocks. This is known as the Kalua O Lapa flow created by lava tubes and depressions near the shoreline. As the Pacific waves come in, they burst through lava tubes, which look more like jagged black lava rock and, with the pressure and force of nature, erupt like fountains.

One nice couple told us exactly where to stand. As Liz and Logan stood there, I took a few photos and videos on my phone, catching the water and the smiles. Wow, what an adventure.

The rest of the day we took remembering our family members and others, took it easy, ate some great Hawaiian food, and of course had some sweet Hawaiian ice with ice cream.

We got up bright and early on the last day of May 2022. We had read that the Road to Hana would take several hours, as it would take us around the mountains rising up in the middle of the island. We were staying in the southwest part of the island and departed around 6:30 a.m. The lava fields we walked the previous day would have been the road to our destination today but are said to be way too treacherous. We passed right by the road to the top of the mountain where we saw Haleakalā from above a few days ago. We had to go around the island, as the mountain is in the middle. Then we passed some great towns and peeked out at the halfway point to Hana. From the top of this jungle, we began our descent to the southernmost point of Haleakala National Park. A construction crew had us stopped for about twenty or thirty minutes. The line of cars started to stack up like a line of ants if seen from the helicopters above. As we were let through, I saw from this two-lane highway the land and ocean some hundreds of feet below. A man was dangling by a few ropes and his own strength to repair an edge of the paved road they were working on. This crew put their lives on the line for tourists like us, another sacrifice on the day after Memorial Day.

The road to Hana was living up to what others warned us about.

The twists and turns of the road made our stomachs ache. At one point a large diesel sixteen-wheeler carrying gasoline came barreling up the road at a speed maybe twice ours. I realized others had driven this road before, but we were moving at a snail's pace, around ten miles per hour, terrified of the cliff's edge. How could I enjoy this paradise with what felt like my inevitable death at the bottom of this cliff? The answer to that question was to drive about two miles per hour. When we did, we realized those behind us had some place to be. I'm sure they recognized us white-knuckling tourists.

The entrance to this park, driving to Hana, really made me think of my mortality. I had read and heard from others that this was the worst drive in the world. They were right. Its pure beauty does not loosen the white-knuckling you put your family through. I also noticed vans were taking others to their destinations. I wondered if those drivers ever get used to the drive.

This highway is aptly dubbed the "Divorce Highway" and has 617 hairpin curves and fifty-nine unforgiving one-lane stone bridges. These one-lane bridges assume humans will decide who goes first if there are moving vehicles on each side wanting to travel in the opposite direction. After counting hundreds of blind spots on the switchbacks, I gave up worrying and relaxed. We passed many waterfalls in the lush jungle while traveling over the one-lane bridges. We finally reached the park entrance at around 11:00 a.m. It was 3:17 p.m. back home, and that drive made it feel like I had driven those three extra hours. Physically it felt like the six- or seven-hour drive from Santa Fe, New Mexico, to Denver, Colorado, we usually do once or twice a year.

The place was the Pipiwai Trail to Waimoku Falls in Haleakala National Park at the southernmost part of Haleakala. As mentioned earlier, this national park recognizes about 75 percent of its 33,265 acres as sacred, with no roads in or out.

The parking lot on this side of Haleakala was full, so we parked in a grassy field overlooking the ocean. We had packed a lunch, so we ate in silence and stared out into the navy-blue ocean. We didn't talk as much as we usually do on these stops, as we had just been through our most traumatic drive in our family's life. By noon, with padded sandals, we were on the four-mile round-trip Pipiwai Trail.

This four-mile hike climbs through a lush bamboo forest to stop beneath the four-hundred-foot Waimoku Falls. The first half mile of constant uphill struggle will flush your sweat glands as you approach Makahiku Falls. The trail here is fenced off, and in the distance we could see the magnificent falls. Makahiku Falls is a two-hundred-foot horsetail waterfall. This point on the trail gave me some time to catch my breath. What a breath to catch in paradise looking at a twenty-story-tall waterfall in the jungle.

Then it was off to what I would call, with a six-year-old son, a difficult hiking trail through a bamboo forest. The wooden boardwalk makes the hike feel easy. The ocean winds whistle through the bamboo on a breezy day, rattle the leaves, and the bamboo stalks creak, clack, and pop! This sound is the most unique sound I've ever heard. I was completely in the moment. To hear a totally new sound at the age of forty-one was amazing. I didn't know that a forest of bamboo popped with its own voice!

How did bamboo get here? We all felt that at any moment a family of pandas would appear. My son even said, "Dad, pandas live in China." He was right.

Some Polynesian voyagers brought many plants with them on their journeys across the Pacific Ocean. The versatile 'ohe bamboo was one such plant. Its purpose was for *'ohe hano ihu*, or nose flute, to start fires, carry water, or split to make irrigation troughs. When immigration to the Hawaiian Islands started to increase, new species of bamboo made their way to Hawaii.

On this first mile into our Pipiwai Trail adventure we all enjoyed the music of this bamboo forest. This natural music was, in my opinion, the epitome of living in the moment. I'm going to make it a practice that wherever I am I can go back to the moment in this bamboo forest and then come back to the present. Let me try it. Yes, it works. Please, find your bamboo forest.

The National Park Service designates this trail as "moderate."

From time to time, we would see a few hikers giving up or taking a break. The park also says the four miles take an hour. Better to give yourself a few hours for this miracle on Earth. Around mile two we could hear the roar of the waterfall ahead and the chatter of voices. People were in awe of this four-hundred-foot tall Waimoku Falls. As we got closer, we stepped into the stream. Logan loves the water and joined the other kids playing in it.

At the end of the trail a sign reads "DO NOT PASS THIS POINT. FATALITIES HAVE OCCURRED." I passed the sign. A few hundred feet into the trail looking above the four-hundred-foot Waimoku Falls, I had never been this close to my destiny. The mist was hitting my neck, and I could see around ten other people who also ignored the sign, as if that death wish sign could speak like the bamboo forest. It must be there for a reason. According to the sign, people have died here.

A family from France was taking pictures. Their daughter, about twenty years old had headphones on and decided to sunbathe under the waterfall, steps from the water cascading down from the 'Ohe'O Gulch. Liz and Logan were not with me, as they stayed back as the sign advised. That was a good decision. Just as I thought of them the sound of a bomb went off. It took me back to 4:00 a.m. in Amsterdam three years ago when, while sleeping among my dreams, someone bombed an ATM machine up the block from where we were staying for my brother-in-law's wedding. I was immobilized, holding my breath. I blinked and took a deep breath. I wasn't in Holland but Hawaii. The bomb that went off was a rock that must have fallen from the four-hundred-foot-high falls.

The French parents couldn't get their daughter's attention, so they swung their beach towels at her. She opened her eyes, took off her headphones, and got mad at them, scolding them in French. As I escaped, stepping over rocks, sand, streams, and puddles, I told myself I would take the signs on other trails in the national parks seriously. If the sign says "BEWARE. BEAR HAVE EATEN PEOPLE HERE," I won't hike in. I'll remember that for the eight national parks in Alaska we must visit.

The danger at the edge was not obvious; after all, the ten or so of us were in paradise. As I got back to the sign, I passed by others taking the same risk. I wanted to tell them, but they were in a trance to get closer, and I had the feeling it was the sense of ". . . and lead us not into temptation, but deliver us from evil . . ." The evil, perhaps, was risking leaving my family. The temptation for my kind of adventurer was inevitable. I had parks to hike, waterfalls to see, and a book, wait, even two books to write. What if I didn't survive? At that moment I knew I had work to do and had to get started. I couldn't wait another ten or fifteen years to write our stories. What if that rock had hit me? Who would write and publish this book?

The moment was clear. When you're put in a situation of life and death, and you have an option that in a moment can just pass you by, your plans change.

I made myself a promise. I'd get back home, write the chapter on paradise, or maybe a few more parks, and publish my book on our national parks.

Logan was eating a granola bar as we rested by a stream soaking in some sunrays and chatting with another child, all of us at a safe distance from the falls. Liz was watching out for him. Their banter was about having fun, taking a rest, eating some snacks, and how funny his new friend was splashing with him in the stream. I asked Logan to take a photo of Liz and me. He did. It was perfect. We were all safe, alive.

Just before departing this end of the trail, I read my family the national park informational sign:

> HALEAKALA NATIONAL PARK – WAIMOKU FALLS – *He wai makamaka 'ole.* Water that recognizes no friend. This describes a dangerous stream or waterfall. The Hawaiian proverb is a warning to always be respectful of the power of natural forces. Flooded streams, waterfalls, and falling rocks

> will not stop for anything in their paths. The beautiful sheer walls of these falls are shaped daily as water chips away one sharp stone after another to fall violently—and without warning—to the ground below. Take photos, but from a safe distance. Waimoku can mean water that cuts, severs, amputates, or breaks in two, as a stream often does after heavy rains.

Wasn't this so true? I wish I would have read this first. If I had, would I still have gone into temptation and steps from that falling rock?

The two-mile hike back was almost all downhill. It was easy on the way back, difficult on the way up, and if you add those together, I guess it could be called a moderate hike. I'd still call it difficult with a child.

The bamboo forest was just as beautiful on the way down. I witnessed a few things in the bamboo forest this time around that struck me as strange. A lady was taking her phone out of her pocket, fumbled with it, dropped it, and as it hit the ground the screen cracked. I had never seen that in real time.

Once again I ran into that French family ahead of us, arguing with each other. It was a family argument that meant more than the near-death experience. Those were signs for me to slow down. SLOW DOWN.

I chuckled as I remembered the song Logan's kindergarten class sang, "The 59th Street Bridge Song (Feelin' Groovy)" from Simon & Garfunkel.

I stopped, and Logan and Liz caught up to me in a few minutes. We had been singing the song all vacation long. We hadn't on this trail, and I belted the start of the second verse. Logan took it away and sang the rest. We were feeling groovy in this bamboo forest.

We were all extremely tired when we got back to the park headquarters and knew we still had another four hours of driving at ten miles per hour on, as Logan put it, "the most rarest road in the world." We saw another trail sign leading to the ocean that was the

Kūloa Point Trail, with the Pools of ʻOheʻo, archaeological sites, and coastal views. Liz and Logan simultaneously shouted, "No thanks!"

I had that darn, horrible thought cross my mind: *When will we ever be here again, TOGETHER?* All vacation we did the democratic vote. I went against that and convinced them it was only a half-mile trail and we just hiked four miles. They looked at me with grins. Instead of getting their approval, I started down the hiking path. They followed, with one condition. This was their last trail of the day.

We hiked into paradise. There were banyan trees that looked alive and ready to give us 250 separate handshakes all at once. We learned how people survived in this area generations ago with fruit trees, farming, and fishing. This easy half-mile circular hike was amazing. At the halfway point we rested on rocks and looked at perhaps the most scenic view I've laid eyes on. The black, soft, sandy beach below, blended into the white crashing waves of the Pacific, and navy-blue hues of the ocean met the bluest sky above. I looked closely at the jungle on the sides of the mountains with a dark green background. Those were the mountains with the rarest road in the world. Would we get a divorce on the way up? Above, ominous clouds looked like they were about to pour rain on us all. On this sunny afternoon we spent hours together in complete harmony. Together in PARADISE. How could this get any better?

On the quarter mile back, we passed by the Pools of ʻOheʻo, or what are known as the "seven sacred pools." The Pools of ʻOheʻo are waterfalls that are part of a stream that flows from the mountain to the ocean. Right under the waterfall, we witnessed where the stream met the ocean. Our family was meeting our destination for the day. Just think if we decided not to take this half-mile hike. Look what we might have missed.

The road back was just as hellish. At one point our vehicle and another got stuck on that one-lane bridge. Yes, that one of fifty-nine single-lane bridges. The driver and I, just handshakes away, agreed that one of us had to back up. As one minute went by, which felt like an hour, a local yelled from his extra-large pickup truck. He started honking, skipped the line, and was now right behind me. The other driver, facing inches away from me, backed up on point. I drove the bridge, and that local zoomed right past about ten other vehicles watching us contemplating our dilemma. This is the tourist's single-bridge dilemma. When on vacation neither tourist can decide, so the locals create the catalyst and must force a decision for them. Time is valuable. I can only imagine if there was an emergency on this divorce road.

We didn't stop anywhere once on the way up or down this hellish road. Our total time driving that one road in and out was about eight or nine hours. When we were well out, we stopped at Mama's Fish House in Paia. However, it was booked for about a week. Make note of that restaurant: "Mama's Fish House." Please make reservations before you get there. That gave us time to walk the downtown area of Paia looking for an alternative. Civilization felt great after the wild ride through the jungle. We sat down at a brand new restaurant. It was Lima Cocina, and this is how it's described on their website:

> Lima Cocina + Cantina is a mix of classic Peruvian cuisine, infused with modern Maui, bringing a casual and exciting new dining experience to the island. Located in Paia, Maui, Lima is Maui's first restaurant and bar, featuring traditional Peruvian cuisine, sourcing local and sustainably farmed produce, meats, and seafood.

One thing that snapped my head around was that every worker here looked like a supermodel. Our blonde, six-foot-four-inch waitress with an Eastern European accent absolutely loved Logan. The manager came out and said the chicken dish I ordered was overcooked. He offered to bring out another delicious chicken dish for me shortly. My wife's fish dinner and Logan's sushi would come out right away. He offered to discount the chicken because of the error. How could I say no? All the people in this restaurant were the most beautiful people I had ever seen. The answer was yes, and just like that, all our food arrived together, steaming hot and delicious.

It was like we earned this beautiful dinner after the worst drive EVER! Forever is a long time, but I don't think I'll ever see a restaurant staff giving us such naturally beautiful hospitality again.

We capped off the downtown walk with ice cream at Artisan Ice Cream that was perfect. This is how their website reads:

> Aloha and welcome to Artisan Ice Cream! We craft fresh ice cream in small batches every day. Our daily scoops use organic milk and cream, organic cane sugar, and organic egg yolks. We've also developed our very own dairy and soy-free vegan ice cream made with coconut cream and coconut milk and other nondairy milks depending on the flavor. Both give a rich, decadent, naturally perfect ice cream. Whether it's homemade lilikoi butter or banana macadamia nut brittle, our entire menu is handcrafted in house. We never use artificial flavors, colors, or preservatives. Artisan Ice Cream is a family business, so what better spot to open shop than right next door to our family's restaurant, Café Des Amis, which opened its doors to Paia way back in 1999. We also partner with Sustainable Island Products to ensure we only serve our ice cream with compostable cups and spoons made from renewable plant-based resources. We're hoping to create a company that's fun to support, work for, and partner with. But really, we just hope you love our ice cream! Aloha! Rich, Paula, Jack and Eloise.

That evening was spectacular. Paia is on my short list to return for a long holiday week next time.

The next morning, Wednesday June 1, 2022, we ventured to Pa'ako Beach. This beach is referred to as the "Secret Cove," as one has to walk between lava walls to enter. If we blinked, we'd pass it by. This cove is between two homes in Mākena in Maui's South Shore. We loved this location so much that we spent around four hours on this beach. Logan immediately made friends with another kid from Oklahoma who had just finished kindergarten. It looked like he was one of three siblings. As I was in the ocean cove, avoiding the inevitable tumble of waves, Liz spoke to the kid's parents. She told me they were all packed and ready to go back home. This was their last beach before the airplane flight. That got me thinking! Soon we would be on our way to the Big Island. I wondered if we'd ever come back as a family to Maui again.

Just then a woman in a wedding dress and her groom in casual khaki pants and a white silk, collared, short-sleeve shirt began to say their vows to tie the knot. This secret cove is not too secret for a wedding ceremony. That's exactly what this lovely couple were doing. Just in front of us in this magical place. Now they were walking around as their photographer and videographer were creating memories for them. I took out my phone and started taking a video of Logan in the cove in the background of this wedding procession.

The bride, with a smile, looked at my phone, realizing she was in a public space, and her groom twirled her around with one arm. Logan stopped in place; his jaw dropped. This was the first time he had ever seen a wedding or so many people all dressed up and celebrating. During the pandemic many if not most weddings had been put on hold. As another ocean wave hit his foot, Logan turned toward the waves and started playing again. It's not every day that you frolic in paradise, make a new friend from Oklahoma, and go to your first wedding. Logan was a lucky man. We were all lucky to be in this secret paradise.

Over the next day we packed our belongings and got ready for the Big Island. Like the family from Oklahoma, we went to the beach one last time before our flight. This beach was Wailea Beach.

Wailea Beach sits below resorts like the Grand Wailea and the Four Seasons. It's lined with palm trees and tourists. We had our last look at Maui's beaches. A sprinkle turned into a light rain. After an hour of solitude watching the waves, we packed up our beach towels and belongings. As the rain started to come down, I rushed out of the beach area and up the cement walkway. Washing the beach sand off my feet, I realized I must have left my phone. Horror set in. How could I find my phone in this rain in the sand? Liz and Logan were now just getting to me. How was I going to explain this one? Luckily, as Liz was gathering her things in the rain, she noticed a phone. At first she thought it was someone else's. It was mine, and she had saved the day.

That got me thinking. In a moment of inattention, I would have lost a lot. More importantly, I would have lost a lot of this book. When I start writing, I use a lot of the photos to remember the details of where we were and how I felt. I'd have twenty fewer pages here about these national parks and the incredible history, places, people, and cultures that surround them.

After a short flight from Maui to Kona we rented a red Toyota 4Runner, and at first it felt very large and difficult to park and maneuver. Then I remembered parking our rented RV in White Sands and Big Bend National Parks and calmed down.

Our next stop was the Waikoloa Beach Marriott Resort. We unpacked our luggage in our room in their Ocean Tower and took in an amazing sunset from our sixth-floor room at the top of the hotel. This was living! We didn't have a kitchen, so we'd be eating out a lot on this island.

Our resort was surrounded by miles and miles of lava rock. The next morning, I got up around 5:30 a.m. and went for a four-mile run. I took a picture of a sign that gave the cultural heritage of this trail. It stated:

> Ancient Foot Trail – Ala Loa Travelers – Much of the ancient *ala loa* (long trail) can still be seen here, meandering through the Kaniku lava flow, alongside the later Alanui Aupuni, the historic Hawaiian Kingdom government road built along the same route. The ala loa was probably used mostly by *maka'āinana* (commoners, people that attend the land), for it passes just inland of the border of the royal sanctuary of 'Anaeho'omalu. Traditional stories speak of "night marchers," a procession of spirits of the dead that passes on these ancient trails during certain nights of the year. Anyone who happens to block their way, or does not address them with the utmost humility, will not live to tell the tale.

If my late mom was with me as a spirit on this path, I said a prayer for her. I didn't want any spirit to be annoyed by my running. Come to think of it, I bet if my mother, Pauline, were still alive, she'd be with us. She loved an adventure, and she would have loved to be here with us to see our twenty-eighth national park together. I'm sure she'd already be out walking this path, thinking of her own mother, Aurora. They both guide me on my journey.

Our first day was a pool day. We got sunburned, ate too much, and walked around our resort. This resort had dolphins we could interact with, a handful of pools, and games to play all around. We played a life-size version of checkers. No one won. We got distracted and moved on to a life-size version of Jenga. We asked Logan if he wanted us to sign the family up for an interaction with the dolphins called Dolphin Quest, but he was okay watching them from a distance. We were good with that as well. We watched the sunset that evening from our sixth-floor view framed by the spine of a fifty-foot palm tree. Words cannot describe the moment. This was the definition of being spoiled.

We got up bright and early the next morning, June 4, 2022, to drive the two hours to Hawaii Volcanoes National Park. We stopped for a flock of about fifty rams crossing the road at Waikoloa Village. Maui had chickens and roosters wandering around; rams were all around the Big Island. We got to the Hawaii Volcanoes National Park sign at 8:30 a.m.

We started this national park adventure when Logan was three months old in Petrified Forest National Park in Arizona. This was our twenty-eighth national park, Hawaii Volcanoes National Park, and Logan was now a little over six-and-a-half years old.

As usual we took pictures next to the park sign. A lush jungle in the background, this sign sat atop lava rock. How precise.

Hawaii Volcanoes National Park encompasses two active volcanoes. They are Kilauea, one of the world's most active volcanoes, and Mauna Loa, the world's most massive shield volcano. This park is by far the world's leading research site for how the Hawaiian Islands were created and the studies of volcanism. In Hawaiian traditions and culture, Kilauea and Mauna Loa volcanoes are considered *wahi kapu* (sacred places) and a source of *mana*, spiritual power. The caldera of Kilauea is considered by some to be the home of the Hawaiian volcano deity Pelehonuamea. Pele is the goddess of volcanoes and fire and the creator of the Hawaiian Islands.

In folklore, Pele travels throughout the many Hawaiian Islands. She appears as either a beautiful young woman or as an old woman, often accompanied by a white dog. If you refuse her requests, then you ultimately suffer her wrath, legend says. Many tales of encounters with Pele include drivers who picked up an old woman dressed all in white on roads in Volcanoes National Park, only to look in the mirror to find the back seat empty. Others say Pele's face was mysteriously in their photos of the lava lake within the crater or molten lava flows. Among the people of the islands, Pele is revered and respected. When these volcanoes begin to erupt, homeowners welcome her and her destruction with ritual offerings.

Volcanoes National Park was established on August 1, 1916, as Hawaii National Park. There are approximately 323,438 acres in Volcanoes National Park. In 2018 there were just north of 1.1 million visitors.

As we entered our twenty-eighth national park, something came over me—a feeling that somehow this place was very special. In my birth year, 1980, this park had been designated as an International Biosphere Reserve and then a World Heritage Site in 1987. This World Heritage Site puts Hawaii Volcanoes National Park in the same category as Mount Kilimanjaro, Machu Picchu, and Sagarmatha (Mount Everest).

The Big Island was the place I asked Liz to marry me. In 2008 Liz and I both ran the San Francisco Marathon with a goal to qualify for the Boston Marathon. I was sixth overall and ran 2:41. Liz, Elizabeth Jaramillo at the time, ran 3:33 for the thirty-fifth overall female. With tears running down her face as she finished, she realized she qualified for Boston. We had accomplished our running goals at age twenty-eight.

To treat ourselves after the San Francisco race, no matter how we finished, we had set up a ten-day vacation to Hawaii.

We had been here long before Logan was born. The day after our marathon we came up to Volcanoes National Park, and around midnight we watched the lava flow, burning red in the dark. I was getting on one knee, sore as it was from the marathon, wedding ring in hand, and realized it was too dark to ask for Liz's hand in marriage. I tucked the ring back into my pants pocket, knowing I would do it somewhere else on this Big Island. That place days later was Akaka Falls State Park.

Memories of this park and images of that night in the dark returned. Had we been here, near that same spot? Now in the light and with a six-year-old we took in the park during the day.

We drove Crater Rim Drive and moments from the Kilauea Visitor Center parked at the Steam Vents at Wahinekapu. As we stepped outside our 4Runner, we saw steam coming out of the ground. The steam from the earth below was warm and windy. It was like a hot, molten cloud rising from the earth. We made the short hike to view Kilauea. At this point, four thousand feet above sea level, we could investigate the caldera. Steam was rising in all sorts of places and looked like a bonfire from a distance. We were witnessing the birth of land. The Kilauea Caldera is an active shield volcano. It has a length of 2.93 miles, a width of 1.95 miles, a circumference of 7.85 miles, and an area of 4.14 square miles. This volcano is gigantic. An average shield volcano has a height of 2.55 miles, making Kilauea about half a mile taller. Half a mile in height is like 2,640 feet or a building that has 264 floors. Again, that's like the size of the tallest building in the world (Burj Khalifa in Dubai at 2,717 feet). Again and again Mother Nature has her way of saying, "Stay out of my way man-made world and enter my reality." Reality soon set in, and after a while we took our steps back from the erupting Kilauea. On this sunny day we didn't see any lava, but we could certainly see the smoke. And where there is smoke, there is surely fire. In this case lava.

We got on the road again and didn't stop until the road ended. In the fifty minutes we drove about twenty-two miles, we went from a temperate climate to a rainy one. We went from the top of a caldera, looking into a volcano, to the lava arches next to the sea. If there's any way to explain driving through land that has seen such extremes, it was this road. There were signs along the road stating what years lava flowed through this land. I'm expecting any day to turn on the news and see this road we traveled turn to lava again. It's not expected, but every now and then it does occur.

The Hōlei Sea Arch is at the end of the Chain of Craters Road. As we got out of our car in the rain, we realized we were the only car there. The light was mysterious and surreal. The rain dissipated as we got to the trail to view this sea arch atop layers and layers of lava rock we were walking on. At every turn we expected to see lava, but it was long gone. Then we saw it. The arches were a thing of another world. In the distance we could see how lava and the strong ocean waves and currents created these majestic natural arches. This stark lava rock formation is about ninety feet high and extends from the steep sea cliffs into the Pacific Ocean. The National Park Service has stated this arch formation is beautiful but temporary and will eventually crumble into the sea. However, others will replace it as the cliff slowly migrates inland. This impressive sea arch was cut into the cliff of an ancient lava flow from about 550 years ago due to differential erosion, which is the difference in the hardness of various layers of lava.

As we walked back, I wondered if this would be the closest our family would get to the lava flow. The answer was yes. A few miles away was the flow of the lava that some estimate ended in 2018. A sign at the end of the road read:

> After 35 Years, the Eruption of Puʻu ʻŌʻō Came to a Dramatic End in 2018 – In the past 500 years, no eruption comes close to matching the duration of Puʻu ʻŌʻō, which first began on the eastern shoulder of

> Kilauea in 1983. Over three decades, the eruption would take the form of 1,500 foot (470 meter) lava fountains, slow-moving molten toes, and spectacular ocean-entry plumes. Lava flows from Pu'u 'Ō'ō covered nearly 56 square miles (144 square kilometers) and added 439 acres of new land to the island's southeastern shore. But as the massive 2018 eruption of Kilauea in lower Puna began, the magma supply to Pu'u 'Ō'ō ceased, bringing an end to over three decades of nearly continuous activity.

The 2018 volcano eruption of Kilauea lasted from May through August. Large lava flow changed the surrounding area forever. These lava flows devastated the local residential areas, destroying more than seven hundred homes. The national park was changed forever as well. The summit area of the park incurred tens of thousands of daily earthquakes, towering ash plumes, and a massive collapse of Kilauea Caldera. The eruption of Kilauea in 2018 was the largest in centuries and coincided with a massive summit collapse. We were now witness to this changed earth around us.

Change always brings differences. When Liz and I were first here, we saw the lava flowing. That year was 2008. Now in 2022, during the day, and with our son Logan, we didn't see any lava flowing. This, too, may change. One day we may be back. The park will go through some changes and again be transformed.

Me and Waimoku Falls

Smoke from a Volcano

Sliding Sands Trail

Our Fam & Waimoku Falls

CONGAREE, NEW RIVER GORGE, AND SHENANDOAH NATIONAL PARKS

THE CAROLINAS AND VIRGINIAS: A LOT HAD CHANGED during the fifteen months since we'd last visited a national park. The world officially announced that the coronavirus pandemic was over. Every now and then you would hear of someone getting the virus who had never had it. With the knowledge of the virus we had gained over the past two years, they survived. Modern medicine could now treat the virus. More than seven million people died worldwide from the virus between 2020 and 2023.

It was now 2023. Masks were no longer mandated, people were traveling all over the world, and it had been a long time since we hit the American road. Logan had finished first grade, Liz had gone back to work, and I was a soccer coach for Logan and six other six-, seven-, and eight-year-old Santa Feans. Although I had only played soccer one year in middle school, there was no coach, so I volunteered as the default coach. It was a fun season. We didn't keep score, so the kids had a blast. They loved the bobblehead soccer ball trophy each received at the end of the season. Logan also played baseball and was cast as a sailor in *The Little Mermaid* musical in the local kids' musical summer camp. We were in the busy family chapters of our lives.

Just like us, my sister Dr. Alicia Warlick, who lives with her family, Randy and Charlotte, in Raleigh, North Carolina, was very busy. Alicia is five years my senior. Charlotte, her daughter, is a few months older than Logan, so they get along and talk the same language. Alicia is an anesthesiologist, so she is always busy or on call. We decided to visit her and from her location rent a car and visit three national parks in the Carolinas and Virginias.

Our first stop was Congaree National Park in South Carolina. Congaree National Park is approximately twenty-seven thousand acres in central South Carolina. It is around twenty miles southeast of the state capital, Columbia. This national park preserves the largest tract of old growth bottomland hardwood forest left in the United States. Some of the lushest trees live and grow here. Also, with trees reaching up to more than 160 feet, this forest has some of the tallest trees on the East Coast, forming the tallest temperate deciduous forest, with large canopies not found anywhere in the world but here. The Congaree River flows through the park. This river flows for approximately fifty-three miles (eighty-five kilometers). The river was named, as well as the park, for the Congaree Native Americans who used to live along it. The Congaree people who fished the waterways in this park were largely killed off by smallpox introduced by the influx of European settlers around 1700.

Prehistoric peoples and their tribes hunted the floodplain of the Congaree River and fished the waterways. These Native Americans had plentiful vegetation and abundant game to hunt. Spanish explorer Hernando de Soto traversed the region in the late 1500s. In the 1600s a fellow Spaniard, Juan Pardo, followed in de Soto's footsteps. I wonder if one day, hundreds of years from now, COVID-19 will be like smallpox. Will we look back and have a shot for babies for new diseases?

Unlike many national parks, Congaree's land was created by a grant. The new settlers obtained these grants of land directly from the

King of England until the American Revolutionary War in 1776 won South Carolinians the right to distribute ownership of the land.

In the 1800s there were many attempts to make the floodplain suitable for farming and livestock, but many failed. There were no successful farmers or ranchers on this wetland. Between 1898 and 1905 the Santee River Cypress Lumber Company, owned by Francis Beidler and Benjamin F. Ferguson of Chicago, acquired much of the low-lying land along the Congaree and Santee River systems. Though many other areas were harvested of their valuable timber, poor accessibility in the floodplain confined logging to tracts near the main rivers. Cypress trees were killed and dried while standing, then floated downriver to the sawmills. What a way to go for trees that may have been over 250 years old. A lot of the logs sank, as the dampness of the floodplain made them too heavy to float at all.

Operations were soon halted around 1914, leaving the floodplain relatively untouched. Beidler and his heirs retained ownership of the area. By the 1950s Harry R. E. Hampton was a member of the Cedar Creek Hunt Club and coeditor of *The State* newspaper. Hampton formed the Beidler Forest Preservation Association around 1961, and because of this advocacy, a 1963 study by the National Park Service reported favorably on the creation of a national monument.

By 1969 the price of timber had skyrocketed. Landowners in Congaree resumed logging operations to cash in. Again the trees of the Congaree floodplain became threatened.

Local citizens, many referred to as tree huggers, advocated for protection of the floodplain. Renewed logging by the Beidlers in 1969 prompted the 1972 formation of the Congaree Swamp National Preserve Association (CSNPA). This group joined forces with the fierce Sierra Club to promote federal legislation to preserve the tract.

South Carolina Senators Strom Thurmond and Ernest F. Hollings introduced legislation in 1975, and on October 18, 1976, legislation passed to create Congaree Swamp National Monument. Congress redesignated the monument Congaree National Park on November 10, 2003, dropping the misleading "swamp" from the name. This was misleading as it wasn't a swamp at all! The floodplain does not have water covering it all year round, which means it is not a swamp. It is one of the most unique floodplains in the country.

From a historic perspective, around this time in 2003, South Carolina rivers were bordered by only twelve thousand acres of old-growth floodplain forest; eleven thousand are preserved in Congaree National Park. Compare this to more than a million acres around South Carolina rivers of the past era. It took three generations to almost decimate a million acres of this unique biodiversity of land. If my math is correct, that is more than a 98 percent decline in river forests in South Carolina over a few generations. There is a direct connection between climate change and the global decimation of other forests like this in South Carolina.

Many who come to this park like to hike, fish, and paddle or canoe the waterways. They look for birds, wildlife, and trees. The park is famous for having well over twenty-five miles of hiking trails, including more than two miles of boardwalk that allows you to explore the floodplains of the Congaree River. Cedar Creek offers canoeing and kayaking trails through a primeval old-growth forest containing some of the tallest trees in Northeastern America. The Congaree Bluffs Heritage Preserve on the park's south side is well visited. This preserve offers many hiking paths that cover more than two hundred acres of hickory, oak, and tupelo forest.

On August 3, 2023, we rented a Camry in Raleigh and drove to Longleaf Campground in Congaree National Park. It was a four-hour drive. We stopped for lunch, for Logan's first Happy Meal ever at McDonald's.

Just an hour before reaching the park we saw a Buc-ee's logo. I had seen a *CBS Sunday Morning Show* about this gas stop. We gassed up. We walked into a madhouse of hundreds of local workers, tourists, and truck drivers. Everyone was heading to the restrooms. If you didn't move fast, you were run over. We grabbed cinnamon-roasted pecans, grown locally, some assorted fudge, and a few Buc-ee the Beaver key chains. We got out just as fast as we got in. This was the Walmart of traveling. One day this company may be as big as the largest corporations in the world. Salaries of all staff positions were posted, with a manager's salary as high as $250,000. We laughed about the experience for a long time. Funny thing is Liz and I were drawn into it, and Logan wanted nothing to do with a Buc-ee T-shirt or toy. Good boy! An hour later we were passing many neighborhoods draped in moss and entering Congaree.

At the entrance to this twenty-ninth national park as a family, we parked the car and took great photos of the large park sign in the rain. We were damp but happy.

In 2018 approximately 146,000 people visited Congaree National Park. This is one of the least visited national parks in the continental US. We were a bit worried we would have to set up our campsite in the rain. We were at campsite number 7 at Longleaf Campground. It was about a half-mile walk from the parking lot. This primitive campground had hiking trails and standing water steps from the campsite. We gathered the tent, chairs, and a few backpacks and within forty-five minutes had everything up and ready for the next twenty-four hours.

As we had reservations with an outfitter for a canoe ride with friends the next day, we drove to South Cedar Creek. This is where the ride would begin and end the next day. As we got to this location, Logan became a bit scared. We walked the dark, damp trail, and out of nowhere we saw a dog.

"Is that a dog?" Liz gasped.

"He might be lost," I said.

"I'm scared!" Logan shouted, and the dog ran away.

We all kept walking on the trail. We saw the dog again, but this time we saw its very large fluffy tail. It wasn't a wild or lost dog. It was a rare fox squirrel. We were amazed. These fox squirrels are the largest tree squirrels native to North America. We kept walking. There was not a human soul for miles. We felt like we were the only ones in the park. At the other campground, there was only one other tent set up, its owners out, maybe on the trail.

We veered off the trail to step into this lower floodplain. I wanted to take a picture standing on a large log. I stepped up on it and in went my foot. This log was so saturated with moisture, my foot crushed it like Shredded Wheat that's been in milk for an hour. The crunch sound echoed and reverberated around the dense, lush forest. It was like a cannon went off. Suddenly two great blue herons surprised us as they flew away. They were searching for crayfish. Crayfish native to the oceans live in abundance here. They burrow deep into the soil, creating what looks like mini volcanic pyramids, thus keeping them safe from such herons and other hungry animals. What other animals were here? We got back on the trail, walked to the car, drove past our campground, and parked at the visitor center. We were too late; it had closed at 5:00 p.m., and we arrived around 6:00.

Instead, we took the most spectacular self-guided 2.4-mile boardwalk tour. The wooden boardwalk was a testament to the miraculous work of the National Park Service. There were twenty points of interest. As we reach each one, Liz read us the story from the guidebook:

> Number 12 – Once a bend in the Congaree River, Weston Lake is now an oxbow lake. Over 2,000 years ago the river gradually changed its course and meandered south, leaving behind Weston Lake. The lake is slowly filling in with clay and organic debris. Freshwater turtles, such as the yellow-bellied slider and common snapping turtle, are often spotted here in the warmer months of the year. All plants and animals in the park are protected. You can help protect wildlife by not handling, disturbing, or feeding them.

"See that fish jump," I shouted as something splashed in the distance. A red fishing bob was hanging in the tree next to us, just off the boardwalk. *This must be where the locals fish,* I thought to myself.

We kept walking.

Liz continued on:

> Number 19 – Just a few miles from here, where the Congaree and the Wateree Rivers meet, a maroon settlement once existed. These settlements were comprised of individuals who escaped slavery on nearby plantations and formed their own independent communities. Rivers provided a means for travel, finding food, and acquiring supplies. Dense vegetation in the floodplain forest, like the twisted roots seen here, provided safety because of the difficulty it posed for slave owners and slave catchers attempting to traverse it in pursuit of those who had escaped.

Logan had a lot of questions about this one. He had never heard about slavery. As it was one of our worst chapters in American history, we explained it to him in terms that a seven-year-old could somewhat conceptualize. He asked if our family had been slaves. We told him the truth. The truth was we had not been slaves.

From the worst case of slavery before we were born to the current climate post-pandemic of Black Lives Matter, police brutality of people of color, and the racial and gender imbalances in our corporate boardrooms, we had a lot to explain, but maybe not all of it to a seven-year-old. It was a brief discussion on slavery, which could have been a bit more than he could understand. Perhaps he got the foundation of the concept of inequality.

We walked past the visitor center, got into our car, the only one in the parking lot, and drove to our campground.

The campground was moist. We ate our sandwiches, and as the sun was setting, we started to see the show in front of us. Flashing fireflies appeared out of nowhere. None of us had ever seen this show. We were amazed. Congaree National Park hosts synchronous fireflies for approximately two weeks between mid-May and mid-June. We were a bit late, early August, but for us it was just as spectacular.

The day wasn't over. Our Presbyterian pastor, friend, and wedding minister Chester was to arrive with his youngest daughter Zia to camp with us. They arrived past sunset, and now it was raining at around 9:30 p.m. We were all a bit sleepy. They settled into our eight-person tent with a divider in the middle, and we talked about the present, past, and future for the next few hours. Zia was amazed at how we loved the fireflies and hadn't ever seen any before. She could see fireflies in her yards in Athens, Georgia.

We all hit the hay. In the middle of the night the pouring rain woke everyone but Logan. He's a heavy sleeper. We had to zip up the tent windows as the rain was now splashing us. We all awoke early in the morning.

Chester cooked us some excellent breakfast burritos. We packed up and drove to the visitor center, now open. I didn't see this the day before, but there was a wooden, carved "Mosquito Meter." It had six levels:

1. All Clear
2. Mild
3. Moderate
4. Severe
5. Ruthless
6. War Zone

We were currently in three. Moderate. We had prepared but still had some bites. Logan, Liz, and I had lathered our bodies with bug spray, and Logan and I wore Bye Bye mosquito bracelets we had found at a DICK'S Sporting Goods in Raleigh. I thank God we were not in a War Zone. Having done extensive research on parks, this was one of my main worries. I was afraid the mosquitos would eat us alive.

Harry Hampton Visitor Center was named for the man who helped save Congaree many years ago. It showed us the wildlife and history, and as we were watching the film about the park, we realized we had to make our 11:00 a.m. appointment for the canoe ride.

Our canoe guide had been growing his hair for three years since the start of COVID. His hair was long like Logan's, and they compared notes. Another family of three joined the five of us. They were from Omaha, Nebraska, and their next stop was Myrtle Beach.

Our canoe ride was spectacular. We started at South Cedar Creek. The ride was slow and perfect for our first family canoe ride: Liz up front, Logan in the middle, and me in the back. The flow of Cedar Creek was moving slowly like molasses. In our first moments in the canoe, we were a little unsteady but quickly adapted. We spotted turtles, herons, and even a few species of snakes. A few other groups passed us from the opposite direction, and the guides, who knew each other, asked if anyone had spotted the one crocodile that supposedly lived in the deep end. We took a break, and our guide traversed us through the floodplain. He explained the feral hogs, who make a mess, floral, and fauna, and showed us that a tall tree that had been struck by lightning was still alive, even cut in half. On previous occasions he said animals had run out of this tree when he approached it. He must have been a butterfly whisperer because one followed him on the river and onto land for about a mile. Too soon it was time to head back home. The four-mile canoe ride took three hours. Our time in Congaree was over. I tipped our guide and asked him one last question: "How can we get to the Congaree River?"

He looked at the ground, as if no one had ever asked that question. "You really can't," he said.

As we were driving to Ashville, our next destination for a few days, we finally saw the Congaree when we drove over the river on Interstate 601. We drove past the large, wide river too quickly.

Our next national park took us to West Virginia. It would be our thirtieth national park together, the New River Gorge National Park and Preserve. We had never been to West Virginia. Our drive on Sunday, August 6, 2023, was four hours from Ashville, North Carolina. New River Gorge National Park encompasses more than seventy thousand acres of land along fifty-three miles of the New River from Bluestone Dam to Hawks Nest Lake in Southern West Virginia. This park is part town, part industry stops, and largely wild with a river through it. A rugged whitewater river flowing northward through deep, spectacular canyons, the New River should be called "Old River," as it is among the oldest rivers on Earth. This river carves the deepest and longest river gorge in the Appalachian Mountains. Think of the Grand Canyon in two billion years. As a result of climate change, as I write this, the world is going through the hottest heat wave on record. Temperatures across the world are peaking at 115 and above. At the same time, in the last year, the skiing was incredible due to so much snow. This summer is sweltering. We are witnessing the coldest, hottest, wettest, and most extreme weather recorded.

The most accepted estimate is that the New River has been on its present course for at least sixty-five million years. The New River was once a longer river called the Teays by geologists. It flowed through Ohio, Indiana, and Illinois and finally emptied into the Mississippi River. Some think about ten thousand years ago the last advance of glacial ice buried most of this river and diverted water of the New River into the Ohio and Kanawha Rivers that were created by glacial action. One other indication of its old age is that the New River flows across the Appalachian Plateau, not around or from it as other streams. The river was there before the Appalachians formed, and these mountains themselves are very old. Some rocks around the New River in this park are as old as 330 million years.

For centuries the gorge remained virtually inaccessible along its entire length. Then in 1872 the railroad opened this isolated wilderness, and the landscape and surroundings began to change. Due to the age of the surrounding rocks, it was a prime place for coal. The railroad bordered the river, making it possible to ship coal to the outside world. Coal mining grew and then exploded here. Towns and villages near the coalfields flourished. In time, like any industry, the bosses were making all the money, and the miners were out protesting. Miners demanded better working conditions. There are many accounts of bitter labor movements; they are recorded in the songs and legends that have become part of our cultural history here. Many of these stories remain, but most of the coal towns are gone. Towns and villages were abandoned when the mines ran out of coal.

This park is a look at nature and what happens to it when a valuable and profitable resource is discovered. From Grandview one sees the rail yards at Quinnimont, where coal was first shipped from the gorge, and the piers of an old bridge that once connected the timber towns of Hamlet and Glade. Hikers on Diamond Point gaze down at the ruins of Kaymoor, one of the earliest New River coal mining towns. In this park, there are also railroad depots, rail yards, rail grades, railroad equipment, and anything one's imagination can conjure up related to the railroads of the past.

On the human side, there are examples of farms, community sites, and homesteads, for this was a working-class state. During the eighteenth and nineteenth centuries these hard-working Americans supplied coal and lumber to our nation to fuel industrialization.

In 1978 New River Gorge was established as a national river and redesignated as New River Gorge National Park and Preserve in 2021. This is one of our newest national parks. It is like a living museum of American life in another time.

Today New River Gorge is known for its excellent recreational opportunities. Many come here to whitewater raft, canoe, hike, rock climb, fish, hunt, bird, camp, bike, and picnic. It is a place to slow down and seek the company of solitude of the natural world.

Our first stop was the Canyon Rim Visitor Center north of Fayetteville, West Virginia. We drove across the New River Gorge Bridge to get there, and it was a wild right-hand turn. I felt like we were going to get hit by a car behind us for slowing down.

This magnificent bridge has a steel arch bridge 3,030 feet long and an arch of 1,700 feet long. This bridge was the world's longest single-span arch bridge for twenty-six years and is now the fifth longest. An average of 16,200 cars and trucks cross this bridge each day. It looks like the Golden Gate Bridge upside down. The canyons below are thick with green forests. It opened in 1977 at a cost of $37 million (equivalent to $131 million in 2021) and may be the main attraction to this park.

There was much to do inside the Canyon Rim Visitor Center. We learned about the park, watched a short film, and bought a few things. There are about three hundred thousand visitors to this center every year. That's about 20 percent of the approximate 1.6 million visitors in 2022 to New River Gorge.

Outside the visitor center is where the real action is. A well-groomed path gives way to a wooden boardwalk. This boardwalk then takes you down approximately two hundred steps. The view of the amazing New River Gorge Bridge is just about the best photo you can take with a bridge; it's a masterpiece. Spanning the New River at a height of 876 feet, it is the third highest bridge in the US. The sounds from the roar of the New River, the birds, the tourists, and the traffic make up the new sound of natural ecotourism.

After our hour-long visit to the visitor center, we checked into our historic bed-and-breakfast in the small town of Fayetteville, West Virginia, about ten minutes away. We had dinner at a farm-to-table restaurant, where I ate a great lamb burger. Across the street was a park with a bronze statue of the Marquis de Lafayette, a French-born general who fought for the Americans during the Revolutionary War. Fayetteville was named after Lafayette. That's also the name of the street I grew up on in Albuquerque. I guess history has a way of following you around.

We walked the town and went to another larger park. A veterans' memorial, cemetery, Little League Baseball fields, and playgrounds allowed us to have another hour of fun before walking the mile and a half back to our historic inn.

Our breakfast the next day was quite good. It was granola blueberry crisp, sausage, and fresh-squeezed orange juice. We handed in our rather large keys and were out to see New River Gorge again. Our first B&B experience as a family was A-OK.

We drove forty minutes or so, again crossing the New River Gorge Bridge, to our destination: Sandstone Visitor Center. It was just past its opening at 9:00 a.m. on a Monday, and we were the first visitors this week. This new center opened in 2003 with a ninety-eight-hundred-square-foot facility featuring a sustainable design concept for energy efficiency and resource conservation. I picked up a telephone and heard the history of an African American railroad worker and the tough work ethic of these men who created the railroad with hard work and determination. It was the voice of the actual worker. I wondered if he was still alive. There is a plethora of natural and cultural history lessons in the exhibits here. We watched a twelve-minute video on the New River and how water is life in this part of the country. It was a good backdrop for our next stop.

Our final stop was Sandstone Falls. We drove past the town of Hinton, West Virginia, to these plentiful low-cascading waterfalls. River flow washed out softer layers below the harder sandstone, creating the larger falls some fifteen hundred feet across. Small islands break the river into smaller falls that drop ten to twenty-five feet. We parked and out we hiked. The sound of the water is like free falling into a misty dream of seascapes. We walked over a mile and what felt like a few hours. The wooden boardwalks lead to the islands, which offer a view of the lower falls. This is one of the most unique botanical ecosystems in West Virginia. This ecosystem is found in only five areas in the state and consists of several southern plant species that have migrated along the north-flowing New River and have adapted to the thin rock-strewn soil and floods that occur here. The New River Gorge itself is home to more than fifteen hundred species of plants and animals. Virginia big-eared and Indiana bats are among the endangered species.

In a country of dwindling natural habitats, migrating neotropical birds depend on this protected place for breeding. Eye-catching red scarlet tanagers and fish-preying great blue herons make their home here.

We crossed the second larger bridge: a mini arch with a steel structure. It brought us to a low-lying island covered with a floodplain forest community and views of the impressive main falls. We took pictures next to the falls from the forest foot trail. There was also a small beach to look out at the river. From the beach we walked up very hard, almost tight Play-Doh-type rocks. This was the sandstone. This was the iconic last stop in this park. Sandstone Falls allowed us to see how this rare ecosystem of islands transforms a mountain stream into a raging whitewater gorge in its final descent through the Appalachian Mountains.

Shenandoah National Park is approximately two hundred thousand acres and stretches for 105 miles on Skyline Drive in the Commonwealth of Virginia. The park is only two hours from our nation's capital, Washington, DC. It lies along the Blue Ridge Mountains in North Central Virginia. In 2020 just over 1.6 million people visited Shenandoah. Some of the rocks exposed in the park date as far back as one billion years and older.

For centuries Native Americans lived and thrived in this Eastern United States mountainous region. The origin of "Shenandoah" is somewhat a mystery. It's almost certainly of Native American origin—possibly meaning "river of high mountains," "silver waters," or even the rather romantic "daughter of the stars."

One legend has been noted as long ago as George Washington. It supposedly was named after an Oneida chief who led Native warriors in support of the colonists in the Revolutionary War.

This land was inhabited seasonally by the Native tribes until the Europeans permanently settled here in the eighteenth century. The new arrivals of Europeans brought to the area farms, apple orchards, and mills, and they quickly began logging these ancient forests.

In the 1930s the government slapped the landowners with eminent domain. The five hundred or so families were resettled. However, many families protested in 1933. Most of the reluctant families came from the central counties. Eventually about forty families were allowed to live out their lives on land that became the park.

Shenandoah National Park was established on December 26, 1935. It was like a late Christmas gift to the American people. Construction, which created a lot of jobs, was up and running for the creation of Blue Ridge Parkway. President Franklin Delano Roosevelt formally opened Shenandoah National Park on July 3, 1936. This was like an early Fourth of July party.

Like many places in the United States the lodges in this park provided only segregated lodgings and restaurants for whites and

Blacks. However, after World War II in 1945 the National Park Service mandated that all concessions in all national parks were to be desegregated. This was a huge step forward in what would become the Civil Rights Movement in the early 1950s.

If you love camping, Shenandoah offers 196,000 acres of backcountry and wilderness camping. While in the backcountry, campers must use a "leave no trace" policy that includes burying your poop and not building any campfires. Because of bears and wildcats, campers must suspend their food from trees. Think "Hey, Boo-Boo" from *Yogi Bear*. There are also a lot of waterfalls in the park, some as high as ninety feet.

On Monday, August 7, 2023, we drove the four-plus hours from New River Gorge to Shenandoah. We arrived at Big Meadows Lodge, our home for the next two days, and settled into our room. We immediately took a short walk to the overlook at Blackrock Summit. We marveled at the Shenandoah Valley below. In the distance we could see Massanutten Mountain. The view was amazing. The smell of nature was all-encompassing.

A storm was brewing, and we had been warned when we entered the park. The walk back to our room was like going through three seasons. Summer changed to fall and quickly to winter. Luckily, we made it home safe. Lightning, followed by one of the loudest thunderbolts I've ever heard, made the whole lodge shake and all the power go out. Thankfully, steps from our room was a twenty-foot-high backup generator to restore power. However, the whole park would be out of electricity. The only gas station was unable to function, and the visitor center had no electricity. This was the real deal. The storm would go on to roll into our nation's capital on its destructive path and would kill two people and leave millions without power.

Ten minutes after the thunderbolt our generator was keeping us comfortable. We had dinner upstairs, watched fog rolling in, and then rolling out, opening up for the sun to shine for the 8:20 p.m. sunset. It was all over in about thirty minutes.

We woke up a few times in our cabin-like room, and for the first time this summer we were a bit cold with temperatures in the sixties.

By 8:00 a.m. we were on our first hike of the day steps outside our door. We took in the three-mile (five-kilometer) Lewis Falls Trail hike. We were happy it was part of the famous Appalachian Trail. We had read many books and heard many stories from friends about hiking this trail. This trail is twenty-two hundred miles, going from Georgia to Maine. The first thing that struck us was how damn rocky the trail was. We really had to pay attention. Logan tripped once. He and I also recognized the plentiful acorns scattered everywhere. We gathered only the best, and later in the day Logan played with them in our room like they were action figures. One day we will place them in our bathroom like folks arrange seashells. The actual falls were a bit melodramatic, and as we came upon them the wind made it a bit dangerous. This hiking loop would again connect us to the Blackrock Summit we hiked to the previous night. It was still as impressive in the early morning daylight. We returned to our historic Big Meadow room and rested up. Around noon we all got hungry and drove to Skyland, ten miles away from Big Meadows. Its origin was Skyland Resort, which predated Shenandoah. However, its modern architecture makes the dining room look brand new. The large windows allow you to eat looking out on the best view in the park. We wanted to take a horseback ride, and the stables were just below our lunchroom. As we parked, we only saw horses, no people. They were closed for the day, another victim of the storm.

The Shenandoah website read, "Power Outages – Big Meadows Wayside and Lewis Mountain Campground area: There are lots of disruptions from last night's heavy storms. Big Meadows Wayside is without power and is closed. There is NO fuel service. There is also no power in the Lewis Mountain Campground area. Crews are working to restore services."

As we said goodbye to the horses, we also realized Logan was too small to ride, according to their height requirement.

We then went to the visitor center and bought Logan a pencil and key chain and Liz a postcard. The power was out, so we could not go through the regular routine of a video and a walk-through. We ran into a lot of people with dogs all over this park.

Road signs said it was unlawful to feed wildlife. However, the night before, I saw a deer trying to eat apples from an apple tree, and I picked a few, and the deer ate them off the ground. My family got mad at me, thinking I was breaking the law.

My law of nature is to feed the hungry. I always tell my son the number one rule for a beast (our two-year-old golden retriever) is to feed the beast. I think the hungry deer liked me. It definitely wasn't afraid of me.

At the cabin Logan was back to playing with his acorns. An hour later we were playing catch with our mitts and a few baseballs in the large meadow next to the amphitheater at Big Meadows. Logan was getting the hang of pop-ups and pitching well. Although he may be a natural, it's just nature when you practice every day. In your backyard or America's. A group of Amish teenagers set up a volleyball net and played next to us. Logan asked what language they were speaking. I think it was a dialect of English.

Just before sunset that evening, we put in a few more miles of hiking. We were the only car parked at the visitor center and walked the Dark Hollow Falls Trail and the Story of the Forest Trail. We came upon three deer, one being a cute little spotted fawn. Our hike ended at the Big Meadows campground. It looked amazing, and people were getting ready for dinner and the night ahead.

The sunset this night with its yellow, pink, and purple hues went well with the green all around. It was nature's masterpiece.

South Cedar Creek Canoe Adventure

Congaree sign in the rain

The river awaits

New River Gorge Bridge

New River's last sandstone

Sandstone Falls

Heaven

REFLECTIONS

LIFE IS SHORT. IF YOU THINK TWICE, YOU MIGHT NOT TAKE the opportunity for the mountains to call you. When they do, pick up your boots and go.

National parks are a cornerstone of who we are as an American culture. When our son was born, a goal of visiting all the national parks called me. Our journey has been a miraculous one.

From the time Logan was just two months old and visiting Painted Desert and Saguaro National Parks, we understood this goal would take on a life of its own. Our baby Logan in pictures at Rocky Mountain National Park calls to us every time we think of our boy. From a toddler in Grand Canyon National Park to a child traversing the most magnificent hikes in the Grand Teton, our son has been very lucky. So have Liz and I. Our marriage has strengthened, and my soul has been regenerated.

These mountains, oceans, rivers, deserts, and valleys have taught us more than we can teach them. We accepted mortality when my mom passed and felt her presence before and after her death in each and every hike and boat ride and think of her favorite winged dragonfly when they fly around us in many parks.

The worldwide pandemic came and went. It wasn't time to slow down our journey and goals. We actually went to more parks when the world stopped and at any moment seemed like it could have ended.

Take it from me: When the national parks call, don't let anything get in your way. Just go.

INDEX

A

B

C

D

E

F

G

H

I

J

K

L

M

N

O

P

Q

R

S

T

U

V

W

Y

Z

ABOUT THE AUTHOR

Antonio Lopez had an idea to take his small family to every national park. That's how *National Parks,* came about. Antonio grew up in Albuquerque, moved out of New Mexico for seven years, and now lives in Santa Fe, New Mexico with his family. He works as a financial advisor and in his writing, he explores our national parks.

Photo © Daniel Quat Photography

Connect with him online:
https://lopeznationalparks.com/

THANK YOU!

Thank you for reading! If you enjoyed this book, please leave a review on Amazon, Goodreads, BookBub, The Story Graph, or anywhere else you like to track your recent reads. Alternatively, you could post online or tell a friend about it. This helps our authors more than you may know.

- The Team at Torchflame Books

Follow Torchflame Books for news about our authors and upcoming new releases @TorchflameBooks.

Find your next great read at www.torchflamebooks.com.

www.ingramcontent.com/pod-product-compliance
Lightning Source LLC
LaVergne TN
LVHW020532100826
845148LV00010B/1432